THE DIALECT OF CUMBERLAND

WITH A CHAPTER ON ITS PLACE-NAMES,

BY

ROBERT FERGUSON,

AUTHOR OF THE TEUTONIC NAME-SYSTEM, RIVER-NAMES OF EUROPE, &C.

FACSIMILE REPRINT 1998
LLANERCH PUBLISHERS
FELINFACH

ISBN 1 86143 050 7

TO

PHILIP HENRY HOWARD, Esq., F.S.A.,

OF CORBY CASTLE, CARLISLE,

WITH THE HIGHEST REGARDS OF

THE AUTHOR.

PREFACE.

T E importance of our local dialects as a collateral aid in the study of the English tongue needs not now to be asserted. Without reference to those various forms of speech, out of which one has by dint of circumstances become crystalized in the standard tongue, the language can no more be clearly illustrated than it could be were we to omit to compare it with the cognate languages of Europe.

The folk-speech of Cumberland has—thanks to the patriotic interest which her sons take in all that belongs to her—had a more ample share of recognition than generally falls to the lot of provincial dialects. Its humour and its pathos, its "canniness"—quaintness with a touch of cynicism—have been ably illustrated in prose, and its rhythmical qualities attested in verse, by the writers whose names appear on the subjoined list. What remains to be done—and towards which I now offer my contribution—is the etymological analysis of its constituents, with a view to ascertain the position which it occupies as regards the standard language, and as regards the other dialects of Scotland and Northern England.

The most complete collection of Cumberland words is that made by Mr. Dickinson, to whom we are indebted for the rescue from that oblivion to which advancing education and the spread of inter-communication threaten to consign all provincial dialects, of a number of words, many of which are of great etymological interest. That the list is not by any means yet complete, the extent and importance of the supplement published by him within the space of eight years goes a long way to suggest. The work of Mr. Dickinson I have taken, then, as the basis of my undertaking, adding such words as I have been able to collect from other sources. I have omitted all words that seem to me to be unimportant variations from the standard language, or that do not call for any etymological observation, my object being to avoid as much as may be interference with the labours of others.

The most thorough investigation which has as yet been made of any northern dialect is to be found in the work lately published by Mr. Atkinson, under the auspices of the Philological Society, on the dialect of Cleveland. This work, which it may be said for the first time on a complete scale exhibits a dialect of the north as illustrated in the light of modern philology, I have taken as the more especial basis of comparison so far as regards the dialects of northern England; and the great work of Jamieson for comparison with the Scottish dialect. Among the other works to which I am indebted, Mr. Wedgwood's lately published Dictionary of the English Language, in which for the first time the provincial dialects find their due place, has afforded me the most important assistance. Also the Icelandic Dictionary, now in course of publication, which was begun by the late Mr. Cleasby and continued by the learned Icelander, Mr. Vigfusson, has afforded me many valuable suggestions, which, however, in several cases were not in time to appear otherwise than as after-notes.

I have added a chapter on the local etymology of the district, a subject very closely connected, it will be seen, with the speech of the people, and for which previous investigations have to some extent prepared me.

ROBERT FERGUSON.

Morton, Carlisle,
February, 1873.

Also published by Llanerch:

THE SECRET VALLEY
or how Lakeland people held out against the Norman Conquest
Nicholas Size

THORSTEIN OF THE MERE
a saga of the northmen in Lakeland
W. G. Collingwood

THE BONDWOMEN
the sequel to *Thorstein*
W. G. Collingwood.

THE LIKENESS OF KING ELFWALD
Northumbria and Iona in the early viking period
W. G. Collingwood

NORTHANHYMBRE SAGA
the kings of Northumbria
John Marsden

TALIESIN POEMS
includes the poems to Urien of Rheged
Meirion Pennar

For a complete list of ca.300 titles, small-press editions and facsimile reprints, write to LLANERCH PUBLISHERS, Felinfach, Lampeter, Ceredigion, SA48 8PJ.

CONTRACTIONS AND AUTHORITIES.

Dick.   A Glossary of the Words and Phrases of Cumberland. By William Dickinson, F.L.S.
London and Whitehaven, 1859.
Supplement. 1867.

West. and Cumb. Dial.   The Westmorland and Cumberland Dialects; with a Glossary. London, 1839.

Songs and Ballads of Cumberland. Edited by Sydney Gibson. London and Carlisle, 1846.

Folk-speech, Tales, and Rhymes of Cumberland and Districts Adjacent. Ay Alex. Craig Gibson, F.S.A. London and Carlisle, 1849.

Cummerland Talk; being Short Tales and Rhymes in the Dialect of that County. By John Richardson. London and Carlisle, 1871.

Hutchinson.   The History of the County of Cumberland. By William Hutchinson, F.S.A. Carlisle, 1794.

Hall.   A Dictionary of Archaic and Provincial Words, By J. O. Halliwell, F.R.S. London, 1850.

Jam.   Etymological Dictionary of the Scottish Language. By John Jamieson, D.D. Edinburgh, 1808.

Wedg.   A Dictionary of English Etymology. By H. Wedgwood, M.A. London, 1867.

Pr. Prv.   Promptorium Parvulorum sive Clericorum. Dictionarius Anglo-Latinus Princeps. Edited by Albert Way, A.M. London, 1864.

A Glossary of North-country Words in Use. By John Trotter Brockett. Newcastle-on-Tyne, 1825.

J. K.   A New English Dictionary. By J. K. (John Kersey.) London, 1702.

x.   CONTRACTIONS AND AUTHORITIES.

Atk. or *Clev.* A Glossary of the Cleveland Dialect; Explanatory, Derivative, and Critical. By the Rev. J. C. Atkinson. London, 1848.

Lonsd. Glossary of the Dialect of the Hundred of Lonsdale North and South of the Sands. By the late Robert B. Peacock. Edited by the Rev. J. C. Atkinson. London, 1869.

Crav. The Dialect of Craven. By a Native of Craven. London, 1828.

Prior. Popular Names of British Plants. By R. C. A. Prior. London, 1863.

Layamon. Layamon's Brut, or Chronicle of Britain. Edited by Sir F. Madden. London, 1847.

P. Pl. The Vision and Creed of Piers Ploughman. Edited by Thos. Wright, M.A. London, 1856.

Worsaae. The Danes and Norwegians in England, Scotland, and Ireland. By J. J. A. Worsaae. London, 1852.

Philological Essays of R. Garnett. London, 1859.

Cotg. A Dictionary of the French and English Tongues. By Randle Cotgrave. London, 1632.

Cleasby. An Icelandic-English Dictionary. By the late Richard Cleasby. Enlarged and completed by Gudbrand Vigfusson. Oxford.

Hald. Biörn Haldorsen. Icel. Lex.   1814.

Ihre. Gloss. Suio-Gothicum. Joh. Ihre.   Upsal, 1769.

Rietz. Ordbog öfver Svenska Allmoge-språket af Joh. Ernst Rietz.   Lund., 1868.

Richt. Alt Friesisches Wörterbuch von Dr. Karl F. Von Richthofen.   Göttingen, 1840.

Outzen. Glossarium der Friessichen Sprache von N. Outzen. Kopenhagen, 1837.

Kil. Etymologicum Teutonicæ Linguæ. C. Kilian.   1777.

Hamb. Idiot. or *Richey.* Idioticon Hamburgense von M. Richey, P.P.   Hamburg, 1755.

Holstein. Holsteinisches Idiotikon. Schüsze.   Hamburg, 1800.

Danneil or *Brem. Wtb.* Bremisch-Niedersachsisches Wörterbuch. Danneil.   1768

CONTRACTIONS AND AUTHORITIES.

Henneberg.	Hennebergisches Idiotikon. W. F. H. Reinwald. Berlin and Stettin, 1793.		
Swiss.	Stalder. Schweitzerisches Idioticon. Aarau, 1812.		
	Dictionary of the Welsh Language. By Wm. Owen. London, 1803.		
	Dictionary of the Gaelic Language. By the Highland Society of Scotland. London and Edinburgh, 1828.		
Williams.	Lexicon Cornu-Britannicum. By the Rev. R. Williams, M.A. London, 1865.		
	A Dictionary of Cornish Names. By the Rev. John Bannister, L.L.D., Vicar of St. Day. London, 1872.		
	Transactions of the Philological Society: Dr. Guest—vol. ii., p. 155; vol. v., pp. 169, 185. A. Gurney—vol. vii., p. 29. Rev. J. Davies—vol. vii., p. 210.		
Eichhoff.	Parrallele des Langues de l' Europe et de L' Inde. Eichhoff. Paris, 1836.		
Bav.	Bavarian.		
Boh.	Bohemian.		
Dan.	Danish.	*Dial. Dan.*	Provincial Danish.
Dut.	Dutch.		
Fin.	Finnish.		
Fris.	Frisian.	*N. Fris.*	North Frisian.
Fr.	French.	*Pr. Fr.*	Provincial French.
Gael.	Gaelic.	*Obs. Gael.*	Obsolete Gaelic.
Ir.	Irish.		
Ital.	Italian.		
Norw.	Norwegian.		
North.	Northumberland.		
Prov.	Provencal.		
Pres.	Preseent.		
Pret.	Preterite.		
Priv.	Privative.		
Sco.	Scotch.		

CONTENTS.

Glossary 1–175
Additions and Corrections 177–188
Obsolete and other Terms found in
   Names of Places 189–213
General Observations 214–230

ERRATA.

P. 26. For Germ. *haufen* read *kaufen*.
   50. For Dan. *gfen-vei* read *gjen-vei*.
        For *gammarel* read *gommarel*.
116. For Dan. *scaldet* read *skaldet*.
126. For Crav. *slaiu* read *slain*.
164. For *splendid* read *splendit*.

GLOSSARY

OF THE

CUMBERLAND DIALECT.

A.

AAMAS. *sb.* Alms, "in former times a handful of oatmeal or a slice of brown bread."—*Dick.* Ang.-Sax. *ælmesse*, Dan. *almisse.*

ABACK. *prep.* Behind.
Ang.-Sax. *onbæc*, Old Norse *ábak*, (á=on). Old Norse *á fialla baki*, behind the mountains, or as we should say, *aback o' the fells*.

ABACK-O'-BEYONT. At an indefinitely great distance.
Euphony seems to have been the cause of the retention of *beyont* in this case, the usual Cumb. word being *ayont*, which, as elsewhere noted, (see *afore*), may be due to Scand. influence.

ABLE or YABLE. *adj.* Generally, if not invariably, used in the sense of property, an "able man," signifying a man in good circumstances. So the Old Norse *afla* denotes both to be able and to possess or acquire, while "in the Mod. Scand. idioms there are no traces left of the idea of force."—*Cleasby.* In the present dialect of Norway *avle* signifies to harvest.

ABOON, ABUIN. *prep.* Above.
Ang.-Sax. *abufan*, whence by sync. *aboon*.

ABREED. *vn.* To spread or extend.
Ang.-Sax. *abredan*, to draw out.

ACK. *vn.* To take thought about, to lay to heart.
"Neer *ack*—there's nae hard laws in England
Except this bit thing aboot game."—*Miss Blamire.*
Old Norse *akta*, Ang.-Sax. *eahtian*, to consider, meditate, Germ., Dut. *achten*, to mind, care for.

ADDLE. *va.* To earn.
Old Norse *ödlaz*, to obtain, acquire, Ang.-Sax. *edleanian*, to requite.

B

ADLINS. *sb.* Earnings.
Ang.-Sax. *ædlean*, recompense.

AFORE. *adv.* Before.
The Ang.-Sax. has both the prepositions *be* and *on*, while the Scandinavian idiom has only the latter. Hence the use in our dialect of *a* (Old Norse *á=on*) instead of *be*—as in *afore, ahint, atween, ayont*, instead of *before, behind, between, beyond*, may, as suggested by Cleasby, be due to Scand. influence.

AGAIN or AGEAN. *prep.* Against.
Ang.-Sax. *ongean*, against.

AGATE or AGEAT. Literally on the road (Old Norse *gata*, road or way), but used in the general sense of being astir, going about.

AGLEE. *adv.* To look aglee is to look to one side or askance.
" Sae fine she goes, sae far *aglee*,
That folks she kenned she cannot see."—*Miss Blamire*.
Clev. *gleg*, to cast side-looks, glance furtively.
Atk. refers to Old Norse *gluggr*, Dial. Swed. *glugg*, opening, window, eye, Dial. Swed. *titta uuner glugg*, to look askance.

AGLET. *sb.* The metal point at the end of a boot-lace.
Fr. *aiguillet*, a dimin. of *aiguille*, a needle. (*Aiguille* is properly a point on the end of a lace for drawing it through the holes). Hence *eylet* or *aylet-hole*, properly *aglet-hole*.

AHINT. *adv.* Behind. See *afore*.
This word in Cumb., as noted by Atk. of Clev., has the *i* short as in Germ. *hinten*.

AIRD, ARD. *adj.* Applied to land in its primary signification seems to mean high. Gael. and Ir. *ard*, high, cognate with Lat. *arduus*, Sansc. *ærd*, to elevate. In a secondary sense, dry or parched, "such lands being dry or parched only because they lie high."—*Boucher*. "I never heard the term in Cumb."—*Dick*.

AJYE or AGEE. Crooked, awry.
Gee is to move, turn round, Swed. *gaa*, to turn, hence *agee*, (*a*=on) is awry.

ALLAN. *sb.* A piece of land nearly surrounded by water. Apparently the same word as *island*, from Ang.-Sax. *eáge, eáh*, eye. Unless we can think of Welsh *elin*, angle, elbow, in the sense of a piece of land surrounded on two sides by water.

ALODDIN. Not engaged, open to an offer.
From *a* negative, and Old Norse *lada*, Ang.-Sax. *láthian*, to invite, send for.

AMELL. *prep.* Between or among.
Old Norse *âmilli*, Dan. (South Jutland) *amelle*. Nearly, if not quite obsolete in Cumb. .

AMELL-DOOR or MELL-DOOR. *sb.* A door between the outer door and that of an inner room. See *amell*.

ANENST. *prep.* Opposite to, over against.
Wedgwood refers to Old Norse *giegnt*, opposite, which view is rather strengthened by one of the Scotch forms *anent*.

ANCOME or INCOME. *sb.* More properly *oncome*. A swelling or sore not arising from any external cause, something which "comes on" of itself. Old Norse *âkoma*, (*â=on*) rendered by Haldorsen vulnusculum, by Cleasby a hurt from a blow and also an eruption on the skin.

ANG-NAIL. *sb.* A nail grown into the flesh. Also jags round the nail. Ang.-Sax. *ang-nægl*, a whitlow, a sore under the nail, literally any sore connected with the nail. The root-meaning of *ang* is pressure or contraction, whence the derived meaning of suffering, as in Welsh *angen*, need, want, Lat. *angor*, Ang.-Sax. *ang*, Eng. *anguish*, &c.

ANGLEBERRIES. *sb.* Excrescences on the under parts of cattle. I presume from the same origin as the above *ang-nail*, in the sense of pain or disease.

ANGRY. *adj.* Painful or inflamed, (applied to a wound or sore). Old Norse *angr*, Swed. *anger*, sorrow, pain, Ang.-Sax. *ang*, pain, trouble. The Eng. *anger* was formerly used in the sense of sorrow, trouble, anguish.

ANGS or AWNS. *sb.* The beards of barley or other grain. Suio-Goth. *agn*, Dan. *avn*, Old High Germ. *agana*.

ANONDER or INONDER. *prep.* Beneath, under.
Properly *onunder*, being formed like the Ang.-Sax. *onuppan*, above, by the redundant addition of *on* to *under*. Comp. Germ. *hinunter*.

ANTER. *conj.* In case, perhaps.
"Auntyr or Hap."—*Pr. Prv.* A contraction of *adventure*, or rather of Fr. *aventure*, which occurs in Chaucer in the form *auntre*. Hence the Scripture *peradventure*. "The Aunters (Adventures) of Arthur at Tarn Wathelan" is the title of an old Eng. romance.

ARGY. *vn.* To argue, dispute.
> Might be taken to be nothing more than a corruption of Eng. *argue*. It may, however, as Jam. suggests, be from the Suio-Goth. *jerga*, semper eadem obgannire, ut solent amiculæ iratæ, cognate with Lat *jurgo*, Sansc. *jharc*, to squabble. Westm. *arg.* to argue, Sussex *arg*, to grumble, seem rather to favour this suggestion.

ARK or AIRK. *sb.* A chest, applied more particularly to the large chests used in farm-houses for keeping flour or meal. Ang.-Sax. *earc*, a chest, Old Norse *örk*, Dial. Swed. *örk*, a chest for meal ; Welsh *arch*, Gael. *airc*, chest, cognate with Lat. *arca*, Sansc. *ark*, Wel. *argau*, to enclose.

ARR. *sb.* A scar, mark of a wound.
> Old Norse *örr*, Dan. *ar*, Fris. *aar*.

ART or AIRT. *sb.* Quarter of the heaven, direction or point of the compass.
> "Of all the *airts* the wind can blow."—*Burns.*

> Gael. *aird*, quarter of the heavens, Old Norse *ått*, Germ. *ort*, place, region. Diefenbach suggests a possible connection with Goth. *airtha*, Ang.-Sax. *eorthe*, Eng. *earth*.

ARVEL. *sb.* A funeral feast.
> Suio-Goth. *arfol*, literally "inheritance ale," from the ale drunk on those occasions. The usage in Scandinavia was that no heir could take possession of his inheritance until he had given the arval-feast. *Arf* originally meant cattle, and was then applied to property in general.

ASIDE. *prep.* See *afore*.

ASK. *sb.* The newt or water-lizard.
> Gael. *asc.* adder, Gr. εχις viper. But perhaps rather (*ask=ax*) a contraction of Ang.-Sax. *athexe*, newt.

AT. *conj.* That.
> " There's nit mickle on her—we ken *at* guid stuff
> Laps up i' lal bundles, an' she's lal eneugh."—*Gibson.*

> Old Norse *at*, Dan. *at*.

AT. *rel. pron.* That, which.
> " Ilk lad now hugs the lass he leykes,
> Wheyle some hev half a dozen,
> Unless some wreen ill-natured tykes,
> *At* car'nt if th' lasses wizzen."—*Stagg.*

> Old Norse *at*, qui, who.

AT. *prep.* To. "Ah can dui nought mair *at* it."
> Old Norse *at*, Ang.-Sax. *æt*, at, to.

AT. To, as the sign of the infinitive.
"Aw wad leyke *at* gan to Carel." "Nearly obsolete now, but common in the eighteenth century."—*Dick.* Old Norse *at*, sign of the infinitive,

ATTERCOP. *sb.* A spider's web. Properly the insect itself. Ang.-Sax. *attercoppa*, literally "poison-bag."

AUMRY. *sb.* A cupboard where victuals, &c., are kept, Fr. *armoire*, a cupboard, properly a place where arms are kept, Lat. *armarium* (Diez).

AWE or OWE. *va.* To own, possess.
The older form on which *own* is formed, and which was in use till the time of Elizabeth. Sansc. *ic*, Gr. εχω, Goth. *aihan*, Ang.-Sax. *agan*, to own. As in Clev., most commonly used in the phrase "whee's awe this?" Atk., quoting similar instances in Old Eng. use, takes this to be "who shall *awe* (or own) this?"

AX. *va.* To ask.
Ang.-Sax, *acsian, axian.*

AXLE-TEETH. *sb.* The grinders.
Old Norse *jaxlar*, dentes molares.

AYLET or EYLET-HOLE. A lacing hole in a pair of stays, &c. Properly *aglet-hole.* See *aglet.*

AYONT. *prep.* Beyond. See *afore.*

B.

BACK-BOARD or BACK-BWORD. *sb.* A baking board.
Dan, *bagebord.*

BADGER. *sb.* A travelling dealer in grain, meal, butter, &c. Wedgwood makes *badger* a corruption of Fr. *bladier*, one who carries about corn for sale on mule-back.

BAG. *sb.* The belly. Also the udder of the cow.
Gael. *balg.* bag, belly, Ang.-Sax. *bælg.* bag, wallet, Old Norse *belgr*, inflated skin, leather sack, belly. The tendency of the dialect to drop the *l* in such cases, makes *balg* into *bag*, as *balk* into *bawk.*

BAGGIN. *sb.* Provisions taken into the field for labourers. Either from the bag in which the provisions are carried, or perhaps more probably from the bag (see last word) in which they are to be received.

BAIN. *adj.* Near, convenient, applied to a road; willing, handy, applied to a person. Old Norse *beinn*, direct, straight, Swed. *ban*, a good or even road. Old Norse *beinstr vegr*, Cumb. *bainest way*. As in Scandinavia, where neighbours are sparse, the metaphorical meaning of hospitable grew up as applied to a person, so in our district that of willing or obliging.

BAIRN. *sb.* A child.
Anglo-Sax. *bearn*, Old Norse *barn*. This word, originally common to all the Teutonic idioms, was superseded by *kind* in Germany as early as the 13th cent., and by *child* also at an early period in Southern England. It is still in exclusive use throughout the whole of Scandinavia, as also throughout Scotland and Northern England.

BALK, *pron.* BAWK. *sb.* A beam. Also a ridge of land between two furrows. The Ang.-Sax. *balca* has both these two meanings. The Old Norse has two separate words, *biálki*, a beam, and *bálkr*, a partition. Suio-Goth. *balk*, a ridge between two furrows. In the sense of a beam, the word is also found in the Welsh, and Gael. *balc*.

BAM. *sb.* A falsehood, trick, deceit.
Arm. *bamein*, to cheat.

BANDYLOW or BANDYLAN. *sb.* A woman of dissolute character, a prostitute. Perhaps from Gael. *ban*, woman, and *diol*, hire, recompense, as Eng. *whore*, Ang.-Sax. *hura*, from A.-S. *hyran*, Eng. *hire*, and Lat. *meretrix*, from *mereor*. Unless we may think for the latter part of the word of Wel, *dielw*, vile, worthless.

BANG. *va.* To beat. Also to excell, surpass.
Old Norse *banga*, to beat, *bang*, a hammering.

BANNOCK. *sb.* Thick oat-cake, usually made for the harvest home or kern supper. Gael. *bannach*, a cake, *bannag*, a cake made for Christmas.

BARGH. *sb.* A hill.
Old Norse *biarg*, *berg*, Ang.-Sax. *beorg*, Germ. *berg*, mountain, hill.

BARLEY. *va.* To bespeak, generally used by children at play. "Barley me that," is a form of putting in first claim to anything. Peacock refers to Manx *barelhian*, I had rather, but I doubt whether the ordinary derivation from *parley*, Fr. *parler*, is not to be preferred.

BARM. *sb.* Yeast.
Ang.-Sax. *beorma*, Old Swed. *berma*, Dan. *bærme*, Dut. *barm*.

BASH. *va.* To strike hard, work vigorously.
Clev. *pash.* Dan. *baske,* to beat, cudgel, Swiss *batschen,* to strike with the hand.

BASK. *adj.* Sharply acid.
Old Norse *beiskr,* Swed. *besk,* bitter, acrid, Fris. *basch* and *barsch,* Germ. *barsch,* harsh, sharp, tart.

BASS. *sb.* The perch.
"Bace, fysche."—*Pr. Prv.* *Barsh,* perch, Westm. *Base,* the sea perch, *Hamp.* Ang.-Sax. *bærs,* Dut. *baars,* Germ. *bars, barsch.* This is the old Teutonic word, which has been superseded in English by the French *perche.*

BASS. *sb.* Matting, "originally, no doubt, confined to that made of the inner bark of the linden tree, but now inclusive of other materials, as straw, large rushes, &c."—*Atkinson.* Ang.-Sax. *bæst,* Old Norse *bast,* the inner part of the lime tree. Dan. *bast maatte,* bass matting. The root, like that of *baste,* to sew loosely, is probably found in Sansc. *bandh,* to bind.

BASTE. *va.* To beat.
Old Norse *beysta,* to beat, belabour.

BASTE. *va.* To sew loosely, with large stitches.
"Bastyn clothys, subsuo."—*Pr. Prv.* Old Norse *basta,* to bind into a parcel, Dut. *besten,* leviter consuere, (*Kil.*), Pers. *basta,* to bind, from the Sans. *bandh,* to bind.

BAT. *sb.* A blow, stroke.
Gael. *bat,* to beat, Ir. *batta,* blow, Old Swed. *bædda,* to strike, North Fris. *bat,* to beat, Ang.-Sax. *bat,* club.

BATTEN. *sb.* A bundle or truss of straw.
"I connect this word immediately with *batt,* the pret. of Old Norse *binda,* to bind. Comp. N. D. *band,* a bundle, Norw. *binda,* forming its pret. in *bant* or *band.*"—*Atk.*

BATTEN. *vn.* To thrive.
Old Norse *batna,* to get better, Goth. *gabatnan,* to thrive.

BATTER. *sb.* Dirt or mud.
Sco. *batter,* paste, something adhesive. Wel. *baw,* mud, *bawedi,* nastiness, *budro,* to dirty.

BAZE. *va.* To lift or prize with a lever. See *paze.*

BEADLESS. *adj.* Impatient under suffering.
Old Norse *bid,* endurance, patience, with the priv. term. *less.*

BECK. *sb.* The general word throughout the North of England for a small stream, as *brook* in S. Eng., and *burn* in Scot. Old Norse *beckr*, Dan. *bæk*, Ang.-Sax. *becc*, Germ. *bach*.

BEEK. *vn.* To bask by the fire. Also to heat hazel or other rods to make them bend. Old Norse *baka*, Ang.-Sax. *bacan*, to heat, bake, Eng. *bask* and *bake*, of which the Cumb. word is only another form.

BEEL. *vn.* To bellow.
Old Norse *beljia*, Ang.-Sax. *bellan*, to bellow.

BEESTINS. *sb.* The first milk from a newly-calved cow. Ang.-Sax. *byst, bysting*, of same meaning.

BEET. *va.* To beet the fire or oven is to supply fuel to it. Ang.-Sax. *betan fyr*, Old Norse *bæta elld*, to mend or kindle a fire.
"Beet on the eldin."—*Stagg.*

BELK. *vn.* To belch.
Ang.-Sax. *bealcian*.

BELLY-RYNE or BELLY-RIM. *sb.* The membrane inclosing the intestines. The latter is the correct form, from Ang.-Sax. *reama*, membrane.

BENK or BINK. *sb.* A low shelf or ledge of rocks. Welsh *banciau*, table, platform, Corn. *benc*, bench, Ang.-Sax. *benc*, Old Norse, *bekkr*, bench.

BENSEL. *va.* To beat. Also as a noun, a bounce, a sudden bang. A frequentative of *bounce*, of which the original meaning was to strike. Dut. *bonzen*, Swiss *bantschen*, to beat.

BENT. *adj.* Bleak.
Welsh *ban, bant*, high, Gael. *ban*, bleak, barren. Hence *bent-grass*, the coarse grass that grows on moor land.

BENWORT. *sb.* The daisy. *Bellis perennis.*
The plant generally known by the name of *banewort* is the *ranunculus flammula*, "from its *baning* sheep by ulcerating their entrails" (*Prior.*) Ang.-Sax. *banwyrt* (*ban*, wound, hurt, and *wyrt*, plant) was applied both to the violet and the *centaurea minor*. In the names of plants there is often much confusion.

BERRY. *va.* To thrash corn.
Old Norse *beria*, to beat, *beria korn*, to thrash corn.

BET. *vb.* pret. of *beat.*
   The Southerner makes no distinction between *beat* as the pres. and *beat* as the pret. while the Northerner forms the pret. as *met* from *meet*. Hence this, among the better educated classes, is one of the distinguishing marks of a Northern origin.

BICKER. *sb.* "A small wooden vessel used for porridge, &c."—*Dick.* Stagg uses it in the more generally received sense of a drinking glass. Old Norse *bikar*, Germ. *becher*, a large drinking glass.

BID. *va.* To invite.
   Ang.-Sax. *beódan*, Old Norse *biôda*, (pres. *bid*), Dan. *byde*, to invite.

BIDE. *vn.* To await, stay. Also to dwell, abide.
   Old Norse *bída*, Old Swed. *bida*, Ang.-Sax. *bidan, abidan*, to wait, stay, abide.

BIELD. *sb.* A place of shelter, hut, hovel, a fox's den.
   Old Norse *byli*, a dwelling. In Iceland a den, a lair. The final *d*, (as in *build*, formerly *bylle*), is a phonetic addition.

BIG. *va..* To build.
   Ang.-Sax. *byggan*, Old Norse *byggia*. Hence the term. *by*, (= *big*), of Danish origin, in names of places. as Crosby, Aglionby, &c.

BIGGLE. *va.* To blindfold, *biggly*, blind man's buff.
   "When the boy is blindfolded, another turns him gently round to confuse his ideas of locality."—*Dick.* Hence may be the word, viz., from Dut. *biegen*, Old Norse *beygja*, to turn, to bend, Suio-Goth. *bygel*, a turning. Or it may be the same as *beguile*, Low Germ. *begigelen*, properly to deceive by juggling tricks, from *gig*, expressing rapid motion, the idea in either case being that of confusing the person.

BILLY. *sb..* Brother, comrade.
   Old Eng. *bully.* Jamieson's derivation from *billig*, æqualis, is erroneous. The connections of the word are with Mid. High Germ. *buole*, friend, brother, consort, Dut. *boelen*, to love.

BIR or BUR. *sb.* A sudden and rapid movement, as that of a missile through the air. The same, I apprehend, as *bree*, which we have also in a similar sense. Perhaps to be connected with Welsh *bur,* violence, rage, *bwrw*, to throw, cast.

BISEN or BIZZEN. *sb.* A spectacle or sight in the sense of warning, an example to be avoided. Old Norse *býsn*, a strange and portentous thing, Ang.-Sax. *bisn*, example.

BITTER-BUMP. *sb.* The bittern.
  Apparently a combination of two different names for the bird, one of which appears to be Celtic, and the other Norman-French. The Old Eng. word was *bitour*, from the Fr. *butor*, The Welsh names are *bwn* and *bwmp y gors*, from *bwmp*, a booming. As in Lonsd. the bittern is called simply the *bump*, it seems probable that the Welsh term generally used was simply *bwmp*. Hence by the combination of these two different words would come BITTER-BUMP.

BLADDER or BLATHER. *sb.* Foolish or idle talk.
  Suio-Goth. *bladdra*, to prate, to chatter.

BLAIN. *vn.* To become white, to bleach.
  Old Norse *bleikna*, Dan. *blegne*, to become white.

BLAKE. *adj.* Pale yellow.
  Ang.-Sax. *blác*, Old Norse *bleikr*, Germ. *bleich*, pale, fair. The O.N, *bleikr* was variously applied to the colour of gold, to that of a field of ripe barley, and to the light hair of a baby.—*Cleasby.*

BLARE. *vn.* To roar or bellow.
  Dut. *blaasen*, mugire, Fris. *blarren*, to yell, howl. *Wedg.*, comparing Suio-Goth. *bladdra*, takes *blaaren* to be a cont. of *bladeren*, which seems probable. Such contractions are especially common in Friesic.

BLASH. *vn.* To splash.
  Old Swed. *plaska*, to splash.

BLATE. *adj.* Bashful, shy.
  Old Norse *blaudr*, bashful, properly soft or effeminate, Ang.-Sax. *bleâth*, soft, gentle.

BLEABERRY. *sb.* The bilberry or whortleberry, vaccinium myrtillus. Old Norse *blåber.*

BLEARY. *adj.* Windy and showery.
  Clev. *blear*, to expose oneself to the wind. Old Norse *blær*, a puff of wind, draft of air.

BLEB. *sb.* A bubble.
  Gael. *plab*, a soft noise, as of a body falling into water. The word is employed, first to signify "the sound of something wet or soft falling against anything, and hence to designate the object making such a sound, a lump of anything wet or soft, drop of liquid, bubble, &c."—*Wedg.*

BLENK, BLINK. *sb.* A gleam, as of sunshine.
  Old Norse *blik*, gleam, Germ. *blick*, Dan. *blink*, glimpse, Dut. *blinken*, to shine.

BLITTERT. *adj.* Torn by winds.
Germ. *blättern*, to come off in blisters.

BLOW, BLOWN, BLUE. *adj.* Applied to milk that has had the cream skimmed off. Fris. *blo*, blue, similarly applied to milk, Ang.-Sax. *blǽwen*, light blue.

BOGGLE. *sb.* A goblin or spectre.
Welsh *bwg*, *bwgwl*.

BOGGLE. *vn.* To shy or swerve, as a horse.
Perhaps a frequentative from *bow* or *bog*, used in Old Eng. in the sense of bending one's steps—

"Heo *bugen* ut of France,
Into Burguine."—*Layamon.*

From this form *bow* or *bog*, (Ang.-Sax. *beogan*, *bugan*, to bend,) would be formed the frequent. *boggle*, conveying the idea of imperfectly or partly turning.

BOLDER or BOWDER. *sb.* A large stone rounded by the action of water. Old Norse *bylta*, to roll over and over, *böllr*, a globular body, as produced by rolling over. Dial.-Swed. *buller-sten*, a detached mass of stone, compares with our Bowderstone, a large detached stone in Borrowdale.

BOLDER. *sb.* A loud report.
Dan. *bulder*, noise, uproar, Dut. *bulderen*, to roar, as the wind, Old Fries. *bulder*, noise, bluster.

BOLY. *sb.* A horse with white legs and face.
Welsh *bal*, having a white mark on the forehead, *cefyl bal*, a horse with such mark. From the same origin are Ital. *balzano*, Fr. *balzan*, a horse with white legs, and Prov. Eng. *bawson*, a badger, from its white-streaked face.

BOMAN. *sb.* An imaginary person used to frighten children, Lonsd. *bo*, hobgoblin. Welsh *bo*, bugbear.

BONNY. *adj.* Handsome, pleasing. Used also ironically, as Eng. *pretty*. The etymology of this word, so universally prevalent throughout the North, is by no means clear. Johnson's derivation from Fr. *bon*. is altogether unsatisfactory. Rietz suggests a connection with Swed. *bonnt*, jolly, highspirited. Earle (*Philology of the English language*,) sets forth a theoretical Ang.-Sax. *bonig*. Compare also Welsh *bonneddig*, noble, genteel, which is not far removed in sense, and the change of which into *bondy* and then *bonny*, is easy and simple.

BOON-DAYS. *sb.* Days on which customary tenants are bound to work without pay for the lord of the manor. . Also gratuitous help given by neighbours on the occasion of a man's entering upon a new farm, &c. Old Norse *bôn*, Ang.-Sax. *bên*, prayer, petition. "In writing of the middle ages *bôn* occurs for tribute, as if a thing that was disliked could be rendered less obnoxious by the use of smoothe language."—*Ihre*.

BOOSE. *sb.* A stall for a horse or cow.
Ang.-Sax. *bôs*, Old Norse *bâs*, a stall, more particularly for a cow.

BOOZE. *sb.* A carouse, drinking-bout.
Derived by Wedg. from Dut. *buyzen*, to drink deeply, from *buyse*, a large flagon, Sco. *boss*, a jar or flagon, Old Fr. *bous*, grande bouteille.

BORRAN. *sb.* A cairn, large heap of stones.
Lonsd. *borrel*. Both are probably diminutives from Ang.-Sax. *beorg*, Old Norse *biarg*, mountain, hill, heap.

BOSS. *sb.* A milkmaid's cushion for the head.
Dut. *bos*, bunch, bundle, Germ. *bausch*, bunch, wisp of straw, cushion, Eng. *boss*, projection.

BOTCH. *sb.* A bungle.
The original idea seems to be simply that of mending. Ang.-Sax. *betan*, to repair, Swiss *batschen*, *patschen*, Eng. *patch*, Then that of clumsy or unskilful repair; and finally, that of general bungling.

BOTCHER. *sb.* A drink made by pouring water on the honey-comb after the honey has been extracted. Clev. *botchet*. A corruption of *braget*, from Wel. *bragod*, a fermented drink, *bragodi*, to ferment.

BOUN. *adj.* Ready, prepared, on the point of starting.
"As she was *boun* to go the way forth right
Toward the garden."—*Chaucer*.
Old Norse *bûinn*, prepared, ready, from the verb *bûa*, to prepare, set out.

BOURT. *vn.* To pretend, make believe.
Dut. *boerten*, to jest, sport, Bret. *bourd*, deceit, trick, Gael. *burt*, mockery.

BOWER. *sb.* A parlour.
Old Norse, Ang.-Sax. *bûr*, a chamber.

BRAFFAM, BRAUGHAM. *sb.* A collar for a horse.
Clev. *bargam*. Referred by Wedgwood with much probability to the same origin as the word *hamberwe*, or *hanaborough*, a

coarse horse-collar, made of reed or straw, from *berwe* or *borough*, protection from the *hames*, the two words of the compound being in this case reversed.

BRAID. *vn.* A cow is said to braid during parturition.
I apprehend from Old Norse *breida*, Ang.-Sax. *brǽdan*, to stretch, widen, expand.

BRAID. *vn.* To resemble, take after, used with a prep. *of* or *after*, "He braids o' me," he resembles me. Old Norse *bregda*, used with the prep. *til=to*, to turn out like another. *Honum bregdr til foreldris.* "He braids of his father."

BRAKE. *va.* To beat.
Ang.-Sax. *bracan*, to break or bruise.

BRAKESOUT. *sb.* Inflammatory fever in sheep.
Sco. *braik, braxy.* The former part of the word is from Ang.-Sax. *broc*, Suio-Goth. *brak*, sickness, distemper; the latter part from Ang.-Sax. *súht*, Old Norse *sótt*, disease.

BRANDRETH. *sb.* An iron frame for supporting the baking plate above the fire. Ang.-Sax. *brandred*, a gridiron, Old Norse *brandreith*, a grate, Germ. *brandruthe*, and-iron.

BRANDLING. *sb.* A small kind of trout.
Old Norse *branda*, a little trout. Comp. Manx *braddan*, salmon, perhaps radically allied.

BRANG. Brought, pret. of bring.

BRANK. *vn.* To hold the head affectedly and proudly.
Perhaps connected with Old Germ. *brangen*, Mod. Germ. *prangen*, Fris. *prunken*, to show off, make a parade, Old Norse *braka*, insolenter se gerere, Arm. *braga*, to strut.

BRAN-NEW. *adj.* Quite new.
More properly *brand-new*, new from the fire. So *span-new* and *splinter-new*, i.e., chip-new, new from the workman's tools, "referring in the one case to the newness of a metal instrument—in the other to that of something fashioned out of wood."—*Atk.*

BRANNIGAN. *sb.* A fat puffy infant boy.—*Dick.*
Gael. *brain*, large, big, *bronnach*, big-bellied.

BRANT, BRENT. *adj.* Steep, as applied to a hill.
Old Norse *brattr*, Swed. *brant*, steep.

Brash. *adj.* Rash, headlong.
    Gael. *bras*, hasty, rash, venturesome.

Brashy. *adj.* Weak, delicate, fragile.
    Old Norse *breyskr*, prop. brittle, but used metaph. to express weak or infirm. Gael. *brisg*, Arm. *bresk*, tender, fragile, from the same general root signifying to break.

Brass. *sb.* Impudence.
    Old Norse *brass*, procacitas, (properly *brast*, from the verb *brasta*, to bluster?) The noun is not in the Dict. of Cleasby.

Brat. *sb.* A coarse apron. Also a contemptuous term for a child. Wel. *brat*, a rag, Gael. *brat*, an apron, cloth, Ang.-Sax. *brat*, cloak, clout.

Brattle. *sb.* A loud rattle.
    Ang.-Sax. *brastl*, a noise, crackling.

Brave. *adj.* Worthy, excellent.
    Sco. *braw*. Old Swed. *braf*, Swed., Dan. *brav*, Dut. *braaf*, worthy, excellent, honest, Arm. *brav*, handsome, agreeable, Gael. *breagh*, Ir. *breag*, Fr. *brave*, spruce, fine. Our word would seem to have rather more affinity with the Teut., and the Sco. *braw* with the Celt; it is not easy, however, to define the separation between them.

Bray. *va.* To beat.
    Old Norse *braka*, to beat, subdue, Ang.-Sax. *bracan*, to pound, Dan. *brage*, to crush.

Brazzled or **Brizled.** *adj.* Scorched, applied to peas, scrambled for by boys. Ang.-Sax. *brastlian*, to burn, crackle.

Bread. To be in bad bread is to be out of favour.—*Dick.*
    Bread may perhaps be from Wel. *brawd*, Corn. *breuth*, Gael. *breith*, judgment, verdict, opinion.

Breck. *sb.* A piece of fun, an amusing occurrence, a practical joke. "Joe Tyson teem't a pint o' yal down Danny Towson's back. Wasn't that a *breck*?"—Heard by Mr. Gibson at Dean. Old Norse *brek*, explained by Cleasby as a fraudulent purchase of land, and in the plural as "freaks, especially of children." And certainly the *breck* above referred to is childish enough.

Breme. *vn.* To froth.
    Probably related to Old Norse *brim*, surf.

BREUKT. *adj.* Parti-coloured.
Thus a white sheep with black legs is a *breukt* sheep. Sco. *braikit* or *brocked*. Gael. *breac*, spotted, piebald. Fris. *broket*, *bruiket*, Dan. *broget*, variegated. The word might thus have either a Celtic or a Teutonic origin, though the latter seems preferable.

BRIDE-WAIN. *sb.* A festival held at a wedding, during which various games were held, and a subscription made for the young couple. The custom has become obsolete of late years. The *bride-wain* is properly the waggon on which the furniture and effects of the bride were carried, accompanied by a large cavalcade, to her new home.

BROACH. *sb.* A pin or spindle to wind yarn on. In Clev, also the spire or steeple of a church. The idea is that of something sharp-pointed, as found in Welsh *procio*, to stab, thrust, Gael. *brog*, to goad, prick, Fr. *broche*, spit, Eng. *broach*.

BROB or BROG. *sb.* A straw or twig, stuck in the hat or worn in the mouth, by those wanting to engage in service on the hiring-day, in token of their being open to an engagement. In Lonsd. small branches used to mark out lots of hay-grass, &c., at a sale. Vulg. Ir. *brob*, a straw, Welsh *brigwn*, twig, *brwg*, brushwood.

BROCK. *sb.* The badger.
Old Norse *brokkr*, Ang.-Sax. *broc*, Welsh, Corn., Arm. *broch*, Gael., Ir., Manx *broc*. The origin is the same as *breukt*, *q.v.*, in reference to the animals white-streaked face.

BROON-LEEMERS. *sb.* Nuts browned with ripeness, and ready to drop out of their husks. Atk. shows that *leam*, originally meaning to shine or glance as a ray of light, acquired in Old Eng. the sense of slipping or gliding. Hence *leemers* are "slippers," *i.e.*, out of their husks.

BROT. *sb.* Refuse corn, &c.
Old Norse *brot*, a broken piece, fragment, used especially in the plural. Hence *brot* is properly broken bits, from *briôta*, to break. Comp. Germ. *brack*, refuse, similarly derived from *brechen*, to break; and Clev. *brash*, refuse, from Ang.-Sax. *brysan*, to bruise.

BROT OUT. *vn.* Grain shed from over-ripeness is said to *brot out*. Old Norse *briôta*, to break, used with the preposition *ût*, like our *brot out*. The Ang.-Sax. *hreotan*, observes Cleasby, "was rarely used, and then only in the sense of destroy, demolish, whereas this word is common to all the Scan. dialects, and the Goth. *braican*, Germ. *brechen*, Eng. *break* is unknown to them." Hence this word may be taken to be one of those indicative of Scànd. influence in our district.

BROUGH, BUR, BRUFF. *sb.* A halo round the moon.
"Burwhe, sercle, orbiculus."—*Pr. Prv.* Atkinson's suggestion of Old Norse *baugr*, ring, *rosa-baugr*, a circle round the moon, seems to me less open to objection than he himself considers it. Both of the changes involved—the insertion of a phonetic *r*, and the change of *g* final into *f*, are of frequent occurrence.

BROWSE. *adj.* Crumbly, friable.
Dut. *broos*, brittle. The root is that of Ang.-Sax. *brysan*, Eng. *bruise*.

BRUSEY. *sb.* A coarse, fat person.
Wel. *brwyso*, to grow luxuriantly, *brwysg*, unwieldy, *brass*, coarse, fat.

BUCKLE. *sb.* Condition of body, state of health. To be in prime buckle = to be in first-rate condition. Old Norse *búkr*, Germ. *bauch*, trunk, body without the head.

BULE. *sb.* The bow of a basket or pan.
Germ. *bügel*, bow, any piece of wood or metal that is bent, Dan. *bugle*, *bule*, boss, dint.

BULLHEAD, POWHEAD. *sb.* The tadpole. These are only different forms of the same word, *pow=pull*. Welsh *pwl*, blunt, Gael. *poll-cheannan*, a tadpole. *Pole*, in *tadpole*, is the same word.

BULLISTER. *sb.* The fruit of the bullace-tree.
One might think that it was properly the tree itself—*bullis-ter*= bullace-tree. But the Gael. *buileastair*, bullace—the ending being apparently *tair*, worthless—seems to point to a different conclusion.

BULLSTANG. *sb.* The dragon-fly.
The Welsh name of the insect, *cwildraw*, derived by Owen from *cwil*, beetle, chafer, and *tarw*, bull, contains a similar allusion. So also the small beetle called the *lady-cow*, has a similar appellation both in French and German. There seems to be some ancient allusion to the bull or cow, the origin of which we know not. The latter part of the word may be from *stang*, a pole, in allusion to the unusual length of the insect's body. The other Welsh name of the insect, *gwäell-neidr*, from *gwäell*, skewer, spindle, knitting-needle, contains the same idea.

BULLYRAG. *vn.* To scold, to reproach.
May he from the same origin as *bully-rock*, a violent, overbearing person, which Wedg. refers to Low Germ. *buller-brook*, of same meaning. Dut. *bulderen*, to rage, scold, threaten, Swed. *buller*, noise, clamour.

BUMBLE-BEE. *sb.* The humble-bee.
Old Norse *bumla*, to buzz, Dut. *bommele*, drone.

BUMBLE-KITE or BUMMEL-KITE. *sb.* The bramble or black-berry. Haldorsen gives a verb *bumbla* (from *bumbr*, the belly), found only apparently in the phrase *bumbullt er hönum*, he has a pain in the stomach. Hence, *kite* meaning belly, *bumble-kite* might be that which gives the stomach-ache, referring to the effect produced by eating a quantity.

BUNNELS. *sb.* The dry hollow stems of the cow-parsnep and similar plants. Clev. *bun, bunnon*. Ang.-Sax. *buna*, cane, reed, pipe.

BUNSIN-COW. *sb.* A cow given to striking.
Dut. *bonzen*, to strike, Eng. *bounce*, of which the original meaning was to strike. A *bunsin cow*, then, is simply a *bouncing cow*, in the old sense of the word.

BUR-TREE, BUL-TREE, BOW-TREE. *sb.* The elder.
Sco. *bur-tree, bun-tree*. The various Teutonic names of this tree, Ang.-Sax. *ellarn*, Low Germ. *elloorn*, Germ. *hollder*, Dan. *hyld*, signify, according to Wedg., "hollow." To the same origin Atk. refers the *bur* or *bore-tree*, viz., Old Norse *bôra*, hole, boring, while the Sco. *bun* (Ang.-Sax. *buna*, cane, reed) still contains the same idea. Our form *bul* may also be from a similar origin, the root *bol* or *bul* signifying originally bubble. There is a tree called *börr* in the Edda, but of what sort does not appear.

BURLER. *sb.* The attendant who carries round the ale at the festivities in the Lake district. Ang.-Sax. *byrel*, Old Norse *byrlari*, ale-bearer, from *byrelian*, to give to drink, (from *eal*, ale, and *beran*, to carry?) The word is supposed by Cleasby to be of Ang.-Sax. introduction.

BUSK. *sb.* A bush.
"Nearly obsolete."—*Dick.* Old Norse *buskr*, Dan. *busk*.

BUT AND BEN. *sb.* The outer and the inner rooms of a farm-house, where there are only two. Used only on the Scottish border. Ang.-Sax. *butan*, without, and *binnan*, within.

BUTTS. *sb.* The short ridges approaching the corner of a ploughed field. Old Norse *butr*, Fris. *butt*, butt, stump, Welsh *pwt*, anything short and thick, Fr. *buter*, to touch at the end, to abut on.

BUTTY. *adj.* Thick at one end.
Prov. Germ. *buttig*, short and thick. See *butts*.

BUT-WELT. *va.* To turn the butt-ends of corn sheaves to the wind to dry. Ang.-Sax. *wæltan*, Old Norse *velta*, to roll or turn.

BYRE. *sb.* A cow-house.
The word by itself signifies simply room, building, Ang.-Sax. and Old Norse *búr*, and originally would have some prefix designating its purpose, as a cow-byre, &c.

BYSPELL. *adj.* Mischievous, full of vice.
The form *byspelt*, given by Brockett, is a nearer approach to the right one, if the word be, as seems probable, properly *be-spilt*, from Ang.-Sax. *spilt*, corrupted, depraved, from *spillan*, to corrupt, the prefix being the Ang.-Sax. *be*, as in *benumbed*, *begirt*, not, in these cases, adding to, or altering the sense. Or, if we might suppose it to have been originally a noun, we may think of Dut. *byspel*, exemplum, proverbium, in a sense like *bisen*, of an example to be avoided.

C.

CAD. *vn.* To mat or felt together.
Thus matted or tangled hair is *caddit*. I take it to be from the Welsh *cyddio*, to join, connect, couple, from *cyd*, *cym*, signifying combination, and cognate with Lat. *cum*, *com*, *con*, Teut. *sam*, *Cad* or *cat* is an older Celtic form, (*Zeuss*, Gramm. Celt.), now found only in some compounds, as Welsh *cad-blyg* = Lat. complic(atio). A Gaelic form is *coimh*, which we seem to have in our word *cumm't*, curdled, applied to milk. The corresponding Teutonic *sam* is similarly used as a verb in the Northern district, as in Clev. *sam*, to compress or knead together, Crav. *sam*, to collect or gather together.

CADGER. *sb.* A dealer in small articles going about with a cart. Referred by *Jam.* to Dut. *katsen*, to run, or cause to run about. *Atk.* also notes Old Norse *kiagga*, to move as one does under a burden. There is also a third derivation which occurs to me as feasible. "I may observe," says *Jam.*, "that in Scotland *cadger* more properly denotes a fish-carrier." So *Brockett* observes that "persons who bring fish from the sea to the Newcastle market are still called *cadgers.*" Now if we can suppose this to have been the original meaning of the word, we may refer to Germ. and Dut. *kaag*, a sloop or small vessel, and to *kedger*, used in Yorkshire for a fisherman. A *cadger* would in that case be one who bought fish from the *cadge* or fishing-boat, and retailed it over the country.

CAFF. *sb.* Chaff.
Ang.-Sax. *ceaf*, Germ. *kaff*, Dut. *kaf.*

CALEVINE. *sb.* A black-lead pencil.
Sco. *keelivine, guillivine. Killow* or *collow* was a word formerly used in Cumberland for black-lead, and is still, according to Halliwell, in Northumberland. It is probably allied to *collow*, an old word for black or smut; also perhaps to Eng. *coal*, the root-meaning being probably black. Comp. Sansc. *kala*, black, with which Benfey collates Gr. $\kappa\eta\lambda\iota\varsigma$, smut, and Lat. *caligo*, darkness. Comp. also *kohl*, a pigment used in the East for blackening the inside of the eyelid. The Old Norse *kâla, quola*, to dirty, make black, is probably the word more immediately connected. The latter part of the word, *vine*, may be from Welsh *gweinio*, to put in a sheath, a *calevine* pencil being thus a pencil of black-lead sheathed in wood.

CAMBREL, CAMMAREL. *sb.* The hough of a horse.
Also a crooked frame for hanging carcases on. *Wedg.* refers it to Welsh *cambren*, a crooked stick, a frame for hanging meat on, from *cam*, crooked.

CAMPLE. *vn.* To argue, reply impertinently.
A frequentative from Ang.-Sax. *campian*, Dut. *kampen*, to fight, contend.

CANNY, CONNY. *adj.* Agreeable, pleasant, sensible, careful, well-behaved. This word, in the North, as in Scotland, has a great variety of meanings. *Jam.* produces no fewer than eighteen; but the general scope of the word is something combining agreeableness of disposition with propriety and carefulness. The Old Norse *kænn*, peritus, solers, covers a good deal of its meaning, while the noun *kænska*, comis sapientia, pleasant good sense, gives as close an equivalent as can be found. *Atk.*, however, separates *canny* and *conny*, giving the latter rather the sense of personal beauty, and referring it to Dan. *kjon*, pretty. Moreover, the Gaelic *cannach*, kind, pretty, comely, and Ir. *caoin*, good-tempered, agreeable, are words for which a claim might be put in.

CAP. *va.* To excel, to be pre-eminent, whence CAPPER, one who takes the lead of his fellows. Old Norse *kappa*, to strive, contend, Jutl. *kappi*, a champion.

CARL. *sb.* A coarse and rough fellow.
Old Norse, Dan., Swed. *karl*, Ang.-Sax. *ceorl*, a man, male, old man. As *churl* represents the Ang.-Sax., so *carl* the Scand. form, both in a derogatory sense.

CARLINGS. *sb.* Grey peas soaked in water, and eaten on Care-Sunday, whence probably the name.

CARR. *sb.* A flat, marshy hollow.
Old Norse *kjarr*, Suio-Goth. *kærr*, Dan. *kær*, a marshy place.

CAT-TALK. *sb.* Small-talk, chit-chat.
It seems probable that *cat* is the same as *chat*, especially if that word be, as Skinner has it, from the French. In the dialect of Picardy, whence most of our French was derived, a hard *c* generally corresponds to the soft *ch* of ordinary French.

CAT-MALLISON. *sb.* A dog given to worrying cats.
Old Fr. *malison*, a curse.

CAWKERS. *sb.* The irons on the toe and heel of a clog or wooden-soled shoe. Comp. Lat. *calceus*, shoe, *caliga*, half-boot worn by soldiers and studded with large clumsy nails called *caligares*. Also Lanc. *coaken*, a blow from a horse's shoe, Dan. *kok*, hammer, &c.

CHAFTS. *sb.* The jaws.
Old Norse *kiaftr*, Suio-Goth. *kaft*, Dan. *kiaft*. In Denmark the word is vulgarly used for a person, *ikke en kiaft*, not a person.

CHAP. *sb.* A male, man or boy.
From *chaft* or *chap*, similarly (see above) used in Denmark.

CHATS. *sb.* Small branches only fit for fuel, and metaphorically applied to stripling youths. The original sense of the word, which is common, with slight variations, to several dialects, is that of young shoots. Ang.-Sax. *cith*, a young tender shoot, Swiss *kide*, twig, Prov. Eng. *chits*, the first sprouts of anything, Dut. *keesten*, to sprout. The word *chat* is applied to a boy, as elsewhere *chit* to a girl, in the same sense as when we speak of a sprig of nobility.

CHEG. *vb.* To chew, champ with the teeth.
Comp. A.S. *ceac*, Swed. *kek*, jaw, Welsh *ceg*, mouth; *cegu*, to mouth.

CHERTS. *sb.* The first blades of grass in spring.
Properly, I think, *cheets* or *chits*, tender shoots, "the firs sprouts of anything."—*Hall.* See *chats.*

CHIBIES. *sb.* Onions.
Fr. *cive*, a leek, Lat. *cepa*, onion, Ang.-Sax. *cipe*, onion, Welsh *cibellys*, chive garlic. This may be a word of the class referred to by Dr. Guest (*Phil. Soc.* iii. 169) as probably derived by our ancestors from the Romans through the Celts, prior to the Saxon settlement in the British Isles.

CHIEL, CHIELY. *sb.* Fellow, companion, generally used with more or less of familiarity, and with a sense of waggery.
" Play up, old *chiel*, a rantin' reel."—Upshot, *Lonsdale.*

Gael. and Ir. *ceile*, Corn. *cele*, Manx *cheilley*, Welsh *gilydd* and obsolete *cilyd*, fellow, companion, the root of which is found in Sansc. *kil*, to bind. The origin of this word seems to have escaped the observation of Jamieson.

CHIGGLE. *vn.* To cut wood, &c., unskilfully.
Perhaps formed as a frequentative from *chick*, which, originally derived from the sound of a blow or crack, acquired in Old Eng. the sense of crack, flaw.—*Wedg.* Comp. also Fr. *chiqueter*, to cut, gash, hag.

CHILLIPERS. *sb.* Nuts or small coal.
Perhaps from Welsh *chwilfriwio*, to shatter, break to pieces.

CHIP. *va.* To trip up, a term used in wrestling.
Old Norse *kippa*, to trip up, Germ. *kippen*, to tip over.

CHIP. *sb.* The various modes of throwing an adversary in wrestling are called *chips*. See above. Comp. also Welsh *chwip*, a quick flirt or turn.

CHIRM. *vn.* To chirp.
Ang.-Sax. *cyrman*, to cry, scream.

CHOCK-FULL. *adj.* Full to the top.
Swab. *schoch*, a heap, *g'schochet voll*, chock-full, full to overflowing.—*Wedg.*

CHOOP. *sb.* The fruit of the wild rose.
Norw. *kjupa*, another form of Ang.-Sax. *hiop*, Eng. *hip.*

CHOWL. *sb.* The fleshy part of the cheek.
Ang. Sax. *coole*, Gael., Ir. *giull*, cheek, jaw.

CHUNS. *sb.* The sprouts of the potato.
Seemingly referable to Goth. *kuni*, Old High Germ. *chunni*, Old Sax. *kunni*, Ang.-Sax. *cyn*, race, family, offspring, the root-word of which signifies to beget or produce. The Welsh *chwyn*, a weed, in the sense of something springing up of itself, may be related.

CHUNTER. *vn.* To murmur, mutter inaudibly.
Probably formed from *cutter*, to whisper low, with the introduction of the nasal, to express the idea of a dull, muffled sound. Similarly *clanter* from *clatter*.

CHUR. *sb.* The subdued growl of the dog. Also the note of the fern-owl or night-jar. Old Norse *kurra*, to murmur, Dut. *kirren*, Norw. *kurra*, to coo, as a dove. Comparing the Suio-Goth. *kuttra*, it seems rather probable that the Old Norse *kurra*, and the other verbs referred to, are a contracted form of it. Compare our *cuttery-coo*, the note of the dove.

CLAG. *vn.* To stick to, adhere, as a viscid substance.
Old Norse *kleggi*, a close or compressed mass, Dan. *klæg*, viscid, sticky, Ang.-Sax. *clæg*, clay.

CLAM. *vn.* To satiate, to cloy.—*Dick.* To starve with hunger.—*West. and Cumb. Dial.* Clev. to pinch, compress. The last is the original meaning, from Old Norse *klemma*, Suio-Goth. *klæmma*, Germ. *klemmen*, to compress. It is curious that the same word should have acquired, in our district, the sense both of repletion and starvation, starting from the same original idea of pinching or compressing.

CLAMMER. *sb.* A yoke for the neck of a cow, to prevent her leaping hedges. Germ. *klammer*, a cramp, brace, hold-fast, from *klemmen*, to compress.

CLANTER or CLONTER. *vn.* Applied chiefly to the noise made by the iron-bound *clogs* worn by the Cumbrians. Apparently formed from *clatter*, with the introduction of the nasal to express a rather duller sound than *clatter*. So *chunter* from *cutter*. Comp. also Dut. *klant*, clod.

CLAP-BREAD. *sb.* Oaten or other cakes beat or *clapped* out with the hand. Dan. *klappe-bröd*, thin cakes beaten out with the hand.

CLART. *sb.* Dirt of an adhesive character, anything sticky. Formed like *slair*, *glair*, words of a similar meaning in the Northern dialects, upon Old Norse *leir*, mud, mire, which we may trace through the Welsh *llai*, mud, to Sansc. *li*, liquescere.

CLASH. *sb.* Idle gossip. Also a tale-bearer, scandal-monger. Vulg. Germ. *klatsche,* a gossip, tale-bearer.

CLAT. *sb.* Has both the two meanings of the above *clash.* Clev. *clat,* to chatter or prate. Comp. Old Norse *klid,* garritus. Sansc. *clad,* to resound.

CLAVER. *vn.* To climb. Or rather to clamber or scramble, the idea of both hands and feet being involved. Old Norse *klifra,* manibus et pedibus clivum ascendere, Dan. *klavre,* to clamber.

CLECKIN or CLEEKIN. *sb.* A brood of chickens, &c. Clev. *cletch.* Old Norse *klekja,* to sit, as a bird. Dan. *klække.*

CLEG. *sb.* The common horse-fly.
Old Norse *kleggi,* Norw. *klegg,* horse-fly. From the sense of sticking. See *clag.*

CLEPS. *sb.* Tongs for pulling up weeds.
Lonsd. *clip,* to clasp. Ang.-Sax. *clyppan,* Old Norse *klipa,* to grip, catch.

CLEUGH (*pron.* CLEUF). *sb.* A cleft or ravine.
Ang.-Sax. *clough,* a cleft, Old Norse *kleyf,* fissura rupium.

CLIART. *adj.* Having the lungs adhering to the ribs (of cattle). The word would seem to be the same as Sco. *clyred,* having tumours in the flesh, Dut. *klier,* a hard swelling, though the word has acquired with us a somewhat different meaning.

CLICK. *va.* To snatch sharply.
Thus, in reference to three tributaries of the Eden, a Cumberland rhyme says metaphorically,

"Eamont, Croglin, and Cockley Beck,
Eden *clicks* them a' by the neck."

The origin is not very clear. Comparing Fris. *klick,* verber, ictus (*Kil.*), Fr. *claque,* East. *click,* a blow (*Hall.*), it might seem that the original meaning was that of striking. Atkinson, however, takes a different view, citing the Jutl. *klække ved,* to stick tight to, hold fast by, as closely resembling the use of our word, especially in the phrase *click hod.*

CLINK. *sb.* A blow. Also a jingling sound.
Dut. *klinken,* to sound, tinkle, *klinkslag,* a blow with the hand.

CLIP. *va.* To shear sheep.
Old Norse *klippa,* Dan. *klippe,* to cut, clip.

CLOCK-HEN. *sb.* A hen about sitting.
Dut. *klok-hen,* a brooding-hen.

CLOCK. *sb.* A general name for a beetle, as a black-clock, water-clock, &c. Sco. *golach,* used precisely in the same manner. Old Norse *klûka,* a beetle (in *brunn-klûka,* the dytiscus or water-clock), Swed. *klocka,* an ear-wig, Mid. High Germ. *kuleich,* Bav. *kieleck,* a beetle. Jamieson has *forchargollach,* an ear-wig, as a Gaelic word, and in the Dict. of the Highland Soc. I find *collag-lion* with the same meaning. There seems no doubt that these, Celtic and Teutonic, are all different forms of one original word, but while the Sco. *golach* seems to be from the Gaelic, our *clock* seems most probably of Scandinavian origin.

CLOG. *sb.* A shoe with soles of wood plated with iron, in common use in Cumberland. *Wedg.* refers it to *clog* in the sense of a block or clumsy piece of wood, and compares it with Germ. *klotz-schuh,* Dan. *klods,* a clog or wooden shoe. In like manner, from Ital. *zocco,* a log, *zoccoli,* clogs, pattens.

CLOOT or CLOUT. *sb.* A blow, buffet.
Dut. *kloteren,* to strike.

CLOT. *sb.* A clod.
Dut. *klot,* globus, Fries. *klot,* clod.

CLOT-BUR. *sb.* The burdock.
Clote, Chauc. and Pr. Prv. Ang.-Sax. *clate,* Germ. *klette,* Dut. *klissen,* a bur, Fries. *borre, burre,* Dan. *borre,* a bur. The word then would seem to contain a reduplication.

CLOTCH. *va.* To shake roughly.
Germ. *klitschen,* to flap, clash, slap, Dut. *klutsen,* to beat together, as eggs.

CLOT-HEAD. *sb.* A blockhead, clod-poll.
Germ. *klozs-kopf,* a clod-pate.

CLOWE. *va.* To scratch, beat.
Dut. *klouwen,* to beat soundly.

CLUDDER. *vn.* To crowd together.
Dut. *klotteren,* to coagulate. Comp. also Welsh *cluder,* heap.

CLUNCH. *sb.* A heavy, stupid person.
Dut. *klonte,* clod, Swed. *kluns,* lump, Germ. *klunker,* clod.

COBBY. *adj.* Headstrong, obstinate.
Dut. *koppig,* obstinate.

COB. *va.* To beat or thump.
: Welsh *cobio*, to beat.

COBBLE, COBBLE-STONE. *sb.* A rounded stone such as are used for paving. Norw. *koppel*, a cobble or round stone. Old Norse *koppu-steinn*, a boulder.

COCK-LOFT. *sb.* The top garret.
: Welsh *coeglofft*, a garret, from *coeg*, empty.
: "See dancin' we'd hev i' th' *cock-loft*."—*Anderson*.
: The cock-loft, as an available empty room, is often used for dancing.

COCKLY. *adj.* Shaky, unsteady, easily moved.
: Lanc. *kegly*. Brockett gives also the form *cogly*. Old Norse *kogla*, Germ. *kugeln*, to roll, Dan. *kugle*, Germ. *kugel*, a ball. Dan. *kegle*, nine-pin. Welsh *gogi*, to move, to shake.

COD. *sb.* A pillow or cushion.
: Old Norse *koddi*, Swed. *kudde*, a cushion, Ang.-Sax. *codd*, a bag.

COCKS-WUNTERS. A clipped oath, God's wonders.

CODDLE. *va.* To clasp in the arms, to embrace.
: I am disposed to connect our word with Welsh *cydio*, to join, to couple, from *cyd*, *cyf*, *cym*, combination, other and older Celtic forms of which are *cad* and *cod*, the latter found in Welsh *codi*, a concubine (if we may trust *Bullet*). From the form *cod* would, as a frequentative, come *coddle*.

COLLOPS. *sb.* Sliced pieces of meat.
: Suio-Goth. *kollops*, slices of meat softened by beating before cooking, the origin of which may be found in Prov. Germ. *klopps*, a dish of meat made tender by beating, from *klopfen*, to beat.

COLERAKE or COWLRAKE. *sb.* An iron scraper.
: Coole-rake.—*Pr. Prv.* See *cowl*.

CON. *sb.* A squirrel's nest.
: Lonsd. the squirrel itself. It would seem rather probable, from the Welsh *cont*, tail, that there has been some such Celtic word for the squirrel.

COOMB. *sb.* A hollow place surrounded by hills.
: Ang.-Sax. *comb*, a valley, probably adopted from the Celtic. Welsh *cwm*.

COO-CLAP. *sb.* The firm dung of the cow.
: Welsh *clap*, mass, lump.

Coo-swat. *sb.* The semi-fluid dung of the cow.
Lonsd. *coo-squat.* Dial. Dan. *squatte,* to spirt, splash, *squat,* a slop. In Derbyshire *squat* signifies to spot with dirt.

Coo-plat. *sb.* The same as *coo-swat.*
Dial. Dan. *ko-blat,* from *blat,* drop, blot.

Cop. *sb.* Top, peak.
Ang.-Sax. *copp,* Germ. *kopf,* Welsh *cop,* head, top.

Coppy-stool. *sb.* A small round stool.
Derives its name, like cup, Ang.-Sax. *copp,* from its round form.

Copt. *adj.* Pert, set up, saucy.
Lonsd. *cop,* to be saucy. Dut. *koppig,* self-willed, Fin. *kopeen,* to be conceited or set up.

Corby. *sb.* The carrion-crow.
Fr. *corbeau.* See *gorlin.*

Corker. *sb.* Something very appropriate to the point, a settler. Perhaps from the idea of corking up, settling the matter. Or possibly from Welsh *corc,* compact, neat, smart, whence *corcen,* a smart girl.

Corp. *sb.* A corpse.
Gael. and Ir. *corp,* Welsh *corff,* corpse, body, Lat. *corpus,* Sansc. *garbhas.*

Cot. *vn.* "To wait upon a sick person, to saunter about home."—*Dick.* Clev. *cot,* "to cook for one's self, to do one's own household work." *Atk.* refers it to the same source as O. N. *kot-karl,* a poor cottager, Dial. Swed. *kutur,* a poor lodger in a cottage, one who has to do everything for himself.

Cotter. *vn.* To entangle, mat together.
Wedg. collates a number of words in which *cot* has the sense of something matted or clotted. I think that the origin is to be found in Old Celt. *cat, cod, cot,* Welsh *cyd.* See *cad.*

Cottit. *adj.* Short-tempered.
Apparently from Welsh *cwt,* Corn. *cot, cut,* short.

Coup. *vb.* To barter, to exchange.
Old Norse *kaupa,* to traffic, to barter. Germ. *haufen,* to purchase.

Coup. *va.* and *n.* To upset, overturn. Also to fall.
Atk. thinks that from the sense of exchanging, that is, of one dealer turning over articles to another, comes the sense of a literal turning or upsetting. But it is certainly a re-

versal of the ordinary process to derive a direct sense from a metaphorical one, and if the two words are the same, the sense of falling or upsetting must be the original one. Now Cleasby connects Old Norse *kaupa*, to traffic, to barter, with Goth. *kaupatjan*, to strike in the face. " The bargain was symbolised by striking; hence to *strike* a bargain." Comparing Goth. *kaupatjan* with Gr. κυπτω, pronus sum, inclino me, it seems probable that even the sense of striking is not the original one, but rather that of falling, as in the Greek above, in Sansc. *kûp*, to fall, Lat. *cubo*, Gael. *cub*, to crouch, bend, lie down, and in our *coup*. And that the Germ. *kippen*, to tip over, upset, and Old Norse *kippa*, to trip up, are probably modified forms of that lost verb from which our word is more immediately derived.

COUP. *sb.* A small country cart.
From its being emptied by *couping* or being tilted up. Germ. *kip-karren*, a tilting cart.

COW. *va.* To subdue, bring under restraint.
Old Norse *kuga*, Dan. *kue*, to restrain, subdue.

COWDY. *adj.* Frolicsome, in high spirits.
Old Norse *kâtr*, Dan. *kaad*, wanton, frolicsome.

COWK or GOWK. *sb.* The core, as of an apple.
Ang.-Sax. *geolca*, yolk, as of an egg.

COWL. *vb.* To rake together.
Sansc. *kul*, to gather together, Fr. *cueillir*. The above show the connections of our word, though its more immediate parentage cannot be traced, if it be not directly from the French.

COW'T COW, COWIE. *sb.* A cow without horns.
Cow't is properly *cowl't*, Clev. *cowl*, to clip or cut short. Old Norse *kollôtr*, without horns, docked, Suio-Goth. *kulla*, to clip or cut. And *cowie* corresponds with Old Norse *kollr*, a ram without horns, Swed. *kullig*, hornless.

COW'T DYKE. *sb.* An earthen fence without growing wood. Properly *cowl't dyke*. See above.

COW'T-LORD. *sb.* A pudding made of oatmeal and lumps of suet. *Cowde*, a lump, occurs in the *Pr. Prv.* It seems to be connected with Old Norse *hula*, a lump. Or perhaps, rather, with the corresponding verb, as a past part., signifying lumped. The latter part of the word may be *lard*, suet, *cow't-lord* then signifying lumped suet,

COWPRESS. *sb.* A wooden lever.
Properly *cowl-press*, from, according to *Atk.*, Old Norse *kylfa*, Germ. *keule*, a strong, thick stick (as used for a lever), and Old Norse *pressa*, Eng. *press*. Comp. also Gael. *cuaill*, Wel. *cogail*, cudgel, truncheon.

CRACK. *vn.* To boast. Also to tell stories and generally to converse. The former sense, which is common to various dialects, and found also in Early Eng., is the original one. From *crack*, in the sense of a loud report. So Fr. *craquer* was used in a similar sense, se vanter mal a-propos et faussement.—*Menage.*

CRAD, CRADAGH. *sb.* A troublesome child.
Seems to be connected with Gael. *cradh*, to vex, torment.

CRAG. *sb.* The face or countenance.
"A word of the mountain vales."—*Dick.* From the example which he gives,—"He hung a lang *crag* when t' news com,"—it may be taken to mean more especially jaw. Welsh *crogen*, jaw, from *crogi*, to hang.

CRAMMEL. *vn.* To walk with difficulty, or as if the feet were sore. Germ. *krabbeln*, Dan. *kravle*, to scramble. A similar interchange of *m* with *b* or *f* is seen in Eng. *scramble*, Cumb. *scraffle*. It seems probable that our *crammel* represents the word on which, by the prefix of *s*, is formed Eng. *scramble*.

CRANKY. *adj.* Ailing, infirm.
Old Norse *krankr*, Dan., Swed., Germ. *krank*, sick, feeble.

CRANKY. *adj.* Checked, applied to the linen material formerly extensively used for shirts, aprons, &c. The idea is that of bending at right angles. Old Norse *krækia*, deviare, Dut. *krinkelen*, to turn, to bend, *kringelig*, full of turnings.

CREE. *va.* To crush, to bruise.
Fris. *kröge*, Dan. *kroye*, to crush.

CREEL. *sb.* An old-fashioned horse-pannier, a wicker basket used by fishermen. Gael. *criol*, Ir. *kril*, a basket or coffer. Old Norse *krili*, basket, from *krila*, to plait, to weave.

CREWEL. *vb.* To cover a ball with parti-coloured worsted. Properly *crewel* is a ball of worsted. Germ. *knäuel*, Low Germ. *klevel*, a ball of thread. The interchange of liquids in this class of words is very common.—*Wedg.*

CRINE. *va.* To scorch, shrivel.
Welsh *crino*, Gael. *crion*, to wither, dry up.

CRINKELTY-CRANKELTY. *adv.* Very crooked, full of twistings. Dan. *kringel*, crooked, Dut. *krinkelig*, full of turnings.

CROBBEK or CROVVIK. *sb.* A disease of the stomach in cattle, occasioned by change of pasture. Probably *crop-vik*, from *crop*, the stomach, and Old Norse *vig*, wound, hurt.

CROBS, CROB-LAMBS. *sb.* The worst of the flock.
One might think of Eng. *scrub*, in the sense of something worthless, Dan. *skrab*, scrapings, trash. Or the sense may be that of feebleness and decrepitude, derived from shrivelling or crookedness, as Welsh *crab*, wrinkle, *crebach*, shrunk, withered, Gael. *crub*, to crouch, *cruban*, crooked creature.

CROCK. *sb.* An old ewe.
Gael. *crog*, a ewe past bearing, *crogan*, a shrivelled old woman, Eng. *crone* (which also means an old ewe). The root is probably the same as that of *cranky*, ailing, infirm, Sansc. *krik*, to become thin or lean.

CROFT. *sb.* A field or inclosure near a house.
Ang.-Sax. *croft*, a small inclosed field.

CROFUL. *sb.* A very lean person is said not to have a "*croful* of flesh" upon him.—*Dick.* I take it to mean handful, from Gael. *crog.* hand, paw, a word generally used, as in the present case, with something of a contemptuous sense.

CROOSE or CROWSE. *adj.* Brisk, lively.
Jamieson suggests Suio-Goth. *krus,* Germ. *kraus,* signifying curled, comatus, as the origin of this word. Ihre gives Suio-Goth. *krauskopff,* literally "curled-head," as denoting an irritable or excitable person.

CROP. *sb.* The stomach.
Old Norse *kroppr*, the trunk, body without the head. Probably formed by metath. from *corp*. Ir. *corp,* Lat. *corpus,* Sansc. *garbhas.*

CROTTLES. *sb.* Small lumps.
Sco. *crote*, the smallest particle. Welsh *crwd*, a round lump, whence also Fr. *crottes*, the globular droppings of sheep. From the same general origin as *curds* or *cruds, crowdy,* &c. Old Norse *gru, kru,* crowd.

CROWDY. *sb.* Oatmeal mixed with the fat of broth.
Suio-Goth. *grod*, Old Norse *grautr*, porridge made of meal and water, Ang.-Sax. *grut*, meal, Welsh *crwd*, a round lump.

CROWKINS. *sb.* Greaves from melted fat.
Probably for *crowdkins.* See *crowdy.*

CRUD. *sb.* Curd, of which it is the older form.
"*Cruddes* of mylke."—*Palsg.* See *crottles* and *crowdy.*

CRUNE. *sb.* The subdued roar of the bull.
Sco. *crune* "signifies the murmuring or groaning noise made when they want food, are pained, or dissatisfied on what account soever."—*Jam.* Dut. *kreunen*, to groan, to whimper.

CUM-METHER. *sb.* A god mother.
Sco. *cummer*, gossip, companion. Jamieson refers to Fr. *commere*, god-mother. Comparing the Ang.-Sax. *cum-pæder* (*cum-fæder ?*), god-father, ours seems a different word, from Ang.-Sax. *cuma*, comer, stranger.

CUMM'T MILK. *sb.* Milk curdled with rennet, and seasoned with spices.—*Dick.* Lanc. *cummed milk.* From Gael. *coimh*, Ir. *coim*, signifying combination, corresponding with Lat. *cum*, Welsh *cyd*, *cym*, and Teut. *sam*, the idea being that of coagulation. Thus our *cummed* milk corresponds with the Yorks. *sammed* milk, the one being a Celtic, and the other a Teutonic form of the same original word.

CURROCK. See *kirrock.*

CUSH! CUSH! *intj.* A call note for cattle.
Old Norse, Fris. *küs! küs!* similarly used. See *cushie.*

CUSHIE. *sb.* A pet or familiar name for a cow.
Old Norse *kussa*, Icel. *kusa*, "a colloquial diminutive, frequent in modern use."—*Cleasby.* Hence the call "*cush, cush.*"

CUTS. *sb.* Small pieces of straw or paper of different lengths used in drawing lots. "Cut or Lote."—*Pr. Prv.* Welsh *cwtws*, lots.

CUTTER. *vn.* To whisper, talk softly.
"I' th' pantry the sweet-hearters *cuttered* queyte soft."
Anderson.
Suio-Goth. *kuttra*, to chatter, Swed. *kuttra*, to talk low and in secret. A frequentative form of Dut. *kouten*, Ang.-Sax. *cwêthan*, &c., to talk.

CUTTY. *adj.* Short.
Welsh *cwt*, Corn. *cot, cut*, Gael., Ir. *cutach*, short.

CWOLY, COLIE. *sb.* A shepherd's dog.
Sco. *collie.* Gael. *cuilean*, dog, hound. Properly an appellative, it is used, like Tray, as a proper name.

"If hares were as plenty as hops,
I durstn't fell yan for my life, man,
Nor tak't out o' auld Cwoley's chops."—*Miss Blamire.*

So in *Chaucer—*

"Ran *Col* our dog, and Talbot, and Gerlond."

Similarly, it seems to me by no means improbable that Tray, now preserved only as a proper name, and that more especially in legend or poetry, may have been an ancient appellative, signifying runner, from Sansc. *trag*, Gr. τρεχω, Goth. *thragian*, to run, and of which also in the Celtic branch a trace is found in the obs. Ir. *traig*, Gael. *troigh*, foot. We find from Martial that *vertragus* (in some editions incorrectly *vertagus*) was the name of a hound imported from Britain—

"Non sibi, sed domino, venatur *vertragus* acer,
Illæsum leporem qui tibi dente feret."

And also Arrian (De Venat.) remarks that swift-footed dogs were called in Britain *ouertragoi*. Gluck explains *vertrag* as swift-footed, from *trag*, as above, and the intensitive particle *ver, gwer*, present Welsh *gor*. If we might suppose the prefix to be the same word as the Welsh *guare*, Corn. *gware*, to play, sport, it would give to *vertrag* the appropriate meaning of a "sporting dog," suggesting the possibility of a word *trag*, whence possibly our *Tray*—for a dog in general.

D.

DADDER, DIDDER, DODDER. *vn.* To shake, tremble, shiver. "Dyderyn for colde."—*Pr. Prv.* "A'll tak sum o' that *dadderin'* stuff," Mr. Gibson heard a Cumberland youth say at a supper table, indicating at the same time a shape of jelly. Old Norse *datta*, to vibrate, Germ. *zittern*, Dut. *sitteren*, Old Norse *titra*, to shiver.

DAFFIN. *vb.* Joking, bantering.
The sense of folly enters conspicuously into our word, which seems to be from the verb *daff*, explained by Jamieson as "to

be foolish." Clev. *daff* means also coward, dastard. Old Norse *daufr*, deaf, stupid, *deyfa*, to make blunt, to stupify, Dut. *dof*, dull, Old Norse *tæpr*, imperfectus, cui aliquid deest, *Gud. And*.

DAFT. *adj.* Simple, half-witted, stupid, or foolish.
Ath. takes *daft* to be the past part. of the above verb *daff*. Comp. also Swed. *tafatt*, stupid, awkward, Bav. *täppet*, foolish, Old Swed. *tafatt*, adv. inepte, the adj. being probably lost.

DAGGY. *adj.* Drizzly.
Clev. *dag* or *deg*, to drizzle. Old Norse *deigr*, moist. "In Iceland," observes Cleasby, "as applied to the weather, it implies less than wet and more than damp." This is exactly the meaning it has with us."

DALE (pron. *deall*). *sb.* Valley.
Ang.-Sax. *dâl*, Old Norse *dalr*, Germ. *thal*. The origin is Ang.-Sax. *dêlan*, Old Norse *deila*, to divide, separate, in reference to the valleys as divisions between the mountains. *Dale*, observes Menage, has still in Normandy the meaning of a channel, gutter, or trough, through which water is carried away, which—the dale forming the channel by which the water is carried away from the mountains—he takes to be a relic of the Scand. *dalr*. But it seems rather to be a relic of another Northern word *dæla*, a kind of groove through which the bilge water is carried out of a ship, present Norw, *döla*, a groove-formed trough, eaves, a trench.

DALES-MEN. *sb.* The inhabitants of the dales.
"Icelanders say *dala-menn*, 'dales-men,' as in Eng. lake district."—*Cleasby*.

DANDER. *vn.* To hobble, to wander listlessly.
Sco. *dander*, *dandill*, to saunter. Germ. *tândeln*, to trifle, loiter.

DALLY. *sb.* A tee-totum.
Old Eng. *daly*, a plaything, from Lat. *talus*, the ankle-bone of animals, then a die to play with.—*Wedg.*

DANDER. *sb.* Passion, excitement. A person in a passion is said to have his *dander* up. Perhaps, along with *tantrum*, from Welsh *tant*, spasm, throb, the idea of which seems to be tension, *tannu*, to stretch, throb.

DANG. *va.* To strike, thrust, push.
Dynge.—*P. Pl.* Old Norse *dengja*, Swed. *dänga*, to bang, thump.

DARK. *vn.* To lurk, listen in the background.
Sco. *darn*, to hide, conceal. Old Eng. *dare*, to lie quiet and still. I rather think that our word may be a corruption of one or other of the above, formed from a striving after a meaning when the original word came to be forgotten. The Sco. *darn* is from Ang.-Sax. *dearnen*, to hide; the Old Eng. *dare* Wedg. connects with Low Germ. *bedaren*, to be still and quiet.

DAVE. *va.* To soothe, assuage.
Suio-Goth. *dofwa*, to benumb, deaden, Swed. *döfva*, to mitigate, alleviate.

DAWD, DODE. *sb.* A lump of anything.
Old Eng. *dot*, a small lump. Fris. *dodd*, a lump.

DAZED. *adj.* Benumbed, stupified. Also as applied to pastry, half-baked. Old Norse *dasadr*, exhausted, worn out, Ang.-Sax. *dwæs*, Dut. *dwaas*, dull, heavy. As applied to pastry the sense is that of heaviness.

DEAL or DALT. *sb.* A share in common land.
Ang.-Sax. *dæl*, Old Norse *deild*, a share or division, Ang.-Sax. *dælan*, Old Norse *deila*, to divide. Menage remarks that *dale* and *delle* are still used in Normandy to denote a certain measure of land, no doubt a relic of the Northmen.

DEEF. *adj.* Applied to light grain, also to unproductive land. Ang.-Sax. *deaf-corn*, barren corn, Suio-Goth. *dauf jord*, unproductive land. The word, which is the same as Eng. *deaf*, was widely used in the sense of deprivation.

DEET. *va.* To winnow or dress corn.
Ang.-Sax. *dihtan*, to prepare, arrange, dispose. In most of the other Northern dialects the word is of more general application, in accordance with the Ang.-Sax.

DEEVE. *vb.* To deafen.
Old Norse *deyfa*, Dan. *döve*, to deafen, stun, stupify.

DEFT. *adj.* Handy, neat. Also quiet, silent.
Ang.-Sax. *dæfte*, mild, convenient, neat.

DEG or DAG. *vn.* To ooze, distil.
Old Norse *deigia*, to be moist.

DENSH, DAINSH. *adj.* Delicate, fastidious, squeamish.
Bav. *däntsch*, a delicacy, *däntschig*, fastidious. The origin seems to be Welsh *dant*, tooth, whence *dantaidd*, fastidious, nice, Eng. *dainty*. So Eng. *toothsome*, from *tooth*.

DESS. *va.* To build or pile up, as applied to stacks, &c.
Old Norse *des*, a rick, *hey-des*, a rick of hay, Welsh *das*, Gael. *dais*, heap, rick, stack.

DEVLT. *adj.* Moped, dispirited, impaired in mind.
Old Norse *dvali*, Dan. *dvale*, a trance, state of torpidity, Old Germ. *twĕlan*, to be torpid. Hence *dwalm* or *dwam*, swoon, suspension of the senses.

DIBBLE. *vn.* To plant seed. "Sometimes applied to burying a corpse."—*Dick.* "The syllable *dib*, expressing the act of striking with a sharp instrument, is a modification of Sco. *dab*, to prick, Bohem. *dubati*, to peck, Eng. *job*, to thrust or peck, parallel with *dag* or *dig*, to strike with a pointed instrument."—*Wedg.*

DIKE. *sb.* A hedge. Also a ditch, but rather a dry ditch. This double sense occurs also in the Dut. *dijck*, both agger and fovea, (*Kil.*), and in the Dan. *dige*, ditch and bank. So also Ang.-Sax. *dic*, Suio-Goth. *dike*, ditch and bank. This, observes Ihre, is naturally to be accounted for, as the same earth which is taken out of the ditch, serves to make the mound. The root, if it be the same as that found in Sansc. *dih*, to heap up, would seem to make it appear that the original sense was that of the bank or hedge.

DILL. *va.* To soothe.
Old Norse *dilla*, to lull, as a nurse does a child.

DITT. *va.* To stop up.
Ang.-Sax. *dyttan*, Old Norse *ditta*, to close, to stop up.

DOBBY. *sb.* A hobgoblin.
Perhaps, by transposition of consonants, for *boddy*. Hence same as Sco. *boody*, from Gael. *bodach*, spectre, boggle. The converse transposition appears in Yorks. *body*, a simpleton (*Ray*), probably the same word as our *dobby*. See *dope*.

DOCKIN. *sb.* The dock (plant).
So *hollin* for holly, *ivin* for ivy.

DODDY. *sb.* A cow without horns.
"Doddyd, wythe-owte hornysse."—*Pr. Prv.* Fris. *dodd*, a lump. "To *dod* is to reduce to a lump, to cut off excrescences."—*Wedg.*

DOD. *sb.* The name of many round-topped hills in Cumb. From the same origin as above, in reference to their round, lump-like form.

DOFF. *va.* To undress. To "do off."
In common use in Early Eng. Dut. *afdoen*, to put off.

DOG-DAISY. *sb.* The common daisy.
Dog, in the names of plants, signifies worthlessness.

DOG-PIG. *sb.* A castrated boar.
Welsh *diawg*, slow, lazy, dull (*di*, priv., and *awg*, keenness, desire). Hence of similar meaning to *seg*, a castrated bull. Compare the Craven simile—"As lither (lazy) as a libbed bitch."

DOLDRUMS. *sb.* Low spirits, melancholy.
Gael. *doltrum*, grief, vexation.

DON. *va.* To dress, to put on any article of clothing, to "do on," as to *doff* is to "do off." "Do on clothys, induo."—*Pr. Prv.*

DONKY. *adj.* Drizzly, applied to the weather.
Swed. *dänka*, Dial. Dan. *dynke*, Germ. *dunken*, to make or cause to be damp. *Dank* and *damp* are synonymous, "as syllables ending in *mb* or *mp* frequently interchange with *ng* or *nk*."—*Wedg.*

DONNAT. *sb.* The devil. Also a worthless person.
Dow signifies usefulness or virtue, and *donnat* is probably *dow-nought*, good for nothing, as Germ. *taugenichts*, Dan. *dogenigt*, Dut. *deugniet*, a good-for-nothing person. So we use conversely "nought at dow."

"For dancin' he was *nought at dow*,
But a prime han' for a drinker."—*Lonsdale.*

DOOK. *va.* and *n.* To bathe, dive, duck, or stoop.
Dan. *dukke*, to dive, duck under water.

DOOSE or DOWSE. *va.* To slap with the hand.
Gael. *duis*, the hand, whence *duiseal*, a beating. Comp. also Vulg. Germ. *dusel*, a box on the ear.

DOPE, DOPY, DOBBY. *sb.* A simpleton.
Clev. *dove*, to be heavy and stupid. Fris. *dobig*, simple, half-witted, Suio-Goth. *dofwa*, to have the senses dulled or stupified, Old Norse *dofi*, torpidity, Sansc. *div*, to be dull or sleepy.

DOTTLE. *sb.* The small portion of tobacco left unsmoked in the pipe.—*Dick.* "Dotelle, stoppynge of a vessele."—*Pr. Prv.* Dut. *dodde*, a tap, stopper, plug, Low Germ. *dutte*, Dial. Dan. *dot*, a stopper, Ang.-Sax. *dyttan*, Old Norse *ditta*, to stop, close.

DOUSE, DOWSE. *adj.* Kindly, pleasant, hospitable.
"Aye the *douse* dapper lanlady cried 'eat an' welcome.'"
Anderson.
Fr. *doux, douce.* The original meaning is preserved more closely with us than in Scotland, where *Jam.* explains it as "thrifty."

DOW. *sb.?* Usefulness, virtue.
Ang.-Sax. *dugan*, Dan. *due*, to be of use, to be good or fit for something, Sansc. *dah*, valere.

DOWLY. *adj.* Melancholy, dejected. Applied to a place, lonely, cheerless. Old Norse *dâlegr*, wretched.

DOWP. *sb.* A bay in a lake.
This seems to be a characteristic Scandinavian word. Old Norse *djûp*, the deep sea close to land (whence the name of Dieppe), and then a large bay.

DOWY. *adj.* Down-hearted, dejected.
Perhaps from Welsh *dueg*, melancholy. Or perhaps for *dowly*, Old Norse *dâlegr*, wretched, hapless.

DOZENT. *adj.* Spiritless, stupified.
Among the various related words are Fris. *dôsig*, dizzy, Ang.-Sax. *dysig*, foolish, Dial. Dan. *dase*, to be heavy or listless, *dose*, to be dumb in sense and faculty. The root is the same as that of *dazed.*

DOZZLE. *vn.* To drizzle, applied to the weather.
Prov. Germ. *döseln*, to drizzle.

DOZZLE. *sb.* A lump.
Gael. *dos*, a hump.

DRABBLE. *vn.* To make wet or dirty, to draggle.
"Drabelyn, paludo."—*Pr. Prv.* Old Norse *drabba*, to dirty, Dut. *drabbe*, Dan. *drav*, dregs, Low Germ. *drabbeln*, to slobber, Gael. *drabh*, dregs, *drabach*, dirty.

DRAFF. *sb.* Brewers' grains.
Old Norse *draf*, Ang.-Sax. *drabbe*, Dan. *drav*, dregs, refuse food for hogs, Gael. *drabh*, dregs.

DRAKT. *adj.* Wet.
West. *drakes*, a slop or mess. Old Norse *dreckia*, to plunge in water, to drench. The Welsh *trochi*, to dip, to plunge, seems to be an allied word.

DRAMMOCK. *sb.* A mixture of oatmeal and water.
Probably for *draffock.* See *draff.*

DREE. *adj.* Slow, tedious.
From the sense of what is drawn out, Goth. *drig. driugr,* long drawn out, Old Norse *driûgr-genginn,* taking long to pass (of a road), Swed. *dryg-mil,* a long (or a *dree*) mile.

DREEN. *sb.* The gratified sound made by the cow during milking. Old Norse *dreynja,* Dan. *drone,* Dut. *dreunen,* Germ. *dröhnen,* to roar, to bellow, Sansc. *dhran,* to groan, give out a hollow sound.

DREUVT, DREEAVT. *adj.* Drenched or saturated with water. Probably from the same origin as *drabble,* q.v.

DRIP. *sb.* Driven snow.
Found only in the phrase " white as drip," applied to anything brilliantly white. Old Norse *drif,* driven snow. The phrase itself, *hvit sem drif,* " white as drip," is current in Iceland.

DRUCKEN. *adj.* Drunk.
Old Norse *druckinn,* Dan. *drukken,* drunk.

DRUSH DOWN. *vn.* To rush down, fall down suddenly.
Sco. *thrusch,* to fall or come down with a rushing or crashing noise. Goth. *driusa,* to fall. Prov. Germ. (Henneberg) *drauschen,* to rush.

DUB. *sb.* A small pond or pool.
Old Norse *dapi,* a pool, Fris. *dobbe,* a ditch, puddle, Gael. *dubhagan,* a pond. In Lonsd. Peacock gives the additional meaning of " a deep hole in a river," but this would seem to be an altogether different word, from Old Norse *djûp,* Dan. *dyb,* a deep hole, a word which we also retain, but in a totally different sense. See *dowp.*

DUB. *va.* To prepare a cock for fighting.
Fr. *addouber,* to dress, arm at all points.

DUBLER, DOUBLER, DIBBLER. *sb.* A large plate or dish.
" The *dubler* was brong in wi' wheyte breed an' brown."
Anderson.

Dobeler.—*P. Pl.* It seems probable that the meaning is that of a vessel which requires to be carried in both hands. This is the origin suggested by Schmeller for Germ. *zuber,* tub, in opposition to Germ. *eimer,* Old High Germ. *ainhar,* a pail, a vessel carried in one hand. The author of the Craven Glossary refers for the origin to a Welsh *dwbler*, but though Lloyd gives *dwbler* as a word used in Cardiganshire, it does not appear in any dictionary that I can find, and may be more probably borrowed from the English. Way, in a note to the *Pr. Prv.*, says "the term is derived from the Fr. *doublier*, a dish," which seems more probable, though the only term I find is *double vaisseau*, a caldron or kettle full of hot water (*Cotg.*)

DUDS. *sb.* Clothes, more especially when worn and shabby. Gael. *dud*, rags.

DUFFY. *adj.* Soft, spongy, woolly.
Lonsd. and Crav. *duffel*, a cloth with a rough nap. Old Norse *tog*, the rougher part of a fleece, from *toga*, to draw out. Hence *duffy* is from the same root as *tough*, which, like it, replaces the *g* sound by that of *f*.

DUMP. *va.* To butt with the horns.
Old Norse *dumpa*, Dan. *dumpe*, to strike, to thump.

DUMPY-COW. *sb.* A cow given to striking. See *dump*.

DUNCH. *va.* To nudge with the elbow.
"Dunchyn, tundo."—*Pr. Prv.* Dut. *donsen*, pugno in dorso percutere, Suio-Goth. *dunsa*, impetu et fragore procedere, Dan. *dundse*, to thump.

DUNNECAN. *sb.* A privy.
Perhaps from Gael. *dionach*, reserved, set apart, from *dion*, shelter, covert.

DURDEM. *sb.* A tumult, uproar, disturbance.
Lonsd. *durdem*, *durden*. On the whole, I think the derivation from Gael. *durdan*, murmur, humming, the most probable.

DUST. *sb.* Uproar, disturbance.
Suio-Goth. *dust*, *dyst*, tumult.

DWALLOW. *vn.* To wither, turn yellow with age.
Old Norse *dvali*, Swed. *dwala*, dulness, fainting, stupefaction. The sense of our word has changed from mental torpor to physical decay.

DWAM. *sb.* A swoon.
Properly *dwalm*. Suio-Goth. *dwalm*, a state of torpor, a swoon.

DWINE. *vn.* To wither, pine away.
"Dwynyn a-wey, evaneo."—*Pr. Prv.* Ang.-Sax. *dwinan*, Old Norse *dvina*, to wither.

DYSTER. *sb.* A dyer.
Stands in the same category as *brewster* and *webster*, both words of the Northern dialect, for brewer and weaver. The ending is properly a female one, Ang.-Sax. *estre*, as in *sangestre*, songstress, but the distinction seems at an early period to have been lost, as *whytster*, a fuller, is rendered in the *Pr. Prv.* candidarius, and in Palsg. *blanchisseur.*

E.

EAR. *sb.* The kidney.
The same in North., Suff., and Sco. Old Norse *nyra*, Dan. *nyre*, Germ. *nieren*. A similar anacope of *n* we have in *est* for nest.

EATH. *adj.* Easy.—*West. and Cumb. Dial.*
Old Eng. *eith*, Ang.-Sax. *eath*, easy.

EEN. *sb.* Eyes.
Our word, like the Sco. *een*, retains the old plural.

EFTER. *prep.* After.
Old Norse *eftir*, Dan., Swed. *efter*. The Ang.-Sax. also has both *æfter* and *efter*.

EGG ON. *va.* To incite, stimulate.
Ang.-Sax. *eggian*, Old Norse *eggia*, Dan. *egge*. The root idea, as in stimulate (*stimulus*, a goad) is that of pricking, Ang.-Sax. *ecg*, a sharp point.

ELDIN. *sb.* Fuel, as peat, turf, wood..
"Eyldynge or fowayle."—*Pr. Prv.* Old Norse *elding*, fuel, firing, from *elda*, to kindle a fire.

ELDIN. *sb.* The butter-bur.
The name, like that of the elder, probably contains the meaning of hollow, which is also that contained in *bur*. See *bur-tree.*

ELLER. *sb.* The elder.
Ang.-Sax. *alr*, *ælr*, Germ. *eller*. In the Pr. Prv. *eldyr* or *hyldyr*. See *bur-tree.*

ELSON. *sb.* A shoemaker's awl.
Dut. *else*, Old Dut. *elsene*, awl.

EN. *conj.* Than.
    May be derived from the Old Norse *enn*, than—*meira enn athrir*, "mair *en* others." But we also find in Prov. Germ. (Henneberg) *enn* for *den*—*net mehr enn drei*, "nit mair *en* three." The Old Norse *enn* is formed by anacope from *thenn*, as is the Prov. Germ. *enn* from *denn*. Or in other words it may be said to be the result of defective pronunciation. "The anacope," observes Cleasby, "is entirely Scandinavian,"—which, if it means that it is not to be found in German, is to be qualified by the exception above quoted. Now the question is—is our word derived from the Scandinavian, or is it the result of similar phonetic tendencies within the dialect itself? To this we can give no certain answer, but in any case it is probable enough than these phonetic tendencies in our dialect, (of which another instance is *er* for *nor*,) may be of Scandinavian origin.

ER. *conj.* Nor (used for than).
    "Mine's better *er* thine."

ESH. *sb.* The ash.
    "Esche."—*Pr. Prv.* Ang.-Sax. *æsc*, Old Norse *ask*, *eski*.

ESP. *sb.* The aspen.
    "Espe."—*Pr. Prv.* Old Norse *espi*, Ang.-Sax. *æsp*. "Words that seem to represent the sibilant sound of its ever-moving leaves, as in *asp*, Gr. ασπις, from its hissing."—*Prior*.

EST. *sb.* Nest.
    This word, with which I can find nothing elsewhere to compare, except *ear* for *near*, shows in a still stronger manner the tendency of the dialect (see *en*) to cut off an initial consonant.

ETTLE. *vn.* To aim at, intend, propose.
    Old Norse, Old Swed. *ætla*, to think, purpose.

EZINS or EASINS. *sb.* Eaves of a building.
    "Evese or evesynge."—*Pr. Prv.* Ang.-Sax. *evese*, eaves, *efesian*, to cut in the form of eaves.

F.

FADGE. *sb.* A slow heavy trot.
    Clev. *fadge*, to move as a corpulent person does. Swed. *fagga*, to load, to weight.

FAFFLE. *vn.* To trifle, to saunter.
Dut. *femelen,* Fris. *fample,* Prov. Germ. *fappeln,* to trifle, fumble.

FAG. *vb.* To load, to encumber.
Swed. *fagga,* to load.

FAIN. *adj.* Glad, anxious, fully disposed.
Ang.-Sax. *fægen,* Old Norse *feginn,* joyful, willing.

FAIR. *adj.* and *adv.* Used intensively, altogether, entirely. "It's a *fair* sham," *i. e.*, a complete shame. "There is a remarkable coincidence of sense and application between this word and the Dial. Dan. *fær, fære,* adj. and adv., quoted by Molbech, and explained as meaning greatly, in a high degree, remarkably, *e. g.*, *hun var fære smykket,* she was extremely pretty.—*Atk.*

FALLOPS. *sb.* Rags, untidy dress of a woman.
Seems connected with Dut. *falie,* a loose wide dress of women.

FARLIES. *sb.* Wonders, remarkable things.
Ferly, a wonder.—*P. Pl.* Ang.-Sax. *færlice,* sudden, unforeseen, Old Norse *ferlegr,* monstrous, horrible.

FARNTICKLES, FANTICKLES. *sb.* Freckles on the face, &c. *Farn* is, no doubt, as suggested by *Atk.*, a contraction of *frecken,* Old Norse *frekna,* freckles. And *tickle* is a diminutive of *tick,* a slight mark. *Fantickle* may be only another form, or it may be from Old Norse *fina,* also signifying a freckle.

FARRANTLY. *adj.* Orderly, respectable, well-behaved.
On the whole, I am disposed to accept Morris's derivation from Gael. *farranta,* brave, stout. *Farranta* is from *fear,* a man; and the idea of that which becomes a man, which, in the eyes of the fierce Gael, was courage in the fight, might, as in the case of *mense,* similarly derived, become that of a peaceful propriety of conduct.

FASH. *va.* To annoy, trouble, vex.
Jamieson's conclusion that this word is borrowed directly from the Fr. *facher* (formerly *fascher*) must, in view of its universal prevalence throughout the North, be regarded with some suspicion, and I am rather disposed to agree with *Atk.* in his suggestion of a Scandinavian origin. He suggests Swed. *fiasa* and *fiaska,* and Dial. Dan. *fasse,* all having very much the same meaning of taking useless care and trouble.

FAUGH (pron. *faff*). *sb.* Fallow.
: Ang.-Sax. *fealg*, Dial. Dan. *fælge*, fallow. Our dialect, as usual, suppresses the *l*, and changes the sound of *g* into *f*. Comp. *saugh* or *saff-tree*, the willow, from Ang.-Sax. *salg*.

FAXED-STAR. *sb.* A comet.—*Hall.*
: Ang.-Sax. *feaxed steorra*, a haired star, a comet, from Ang.-Sax. *feax*, Old Norse *fax*, hair, mane.

FEAL. *vn.* To hide.—*West. and Cumb. Dial.*
: Old Norse *fela*, Suio-Goth. *fala, fela*, to hide.

FECKLESS. *adj.* Helpless, inefficient.
: From *feck*, the imperfect of Old Norse *fá*, to attain, acquire (whence I take our word *fue*), *Atk.*, I think rightly, derives Clev. *feck*, ability, efficiency, whence our word *feckless*. From the corresponding Germ. *fähen*, comes *fähig*, capable, effective, which would correspond with *fecky*, which has probably been at some time in use.

FEEK. *vn.* To be restless or anxious, to fidget.
: "Fykynge about in idleness."—*Pr. Prv.* Old Norse *fika*, to make haste, to bustle, Dut. *ficken*, Bav. *ficken*, to switch, move rapidly to and fro.

FEEL. *adj.* Smooth.
: Ang.-Sax. *feolian*, to file, polish, make smooth. In Clev. to "file over" is to smooth over, to cajole. The Ang.-Sax. *feolian*, judging from Old Norse *fága*, Germ. *fegen*, to polish, may be a contraction of *fegolian*. Comp. Fr. *filou*, sharper.

FELL. *va.* To knock down with a blow.
: Ang.-Sax. *fellan*, Old Norse *fella*, to knock down.

FELL. *adj.* Energetic, striving.
: Ang.-Sax. *fell*, fierce, cruel, severe.

FELL-FAW. *sb.* The field-fare.
: Ang.-Sax. *feala-for*, from *fealo*, yellow.

FELL. *sb.* A mountain.
: Old Norse *fjall, fell*, Swed. *fjäll*, Dan. *field*. The word is not found in the Saxon idiom, and its universal use throughout the district may be taken as a proof of Northern occupancy.

FEND. *vn.* To manage or make shift, to be careful and industrious. Ang.-Sax. *fandian*, to try, prove, search out, Dan. *fænte, fente*, to strive, to acquire with toil and care.

FEST. *vn.* To send out cattle, &c., to other farms to be grazed. Old Norse *festa*, to settle, stipulate, make a bargain.

FETTLE. *va.* To fit, arrange, to repair or put a thing to rights. In the general sense in which it is used, it would seem like a frequentative form of *fit*, Old Norse *fitja*, to web, to knit, Suio-Goth. *fittja*, to fasten.

FEUR-DAY, FEER-DAY. *sb.* The break of day.
Dut. *veur-dagh*, tempus antelucanum.

FEWSOME. *adj.* Handsome, becoming.
In Clev. *viewsome*, which is no doubt the proper word; we have also *viewly*, in the same sense.

FIG-FAG or FICK-FACK. *sb.* The neck tendon.
The Germ. and Dut. *fick-facken* both have the sense of fidgetting, making frequent and rapid movements, which seems to be the idea contained in the present word.

FILLY-FAIR. *sb.* "Palm Sunday has long been held as a day of recreation for young people at Arlecdon, and is called *Filly* fair day."—*Dick.* Gael., Ir. *feil*, Manx *fealley*, a holiday, festival of the Church.

FIRE-HOUSE. *sb.* The inhabited part of a farm-stead.
Comp. Icel. *eld-hús*, the "fire-house," or main room of the homestead.

FIRTH or FRITH. *sb.* An estuary, an arm of the sea.
Old Norse *fiordr*, Suio-Goth. *fiaerd*, Dan. *fiord*.

FIRTLE. *vn.* To trifle, to make an appearance of work. Perhaps for *fittle*, (Eng. *fiddle*), from Old Norse *fitla*, to fidget with the fingers.

FIZZLE. *vn.* To work busily but ineffectually.
Clev. to fidget. Swiss *fiselen*, to fiddle about a thing, work in a trifling manner, make a pretence of business.

FLAITCH. *vb.* To wheedle, obtain one's ends by flattery. Dial. Swed. *fleka*, Old Germ. *flechen*, to caress, fondle, fawn, Old Swed. *flikare*, Old Germ. *flechare*, a flatterer, a wheedler.

FLACKER. *vn.* To flap, to flutter. Also to give way to an immoderate fit of laughter. Old Norse *flaka*, to flap. The second meaning is no doubt derived from the first, referring to the shaking of the sides in laughter.

FLACK. *sb.* A square piece of turf.
Lonsd. *flah.* Dan. *flag*, a flat sod of turf, used in some parts of Jutland as a covering for peat and turf stacks.—*Molb.*

FLAN. *adj.* Flat, shallow, applied to dishes, &c.
In Yorks. to *flan* is to widen towards the top, to expand outwards. Old Norse *flenna*, to expand, to stretch out, *flentr*, expanded, *flenn-eygr*, saucer-eyed, Dial. Dan. *flane*, to gape, to stare.

FLANNEN. *sb.* Flannel.
Our word shows the old and correct form, flannel being originally a Welsh manufacture, and derived, no doubt, from *gwlanen*, flannel, from *gwlan*, wool.

FLAY. *vn.* To frighten.
Old Norse *flæja*, to put to flight, terrify.

FLAYSOME. *adj.* Frightful. See *flay*.

FLECKED. *adj.* Spotted, marked, streaked.
And wonderful foweles,
With *fleckede* fetheres.—*P. Pl.*
Old Norse *flecka*, to spot, stain, *fleckottr*, spotted, Germ. *flechen*, to stain.

FLEUZ'T. *adj.* Bruised, fringed, broken into filaments.
Lonsd., Crav. *fluzzed*. Old Norse *flysja*, to split into slices, *flis*, a splinter, Dan. *flise*, to splinter.

FLEER. *vn.* To laugh heartily.—*Dick.*
To have a countenance expressive of laughter without laughing out.—*Brock.* To manifest the feeling or spirit of mocking or scornful ridicule without actually laughing out.—*Atk.* Dickenson's definition is borne out as regards Cumb. in the following :
" They brunt his wig, an' greym't his feace,
And waken't him wi' *fleerin*."—Upshot, *Lonsdale.*
Dial. Dan. *flire*, to smile sneeringly, Nor. *flir*, suppressed laughter.

FLEET. *sb.* Lot, large number.
" The hail *fleet* o' them."—*Dick.* Sco. *fleet*, to abound. Old Fr. *flotte*, a crowd, *flotte de gens*, crowd of people. The origin is probably Teutonic.

FLICK. *sb.* A flitch (of bacon).
Ang.-Sax. *flicce*, Old Norse *flikki*, flitch of bacon.

FLINDERS. *sb.* Fragments, small pieces.
Old Eng. *flitter*, to scatter in pieces. Norw. *flindra*, a shiver of stone or the like. Dut. *flenters*, tatters.

FLIPE. *sb.* The rim of a hat.
Dan. *flip*, tip, corner, extremity.

FLIT. *vn.* To remove from one house to another, generally in the sense of evading creditors, though that sense does not enter into the origin of the word. "It seems almost always to imply the removal of something, *e.g.*, of the out-going tenant's movable property."—*Atk.* Old Norse *flitja*, to carry, convey. Dan. *flytte*, to remove, carry away, shift or change dwelling.

FLYTE. *vn.* To mock, scold, ridicule.
"Flytin or chydin."—*Pr. Prv.* Ang.-Sax. *flitan*, to strive, dispute, quarrel.

FLOFF. *sb.* The lightest of chaff.
Eng. *flue*, *fluff*, down or nap. Low Germ. *flog*, light things that rise and fly in the air, *flog-aske*, light flying ashes. The common change occurs of *g* into *f*.

FLODDER. *sb.* Froth, foam, half-dissolved snow.
Probably allied to *flutter*, Low Germ. *fluddern*, Bav. *flodern*. Wall. *fluturare*, to flutter, as a butterfly or flake of snow. *fluturu*, a flake of snow. Comp. also Dut. *floderen*, to trudge through wet and dirt.

FLOW. *sb.* A bog, quagmire.
Old Norse *flôi*, a marshy fen, from *flôa*, to flood, Prov. Germ. *flage*, a quagmire. This sense of liquidity is exemplified in the case of Solway Flow, by an irruption in the last century, which caused extensive damage and some loss of life.

FLOUGH. *adj.* Wild, skittish, as a young horse.
Applied also, in the case of a person, to wild and reckless expenditure. Swiss *flück*, skittish, applied to a horse, Low Germ. *flugg*, lively and spirited beyond what is becoming. The idea, as also in our words *flighty* and *volatile*, is derived from that of flying.

FLOUGH. *adj.* Cold, boisterous, applied to the weather.
From the sense of flying, as in above. Comp. Fris. *flaag*, a sharp and sudden shower, Low Germ. *flage*, a passing storm of wind or rain, Old Eng. *flaw*, a violent storm of wind.—*Hall.*

FLUET. *sb.* A blow or buffet.
Properly, I think, a slap with the flat hand. Perhaps the same as Old Eng. *flirt,* "a fillip, rap, or flirt." (*Cotg.*) Halliwell has also Prov. Eng. *flatten,* to slap, and *flatte* occurs in *P. Pl.* in the sense of dashing water on the face.

FLUKE, FLOOK. *sb.* A flounder, flat fish.
Ang.-Sax. *flóc,* Old Norse *flóki,* a flat fish.

FLUSTERATION. *sb.* Excitement and confusion.
Clev. *flusterment.* Old Norse *flaustr,* precipitancy, excitement, Walach. *flusturare,* to do a thing in a boisterous or turbulent manner.

FOG. *sb.* After-grass, when the hay has been cut and removed. Welsh *ffwg,* dry grass, (*Garn.* Phil. Ess.)

FOGGY. *adj.* Light, soft, spongy.
Welsh *ffwg,* what is volatile (as dry leaves or grass).

FOISTY, FUSTY. *adj.* Having a close, disagreeable smell, as of dampness or mouldiness. "Fyyst, stynk."—*Pr. Prv.* The origin seems to be Old Norse *fisa,* to blow, also to break wind, whence Old Norse *fýs,* Dut. *veest,* Germ. *fist,* flatus ventris, Low Germ. *fistrig,* ill-smelling, as a peasant's room.

FOOTH. *sb.* Plenty, abundance.
Properly *fulth.* Formed from *full,* as *wealth* from *weal* and *health* from *heal.*

FOOTHY. *adj.* Well off, in good circumstances.
Dick. gives also the sense of liberal, hospitable. See *footh.*

FORBYE. *adv.* Besides, in addition to.
Dan. *forbi,* Germ. *vorbei,* besides, over and above.

FORCE. *sb.* A cascade or waterfall.
Clev. *force* and *foss.* Old Norse *fors,* waterfall, *forsa,* to stream in torrents, Norw. and Mod. Icel. *foss.* "This," observes Cleasby, "is a test word of Scandinavian language and origin." He also refers to a passage in Constant. Porph. De Admin. Imperii, where the Byzantine author gives the names of some waterfalls in Russia, from which it would seem that the Russian word was then βορσί,* or φόρος, (Russia, it must be remem-

---

* Pron. *vorsy* in Mod. Greek. Hence, probably, as well as *foros,* the same word as the Old Norse *fors.*

bered, was colonised by Northmen). It seems probable that Old Norse *fors* is formed from the prep. *fra* joined with the verb *isia*, proruere.

FORDER. *va.* To further, assist, promote.
Suio-Goth. *fordra*, promovere, juvare, Germ. *fördern*, to promote.

FOR-ELDERS. *sb.* Ancestors.
Old Norse *foreldri*, forefathers, Dan. *forældre* (limited to parents).

FORMEL. *vn.* To bespeak.
Old Norse *formæla*, to appoint, Dan. *formelde*, to proclaim.

FORSET. *va.* To waylay.
Ang.-Sax. *forsettan*, to set before, Old Norse *forsât*, an ambush.

FOSPEL-HOLE. *sb.* The print of a footstep on soft ground.
Fospel may possibly be a corruption of *fosper*, i.e., *foot-spor*. Old Norse *fôt-spor*, foot-print. Otherwise I can suggest no explanation, unless we may think of Welsh *fosp*, breach, gap.

FOTTER. *va.* To hummel barley in order to break off the awns. Crav. *fawter.* Sco. *fatter.* The proper word is *falter*, as found in Marshal's Rur. Econ. *Atk.* thinks it "an arbitrary application of the standard word, connected with the interrupted or up-and-down motion of the instrument when in use." I am more disposed to think of Germ. *foltern*, Dut. *folteren*, to put to the rack, torture, torment.

FOWT. *sb.* A fondling, a petted child.
In Clev. also a fool, stupid lout. *Atk.*, however, separates the two words, deriving the former from Lat. *fotus*, and the latter from Old Norse *fauti*, simpleton. I confess, however, to some doubt respecting this—the connection between fondness and folly being so close. Thus the original sense of fond is foolish; we speak of "doting" on one, and through the North "silly thing" is a common term of endearment towards children. I should therefore be disposed to consider the two senses as concurrent, and to make the Old Norse *fauti* the origin of both.

FOZZY. *adj.* Soft and spongy, as frosted turnips.
Pruss. *fossen*, to break up into a spongy mass of ligaments, Dut. *voose*, spongy, *voose raapen*, fozzy or frosted turnips. Old Norse *fauskr*, a rotten, dry log.

FRA, FREV. *prep.* From.
Old Norse *frâ*, (pronounced *frav*).

FRAHDLE. *vn.* To talk foolishly.—*West. and Cumb. Dial.* Sco. *fraydant*, quarrelsome. Welsh *ffraethder*, fluency, wittiness, flippancy, *fregodi*, to chatter, talk gibberish.

FRAINED. *adj.* Freckled, marked with small-pox.
Old Norse *freknöttr*, Dan. *fregnet*, freckled, cognate, it would seem, with Welsh *breck*.

FRAP. *va.* To snap the fingers.
Apparently from Fr. *frapper*, to strike.

FRATCH. *vn.* To quarrel, squabble.
In the Pr. Prv. *fracchyn* is described as the creaking of new carts, &c., and explained by *strideo*. Hence it would seem that the original meaning was that of a harsh grating sound, whence, metaphorically, the jar of quarrel. A varying reading in the *Pr. Prv.* is *frashin*, which corresponds with Sco. *frais*, to make a cracking or crashing noise, and it seems rather probable that this is the original form, in which case the probable origin is Suio-Goth. *fraesa*, stridere. Our word *fractious*, quarrelsome, seems more probably derived from the above *fratch*, than from Lat. *fractus*, to which it is referred by Todd, Jamieson, and others.

FREELIDGE. *sb.* "The freehold privileges belonging to the burgage tenure."—*Dick.* Also (the stones which mark the boundaries of a borough being called *freelidge stones*,) it would seem to apply to the privileges of the borough freemen. Probably the same as Germ. *freilehen*, freenold.

FREM or FREMMED. *adj.* Foreign, strange, unfamiliar.
Ang.-Sax. *fremed*, Dut. *vremmed*, strange, foreign.

FROSK. *sb.* A frog.
"Nearly obsolete."—*Dick.* Frosche.—*Pr. Prv.* Ang.-Sax. *frosc*, Old Norse *froskr*, Germ. *frosch*.

FROUGH, FROFF. *adj.* Easily broken, short in grain.
Seems to be most probably a variation of *froth*, used by Tusser in the same sense. Ang.-Sax. *freothan*, fricare. For similar instances of interchange between *th* and *f*, see *swaith* and *tharth*.

FROW. *sb.* A morose or forbidding-looking woman.
Ang.-Sax. *freo*, Old Norse *freyja*, mistress, lady, woman. Like *queen*, this word, originally a term of honour, has come, in provincial speech, to be used in a contemptuous sense.

FROWSY. *adj.* Coarse, vulgar. See *frow*.

FRUDGE. *vn.* To rub rudely against.
Clev. *fridge*, to rub up or chafe. Lat. *fricare*, Ital. *fricciare*, to rub.

FRUMMETY. *sb.* Barley boiled with milk.
Prop. *frumenty*, from Fr. *frumentée*, a kind of wheat gruel, Lat. *frumentum*.

FRUSH. *adj.* Brittle, crumbly.
Fr. *froisser*, to break, Ital. *frusciare*, to crush together.

FUDDERMENT. *sb.* Warm wrappings or lining.
Old Eng. *fodder*, to line a garment. Old Norse *fóðr*, lining, *fóðra*, to fur or line a garment. Hence, by cont., our word *fur*.

FUE or FEW. *vn.* Used, as elsewhere *shape, frame, offer*, in the sense of showing aptitude for anything.

"I' th' chimley nuik some gay guid hans,
An' gaily ill to slocken,
Fell tui wi' poddingers an' cans,
An' *few't* well to get drukken."—*Lonsdale*.

Sco. *faw*, to obtain, acquire. Probably from Old Norse *fâ*. Dan. *faae*, to grasp, acquire, to be busy, exert oneself, Ang.-Sax. *fôn*, Germ. *fahen*, to catch, seize, to be of effect, whence *fähig*, capable, fit. The imp. of Old Norse *fâ* is *feck*, whence prob. Clev. *feck*, ability, which we seem only to have in the adj. *feckless*.

FULL. *va.* To fill.
Goth. *fulljan*, Ang.-Sax. *fillan* and *fullan*, Dut. *vullen*.

FUR, FOOR. *sb.* Furrow.
Ang.-Sax. *fur*, Old Norse *for*, Dan. *fure*.

FUZ-BAW, FUZ-BALL. *sb.* The puff-ball, a kind of fungus, Fr. *vesse*. The idea seems to be that of rottenness, and the origin the same as that of *fousy*.

FUZZEN. *sb.* Potency, briskness, applied to liquors.
"Germ. *pfuschen*, Swiss *pfusen*, Eng. *fizz*, represent the sound of water flying off from a hot surface, of air and water in intimate mixture and commotion. Hence *fuzz*, having the nature of things which *fizz*." *Wedg*. The word *fuzz* no doubt related to our *fuzzen*, was formerly current in the sense of getting

F

drunk, as also its frequentative *fuzzle*, whence, as a corr., comes our present word *fuddle*. "The University troop dined with the Earl of Abingdon, and came back well *fuzzed*."—*Wood in Todd*.

G

GAB. *sb.* The mouth. Also foolish or idle talk.
Dan. *gab*, Pol. *geba*, mouth. Prov. Dan. *gabe*, over free or chattering talk, Old Norse *gabba*, Ang.-Sax. *gabban*, to mock, cheat, lie.

GAE, GAN, GANG. *vn.* To go.
Ang.-Sax. *gangan*, *gân*, Old Norse *ganga*, Old Fries. *gân*, Dut. *gaan*. As in Clev., *gan* is in Cumb. the most common form.

GAIN. *adj.* Near, direct, convenient, applied generally to a road or way. Old Norse *gegn*, direct, *hinn gegnsta veg*, the shortest way. Dan. *gfen-vei*, short cut.

GALORE or GALWORE. *sb.* Abundance.
"Wi' snaps and gingerbread *galwore*."—Bridewain, by *Stagg*.
Apparently from Welsh *gwala*, fullness, sufficiency, *gwalyo*, to make full, Ir. *gleire*, much, plenty.

GALLY-BAWK. *sb.* The beam or bar across the chimney, from which the pot-hooks are suspended. Literally "gallows-bawk," Old Norse *galga*, gallows. "Compare the Wärend word *gäll-stang*, which I believe has the exact meaning of our word, simply substituting *stang* for *bawk*."—*Atk*.

GAME-LEG. *sb.* A lame or injured leg.
Probably from Wel. *cam*, Corn. *gam, cam*, crooked, Fr. *gambir*, to crook.

GAMMERSTANG. *sb.* A tall, awkward person.
The latter part of the word is from *stang*, pole; the origin of *gammer* is not so obvious. Dr. Whittaker says, *ganger-stang*, a walking-pole. Morris derives it from *gammer*, an old woman, which Jam. also refers to for Sco. *gamareerie*, tall, raw-boned, and awkward. Or the origin may be the same as that of *gammarel*, *q.v.*

GANGREL. *sb.* A tramp, vagabond.
Derived in Cleasby's Icel. Dict. from Old Norse *gangleri*, wanderer. But the termination *rel* is common to so many words in

our dialect, as *haverel, hangarel, waistrel*, &c., that we cannot suppose it to be in this case a transposition of *ler*. The former part of the word is no doubt from *gang*, in the sense of wandering.

GAR. *va.* To compel, make to do.
Old Norse *gera, giora*, to make, do, create. "*Gar* may be garded as the shibboleth of a language wholly or partly Scanddinavian."—*Garnett*. Though it is to be observed, as remarked by *Atk.*, that a similar use of the word to ours is rare in Scandinavia.

GARN. *sb.* Yarn.
Ang.-Sax. *gearn*, Old Norse, Dan., Swed. *garn*.

GARRICK. *adj.* Awkward, stupid. The word is also used as a noun.

"Guidman stuid wraulin at her lug,
An' co't her many a *garrick*."—Upshot, *Lonsdale*.

Gael. *garrach*, homo crassus et obesus, *gorach*, foolish, stupid, *gorag*, a foolish woman.

GARRON. *sb.* A tall awkward horse or other animal.
Perhaps from Wel. *gar*, leg, shank, whence *garan*, a crane, from its long legs. The Gael. has *gearran*, properly a gelding, but from the adj. *gearranach*, horse-like, clownish, one might be disposed to think that it had acquired something of the sense of an awkward horse, in which case it would be the most probable origin of our word.

GARTH. *sb.* An inclosure, generally used in compounds, as *stack-garth, hay-garth*, &c. Old Norse *gardr*, Dan. *gaard*, Ang.-Sax. *geard*, Eng. *yard*, Wel. *gardd*, Bret. *garz*, hedge, garden. Our word, from the compounds in which it occurs, as stack-garth, O. N. *stakk-gardr*, kirk-garth, O. N. *kirkju-gardr*, grass-garth, O. N. *gras-gardr*, a garden, (obsolete, but found in names of places in Cumb.), may be taken to be of Scandin. origin. In O. N. it acquired also the meaning of fortress, whence Novgorod, Belgorod, Pavlograd, names commemorative of the Scandin. colonization of Russia. The old name of Constantinople was Mikligardr, the "muckle garth." *Wedg.* makes the original meaning to be rod, wand, Ang.-Sax. *geard*, whence, "probably from rods or wattle-work affording the readiest means of making fences, a fence, hedge, &c." I rather suppose, however, that these are two distinct groups, the root of the one being to be found in Sansc. *ghær*, to penetrate, and that of the other in Sansc. *gærh*, to inclose.

GATE (pron. *geeat*). A road, street, or way.
Old Norse *gata*, Dan. *gade*, Ang.-Sax. *geát*, Germ. *gasse*. Hence *gate* as the equivalent of *street* in most of the Northern towns.

GATINS. *sb.* Sheaves of corn, &c., set up singly to dry.
Perhaps from Old Norse *gæta*, to tend, take care of, in the sense of things requiring extra attention. Or perhaps for *gastins*, Gael. *gaistean*, a sheaf or bundle of hay, &c.

GAUT. *sb.* A boar pig.
Prop. *galt*. Old Norse *galti*, Dan. *galt*, boar.

GAWKY. *sb.* A stupid and awkward person.
Old Norse *gaukr*, Ang.-Sax. *geac*, simpleton, Old Norse *gick*, Germ. *gauch*, fool, Fr. *gauche*, awkward, Corn. *gocy*, foolish, Gael. *goic*, scoff, taunt.

GAWVISON. *sb.* A foolish person, to which Dick adds the sense of noisy. Clev. *gauby*, *gauvey*, *gauvison*, all with the same sense. Old Norse *geipa*, to talk nonsense, *gapa*, to stare with open mouth, Norw. *gap*, a simpleton.

GAYSHEN. *sb.* An emaciated person, all skin and bone.
Perhaps from Gael. *gais*, to shrivel up.

GEAL. *vn.* To ache or tingle with cold.
Sco. *gell*. Germ. *gellen*, to tingle.

GEALLS. *sb.* Cracks or fissures in timber while seasoning.
Seems allied to *gill*, a cleft or ravine. Old Norse *gilia*, to split or cleave, *giöll*, petra cava.

GEAR. *sb.* Dress, equipment, harness of a cart or plough, property in general. Ang.-Sax *gearwe*, Old Norse *görvi*, gear, apparel.

GEE. *sb.* Gee is the carter's word of command to his horses to turn to the right or from him. To "take the *gee*" is to take affront, and to declare abruptly off. Jam. refers to Swed. *gä*, to budge, to turn round.

GEGGIN. *sb.* A small tub with a long handle.
Gael. *gogan*, a small wooden dish made of several pieces.

GEGGLES. *sb.* A giddy girl.
Crav. *geg*, to walk in a careless manner. The idea is that of restlessness or unsteadiness. Fr. *gigue*, a jig or rapid dance, *gigues*, a giddy girl, Old Eng. *gig.* a top, Swiss *gagli*, a girl

that cannot sit still.—*Wedg.* The root is found in Welsh *gogi*, to agitate, move quickly, whence also Gael. *gogaid*, a fickle woman, Fr. *coquette*.

GETTER. *sb.* One who begets.
Old Norse *getara*, one who gives birth to. In O. N. the word was applied to both parents; with us it is exclusively applied to the male.

GIF. *conj.* If.
Ang.-Sax. *gif.*

GILDER or GILDERT. *sb.* A snare for catching birds.
Old Norse, Old Swed, *gildra*, a snare, gin, trap.

GILL. *sb.* A small ravine.
Old Norse *gil*, Norw. *gil, gjel.* "Brooks and tributary streams flowing through clefts in the fell-side to the main river at the bottom of a vale are in Iceland called *gil.*"—*Cleasby*. This is precisely our *gill*, only the word applies properly, I take it, not to the stream itself, but to the cleft through which it runs. Hald. has the verb *gilia*, diducere, alveum facere, but the verb in that sense is wanting in Cleasby. The modern spelling of *ghyl*, (intended no doubt to show that the *g* is hard), implying as it does that the history of a word, as contained in its form, is of less account in a dialectic word than in one of the Eng. language, is, I hold, reprehensible.

GILT. *sb.* A sow pig that has not yet borne.
Old Norse *gyltr*, Icel. *gilta*, Ang.-Sax. *gilte*, a young sow.

GIMMER. *sb.* A ewe under two years old.
Old Norse *gymbr*, a ewe of one year old, Dial. Swed. *gimber*, a ewe that has not yet borne a lamb.

GINNERS. *sb.* The gills of a fish.
Diefenbach collates *ginners* with *gills*. It seems to be from Old Norse *gjölnar*, gills, the *l* being dropped as usual. Hence *ginners* would be a double plural.

GIRD. *sb.* A fit, as a *gird* of passion or laughter.
Perhaps from Welsh *gyroedd*, drive, impulse, *gyrddu*, to act vehemently. Or from Old Norse *grîd*, æstus animi.

GIRD. *sb.* A hoop formed of an ozier rod bent into a circle. Ang.-Sax. *gyrd*, Old Norse *girdi*, a rod, a twig.

GIRDLE. *sb.* A circular plate to bake cakes, &c., on.
Welsh *greidyll*, a baking plate, from *greidio*, to burn, to scorch. Comp. also Suio-Goth. *grissel*, (prop., according to Ihre, *graedsel*), a baking plate, from *graedda*, to bake.

GIRSE. *sb.* Grass.
Ang.-Sax. *gærs, græs*, Dut. *gars, gras*, Eng. *grass*.

GISS! *intj.* A call for swine. Perhaps for *gris*.
Old Norse *gris*, a little pig.

GLAD. *adj.* Smooth, as of a door on its hinges.
Old Norse *gledia*, to polish, Dut. *glad*, Germ. *glatt*, smooth, polished. The original sense is that of brightness, next comes that of smoothness, and lastly, that of joyfulness.

GLEE. *vn.* To squint.
Low Germ. *glien*, to slip or slide.

GLEGG. *adj.* Smart, quick.
Old Norse *gleggr*, sharp-sighted, whence met. clever, Germ. *glau*, Welsh, Corn. *glew*, sharp, clever.

GLENT. *sb.* Glimpse.
Dial. Swed. *glinta*, to slip, slide. "Grimm supposes a lost strong verb *glintan*, to shine, glance with light, and probably this word which remains with us is the word in question."—*Rietz.* Comp. Dan. *glimt*, glance.

GLIFF. *sb.* A sudden or hasty view, passing glimpse.
Dan. *glippe*, to slip, to miss, to wink, Dut. *glippen*, to slip.

GLIME. *vn.* To look sideways.
Seems rather to be related to *gleyme*, viscus, mucus, than to *gleam*. The sense would then be that of slipping, turning aside, as in Low Germ. *glippen*, to slip, Dan. *glippe*, to slip, to miss, to wink.

GLISK. *vn.* To glisten.
Old Norse *glyssa*, Old Germ. *glizan*, Norw. *glisa*, to glisten. Comp. Lat. *gliscere*, to take fire, begin to burn.

GLOP. *vn.* To stare with open mouth.
Old Norse *glapa*, to stare, gape.

GLOWER. *vn.* To stare, gaze intently.
Old Norse *glóra*, to gleam, stare like a cat's eyes, (Cleasby), Dial. Swed. *glora*, Norw. *glora*, to stare, Dut. *gluren*, to leer.

GLUMPT. *adj.* Sulky.
Clev. *glumpy*. Old Fris. *glupa*, Prov. Germ. *glupen*, to look sullenly, Low Germ. *gluppen*, to look covertly from under the brows. By the insertion of the nasal we get *glump*, and then, dropping the final *p*, Eng. *glum*, Dial. Dan. *glum*, scowling.

GLOUT. *sb.* A lout, clumsy fellow.
Glowt, to look doggedly or sourly,—*J. K.* Dut. *kloete, loete*, homo agrestis. "Perhaps from the notion of a lump or clod." —*Wedg.*

GOAL. *sb.* A deep pool.
Wel. *gwlw*, channel, Swiss *gülle*, Bav. *güllen*, a sink, Eng. *gully-hole.*

GOB. *sb.* The mouth.
Gael. *gob*, ludicrously applied, probably allied to Old Norse *gapa*, Eng. *gape*, &c.

GOFF, GUFF. *sb.* A simpleton.
Perhaps from Old Norse *gufa*, vapour, steam, whence, metaph., a foolish and empty person. Bret. *goap*, mockery, Fr. *goffe*, a simpleton.

GOLLER or **GOLLOW.** *vn.* To shout, halloo, to bark loudly. Old Norse *gaula*, to bellow, Wel. *galaru*, Gael. *guil*, to weep, lament.

GOMMAREL. *sb.* A foolish and awkward person.
Comp. Old Norse *gambra*, to brag, bluster, prate, *gambrari*, bragger, blusterer, *gumari*, a fop, from *gum*, fuss, exaggeration. But if the word be properly *gonerill*, as Brockett has it, which I am rather disposed to admit, then the most probable origin would be Old Norse *göna*, to stare in a foolish manner.

GOOD-FEW. A tolerable quantity, neither very large nor very small. The *Clev.* expression, "a good little," is not in use in Cumb. Ihre refers to a similar use of Suio-Goth. *gudi*, which "adjectivis et adverbiis additum, significationem intendit."

GOODIES. *sb.* Sugar sweetmeats for children.
Dial. Swed. *guttar*, Swiss *guteli*, sweetmeats for children.

GOODLIKE. *adj.* Handsome, good-looking.
Old Norse *godlikr*, good, virtuous. So *goodly*, in its after-use applied to personal appearance, is explained in the *Pr. Prv.* as benignus, benevolens.

GOPE. *vn.* To shout.
Old Norse *gapa*, Eng. *gape*. To *gope* is to shout with open mouth.

GORB, GORLIN. *sb.* An unfledged bird.
Clev. *gorpin*, Sco. *gorbling, gorling, gorbet*. *Gorlin* is properly *gorblin*, or rather *gorbling*, the fundamental word being *gorb* or

gorp, The Sco. *goròle*, to swallow greedily, Gael. *gairbh*, a greedy belly, show, I take it, the origin of the word, which is derived from the characteristic voracity of young birds. The root is to be found in Gr. γράω, comedo, Gael. *gaorr*, to gorge, Dut. *ghieren*, avide petere, (*Kil.*) Hence North. *gormaw*, the cormorant, *gorcrow*, the carrion crow, Old Norse, Germ. *geir*, Dut. *ghier*, vulture, in all of which creatures voracity is the distinguishing feature. Probably also Old Norse *gorbor*, Norw. *gorp*, Lat. *corvus*, Sco. *corby* or *gorby*, raven. And Gael., Ir. *gioraman*, glutton, whence prob. Fr. *gourmand*. The name Geri, of one of the ravens of Odin, appointed to consume the bodies of those slain in battle, is, no doubt, from the same origin, in the sense of voracity.

GORRISH. *adj.* Gross, over luxuriant.
Lonsd. *grosh*. Clev. *grossy*. Old Norse *gróska*, gramen vernans, (*Hald.*), from *gróa*, to grow.

GOWK. *sb.* The cuckoo.
Old Norse *gaukr*, Ang.-Sax. *geac*, Germ. *gouch*, Gael. and Ir. *cuach*. The root is found in Sansc. *cuc*, to cry.

GOWK. *sb.* A simpleton. See *gawky*.

GOWK. *sb.* The core of an apple, &c. See *cowk*.

GOWL. *vn.* To weep, to lament. See *goller*.

GOWPIN. *sb.* The quantity that can be held in the hollow of the hand, or of both hands together. Old Norse *gaupn*, prop. both hands held together in the form of a bowl, then as much as can be taken in the hands held together, (*Cleasby*).

GOWZE. *vn.* To gush.
Old Norse *gjósa*, to gush.

GOYSTER. *vn.* To bluster, laugh loudly.
Perhaps from Old Norse *gussa*, to make a fuss and noise. Or from *gusta*, to blow in gusts.

GRAB. *va.* To sieze, snatch.
Swed. *grabba*, to grasp, Goth. *greipan*, Old Norse *greipa*, Germ. *greifen*, to sieze.

GRAIDLY. *adj.* and *adv.* Proper, decent, well-behaved, orderly, properly. "Seldom heard in Cumb."—*Dick*. Old Norse *greitha*, Norw. *greida*, to prepare, make straight, put in order.

GRAINS. *sb.* The forked branches of a tree, the prongs of a fork. Old Norse *grein*, Swed. *gren*, the fork of a branch, Old Norse *greina*, to separate.

GRATER-FACED. *adj.* Marked with small-pox.
Seems to be from Old Norse *grautr*, Ang.-Sax. *grut*, groats, to which the marks on the face may be resembled. Comp. *Grautnefr*, "porridge-nose," a nick-name in the Icel. Sturlunga Saga.

GRAVE. *va.* To dig, to use a spade.
Ang.-Sax. *grafan*, Old Norse *grafa*, Dan. *grave*, Germ. *graben*, to dig.

GREET. *vn.* To weep, to cry silently.
Ang-Sax. *grǽtan*, Old Norse *gráta* (pret. *grét*).

GREG. *va.* To annoy, to vex, mortify.
Probably nearly allied to *grudge*, which occurs as *gruch* in the *Pr. Prv.* Suio-Goth. *grufwa sig*, (with the var. *grugha*), to grumble.

GRIME. *sb.* Soot, smut.
Dan. *grime*, Norw. *grima*, Dial. Swed. *grima*, a black spot or smut, especially on the face. The word anciently signified a mask, or a hood partly covering the face.

GRIMIN. *sb.* A sprinkling, slight covering, as of snow.
Seems to be from *grime*, in its original sense of a covering easily removed.

GRIPE. *sb.* A dung-fork.
Suio-Goth. *grepe*, Swed. *grepe*, Dan. *greb*, a stable-fork.

GROON (pron. *greeun*). *sb.* A swine's snout.
Old Norse *groen*, beard, beak, lips of a cow, Fr. *groin*, snout of a pig. Metaph. Old Fr. *groing*, cape, promontory, tongue of land jutting into the sea. Hence, no doubt, the name of Grune Point, a projecting tongue of land near Skinburness.

GROOP. *sb.* The gutter behind the cows in a byre.
Growpe.—*Pr. Prv.* Clev. *grip*, Norf. *grup*. Ang.-Sax. *græp*, Old Norse *grof*, Swed. *grop*, ditch, channel, Eng. *groove*.

GROOSAM. *adj.* Grim, forbidding-looking.
Clev. *gruc*. Germ. *grausam*, fierce, terrible, Dial. Swed. *grusam*, dismal-looking, dejected, Dan. *gru*, horror, Germ. *grauen*, to have a horror or aversion.

GROOVES. *sb.* Places out of which coal, slate, &c., has been dug. "Groove or grove, a deep pit sunk to search for minerals."—*J. K.* Crav. *groove*, a mine or shaft. Dut. *groef*, furrow, ditch, groove, Germ. *grube*, a pit, ditch, hole dug in the ground.

GROUTY. *adj.* Smeared, muddy, dirty.
Dut. *gruete*. dregs, *gruyten*, to mud or clean out canals, Norw. *grut*, dregs, *gruten*, thick, muddy.

GRUN. *sb.* Ground.
Old Norse *grunnr*, ground.

GRUNDSWAITH. *sb.* The rag-wort.
Ang.-Sax. *swathu*, swath in mowing. The sense seems to be that of something trailing on the ground.

GRYKE, CRYKE. *sb.* A crevice in a hill-side.
Old Norse *kryki*, corner, recess.

GULL. *sb.* The corn-marigold, *Chrysanthemum segetum*, sometimes called the *goldin*. Clev. *gowland*. Dial. Swed. *gulle-blommer*, "gold-flower," the corn-marigold, Dut. *goudsbloem*, "gold-flower," the common marigold. Welsh *gold*, the corn-marigold, *goldwyr*, the common marigold. Our word may be taken to be from Old Norse *gull*, gold.

GULLY. *sb.* A hollow between two hills. See *goal*.

GULLY. *sb.* A large knife, especially one used for cutting bread and cheese. Gael. *golaidh*, a clumsy knife, Corn. *golye*, Bret. *goulia*, Welsh *gwelio*, to cut or wound. Hence prob. Old Fr. *goue*, a large knife.

GUMPTION. *sb.* Sense, shrewdness, judgment.
Old Norse *gaumr*, heed, attention, *geyma*, Ang.-Sax. *geomian*, Goth. *gaumjan*, to give heed or attention. Clev. has also *gaum*, *sb.* and *vb.*

GUTLIN. *sb.* A glutton.
Guttle is another form of *guzzle*. Old Norse *gutla*, to sound as liquids in a cask, is referred to as the origin by *Wedg.* I doubt, however, whether it is not simply from *gut*.

GYVERSOME. *adj.* Eager, greedy.
Ang.-Sax. *gifer*, greedy.

H.

HAAF-NET. *sb.* A net used on the Solway, respecting which much legal dispute has arisen as to whether it comes under the definition of a "fixed engine." It consists of a pock-net fixed to a kind of frame, which, whenever a fish strikes against it, is hauled above water. It is, no doubt, as Jam. suggests, from Suio-Goth. *haaf*, a net suspended to a frame by which the fish are lifted out, from S. G. *haefwa*, to lift up. Comp. also Old Norse *haafr*, a drag-net, Dan. *haav*, a bow-net, Norw. *haave*, to draw nets through the water, North. *haafures*, fishing-lines, in some of which words, however, there may be an intermixture of Old Norse *haf*, the deep sea.

HACK. *sb.* A pick-axe.
Dan. *hakke*, pick-axe, mattock.

HADDER. *vn.* To drizzle.
Perhaps from Old Norse *hialldra*, to snow.

HADDER. *sb.* Small rain.
Old Norse *hialldr*, a thin snow shower. Comp. also Gael. *adhar*, snow.

HAFFETS. *sb.* Locks of hair on the temples.
Sco. *haffets*, the temples themselves, which seems to be the proper meaning. Jam. refers to Ang.-Sax. *healf-heafod*, in the sense of semi-cranium, *haffet* thus being simply *half-head*.

HAFFLE, HEFFLE. *vn.* To hesitate, be undecided.
Dut. *haperen*, to stammer, hesitate, stick fast, Swed. *happla*, to stammer.

HAG. *va.* To chop.
Dut. *hakken*, Old Norse *hiacka*, Dial. Swed. *hagga*, Germ. *hacken*, to chop, hack.

HAG-CLOG. *sb.* A chopping-block.
Germ. *hack-klotz*, a chopping-block.

HAGGIS. *sb.* A pudding of mince-meat.
Fr. *hachis*, a mess of mince-meat, from *hacher*, to mince.

HAGGLE. *vn.* To fatigue, over-work.
Perhaps a frequentative from Old Norse *hagga*, to put out of order, derange.

HAG-WORM. *sb.* The common viper.
Old Norse *höggormr*, Dan. *hugorm*, viper.

HAIN. *vn.* To preserve untouched, to save.
"To exclude cattle from a field so that grass may grow for hay." *Hall.* Old Norse *hegna*, Dut. *heynen*, to fence around, to protect, Germ. *hägen*, to fence round, preserve.

HAIRLY. *adv.* Hardly.
Prob. from *hair*, in the sense of fineness, as in *hair-breadth*. Sco. *hair*, a very small portion or quantity, as a *hair* of meal, *i.e.*, a few grains, (*Jam.*)

HAKE! *intj.* An expression of defiance.
"*Hake* for a fight!" See next word.

HAKE. *sb.* Provocation, excitement.
"They drank aw t' yell up ivery sup,
Wi' nouther *hake* nor quarrel."—*Lonsdale.*
Bret. *hek* or *heg*, provocation, irritation, *hega*, to provoke, irritate, (whence Fr. *agacer*?) Fris. *hagghen*, to quarrel, Germ. *häkelei*, teazing, provocation. *Hake* is prob. allied to, though not identical with *egg*, to incite; the idea in the latter is that of a sharp point, in the former that probably of a hook.

HAKE. *vn.* To tire, distress.
"As applied to land, it indicates exhaustion, or being overcropped."—*Dick.* Old Norse *heikiaz*, to fail, be wanting, Germ. *hagern*, to become lean, *hager*, lean.

HAKE. *sb.* A lean horse or cow. See above.

HAKE. *vn.* To butt with the horns.
Wel. *hychio*, to thrust, push, Old Norse *hæcka*, elevare.

HAKE. *sb.* A convivial meeting.
Perhaps from Wel. *haig*, crowd, large gathering.

HAKKER. *vn.* To stammer.
Bret. *hak*, stammering, *haketa*, to stammer, Wel. *hecian*, to halt, limp, Dut. *hakkelen*, to falter.

HALE or HELLE. *vn.* To pour.
Old Norse *hella*, to pour.

HALLAN. *sb.* A mud-wall partition within the entrance of a farm-house. *Jam.* refers to Suio-Goth. *haell*, the stone laid at the threshold of a door. But the Germ. *halle*, porch, Eng. *hall*, seems to offer a more natural explanation. As the author of West. and Cumb. Dial. observes, a *hallan* is to a cottage what a hall or lobby is to a large house.

HALLAN. *sb.* The division between two stalls for oxen or horses. Prob. for *halveling*, as a division into two equal parts, like Germ. *theilung*, partition, from *theilen*, to divide.

HAMMER-BLEAT. *sb.* The snipe, (*Dick*).
Properly, as in Lonsd., the note of the snipe. "In the breeding season the note of the male bird resembles the bleating of a goat."—*Dick*. Seeing the frequent interchange of *f* and *m*, I am of opinion that *hammer* is a corruption of Old Norse *hafr*, Ang.-Sax. *hæfer*, goat. Thus *hammer-bleat* would be simply the Ang.-Sax. *hæfer-blæt*, bleating of a goat.

HAMES. *sb.* The wood part of a horse-collar, to which the traces are attached. Flem. *haem*, a horse-collar, Ir. *ama*, collar.

HAMMER-BAND. *sb.* "In old times the horse was yoked to the cart by a rope from the shoulders, and an iron ring sliding on the shaft, held by a pin; this was *hammer-band* yoking."—*Dick*. Comp. Dial. Swed. *hammel-tyg*, (hammel-tie), the yoking of a cart or plough by swingle-trees. I incline to think that our word should be properly *hammel-band*. We see in the case of *hammer-bleat* how strong the tendency is, whenever the meaning of a word has been forgotten, to corrupt it to something which has at least the appearance of meaning.

HAM-SAM. *adv.* Promiscuously, all in confusion.
 "But weddit fwok rare laughing hed,
 I' th' bower wi' yan anither,
 For five or six gat into the bed,
 An' sat *ham-sam* togither."—Upshot, *Lonsdale*.

Sam = Lat. *cum*, Gr. σὺν, Sansc. *sam*, Wel. *cym*, &c., in the sense of combination, is common to all the Teutonic dialects. The Yorks. dialects have *sam*, to collect, gather together, the Sco. has *samin* (Goth. *samana*), adv., together. We have it in the above, in *sam-cast*, applied to two or more ridges ploughed together, and in *sank*, a quantity, collection of things. The prefix *ham* is used only alliteratively, as in *how-strow, helter-skelter, hummle-jummle*, forms to which our dialect is very partial.

HANCH. *vn.* To make a snap, as a dog when he bites.
Old Fr. *hancher*, to gnash or snatch at with the teeth.—*Cotg*.

HANK. *sb.* A knot or loop, metaph. a habit or practice.
Suio-Goth. *hank*, a loop for fastening a gate.

HANK. *va.* To fasten with a loop, tie up a horse.
Old Norse *hanka*, to fasten with a rope.

HANKLE. *vn.* To entangle.
A frequentative of *hank*, *q.v.*

HANNIEL. *sb.* A long lanky person.
Perhaps from Dial. Dan. and Swed. *hannel*, shaft of a flail, (corr. of *hand-vol*), in a metaph. sense, like *gammer-stang*.

HANSEL. *sb.* Prop. *handsel*. The first money received by a seller, as for instance, on opening a new shop. Hence, the first use of anything. Ang.-Sax. *hand-selen*, a putting into another's possession, Old Norse *hand-sal*, the conclusion of a bargain by joining hands. Shaking hands over a transaction was anciently, and is still in Scand., as with us, the token of concluding the bargain.

HANTEL. *sb.* A considerable quantity, a great deal.
According to Wedg., prop. *hankel*, Germ. *henkel*, Norw. *haank*, bunch, cluster of things hanging together.

HAP. *va.* To wrap up, but rather with loose coverings.
"Happyn or whappyn."—*Pr. Prv.* Wedg. supposes it a corruption of *whap* from *wlappe*. I am rather disposed, however, to look for a connection with Clev *hamp*, "an article of clothing which may have been worn next the skin, or at times over the under-clothing."—*Atk.* Dial. Dan. *hempe*, farmer's smock, Old Swed. *hampn*, vestis, indumentum. Perhaps with Old Norse *hjûpr*, sheet, shroud, *hypja*, a large, coarse covering. I suppose a lost verb, from which our word has been derived. See *happins* and *hippins*.

HAPPINS. *sb.* Thick woollen bed-covers.
Perhaps from Old Swed. *hampn*, vestis. indumentum, *hypja*, a large coarse covering. See *hap* and *hippins*.

HAR, HARTREE. *sb.* The stronger post of a gate, on which it swings. Old Norse *hiara*, Ang.-Sax. *hearra*, Dut. *harre*, hinge.

HARD. *adj.* Sour, applied to ale or beer.
Suio-Goth. *hardt*, "applied to liquor, denotes what is beginning to turn sour, *hardt dricka*, hard ale."—*Ihre.* Dial. Swed. *hard*, similarly applied. So by the Romans *durum* was used to denote rough or acid wine, in opposition to *molle*.

HARDEN-CLOTH. *sb.* A coarse linen fabric.
Ang.-Sax. *heordan*, hards, the refuse of tow.

HARNS. *sb.* The brains.
Old Norse *hjarni*, Dan. *hjerne*, cerebrum.

HARP ON. *va.* To keep dwelling on some subject, particularly an unpleasant one. Old Norse *harpa at*, to keep finding fault.

HARRY. *va.* To rob, applied most frequently to birds' nests. Ang.-Sax. *herian*, to ravage, plunder.

HASK. *adj.* Harsh, rough. Keen, dry, as applied to the weather. "Harske or haske."—*Pr. Prv.* Suio-Goth. *harsk*, Dan. *harsk*, harsh, rough, Zend. *husk*, Sansc. *sushka*, dry. It would rather seem, from the Sansc. and Zend., that *hask* is the original form.

HASTER. *sb.* A surfeit, (West. and Cumb. Dial.)
Seems to be from Old Norse *hasa*, to be surfeited with food.

HAUGH. *sb.* Alluvial land by the side of a river.
"A green plot in a meadow."—*Lonsd.* Ang.-Sax. *haga*, field, Old Norse *hagi*, pasture. Note the frequent change of *g* into *f*.

HAUNTED. *adj.* To be haunted to a place is to grow accustomed to it. Fr. *hanter*, to frequent, haunt.

HAVREL. *sb.* A prater, a simpleton.
Suio-Goth. *havar*, garrulous, Dial. Dan. *habbre*, to chatter fast.

HAVER. *sb.* Oats.
Old Norse *hafr*, Dan. *havre*, Germ. *hafer*, Dut. *haver*.

HAWSE. *sb.* Throat, neck, the collar of a mountain.
Haweswater derives its name from a promontory in the middle which divides it into two sheets, connected by a *hawse* or neck. Old Norse *háls*, Ang.-Sax., Germ., Dut. *hals*, neck.

HAYLER. *sb.* An industrious and energetic worker.
Haggler, the upper servant of a farm, *Isle of Wight*, is perhaps related. Then we have *hug*, a job of work, *North.*, which seems to point to Old Norse *haga*, to manage, to arrange, *hagr*, handy, skilful. As a frequentative of *haga* would be *haggle*, contr. *hale*, whence, I take it, the present word.

HAYSTER. *va.* and *n.* To starve, to be pinched with cold or hunger. Also, to pull about roughly. In the latter sense the word seems related to Ang.-Sax. *hést*, Old Norse *hastr*, hot, hasty, violent, Suio-Goth. *hetsa*, Fin. *hasittaa*, to incite, set dogs on, Swed. *hasta*, to hurry one on, &c.

HEADWARK, (pron. *heedwark*). *sb.* The head-ache.
Ang.-Sax. *heafod-wærc*, a hurt or sore on the head, Old Norse *höfud verkr*, head-ache.

HEAF. *sb.* See *hefted*.

HECK. *sb.* A rack for hay, &c. A half-door or hatch-door. Ang.-Sax. *hæca*, hatch, Dan. *hekke*, rack, Dut. *hekken*, gate, rail.

HECKLES. *sb.* The long feathers on a cock's neck.
In Scot. *heckle* is a fly for angling, dressed with a cock's feather, and deriving its name, according to *Jam.*, from its resemblance to a *heckle*, or comb for dressing flax. If the explanation of *Jam.* be correct, the heckles would be so called on account of such flies being made from them. But the converse would seem to be in a more natural sequence, in which case *heckles* may be from Old Norse *hakka*, to elevate, to raise, in reference to the manner in which the feathers stand out when the bird is enraged.

HERONSEW. *sb.* The heron.
Fr. *heronceau*, a young heron.

HEFT. *sb.* Handle, as of a knife. A pretext or excuse, prevarication, deception. Ang.-Sax. *hæft*, Germ. *heft*, Dan. *hefte*, hilt, handle, Swed. *häfta*, to take hold of. The second sense comes metaph., like *handle*.

HEFTED. *adj.* Hefted or heaf-ganging sheep are "mountain sheep let along with a farm, and depastured upon a particular part of a common called a *heaf*."—*Dick*. *Hefted* seems to be from Old Norse *hefda*, to acquire by use or prescription, *hefdadr*, acquired in such manner, and to apply to the right, probably originally acquired by usage, to pasture upon a particular spot. And *heaf* (which is sometimes, in a mistaken spirit of amendment, altered into *heath*) may be referable to Old Norse *hæfi*, meta, scopus, proportio, jus.

HEFTER. *sb.* Used to express the effective disposing, as of an argument, like *clincher*, both words being derived from the idea of firmly grasping. Compare Old Norse *haft*, bond, hand-cuff.

HEIN. *intj.* Be off!
Old Norse *hedan*, away! be off! Ray gives this as a Cumb. word, but I have never heard it used.

HELM-WIND. *sb.* A violent wind which at particular seasons blows from the summit of Cross Fell. It has been generally derived from the *helm* or cloud which rests during the period upon the top of the mountain. It may, however, be possibly open to question whether the word may not properly be *whelm*, Dut. *wemelen*, to whirl, turn round, *helm-wind* being thus the same as *whirl-wind*. Comp. also Sco. "*helm* of weet," a great fall of rain.

HENCH. *va.* To throw by a jerk from the *haunch* or hip.
Old High Germ. *hlancha*, whence Fr. *hanche*, hip.

HERPLE. *vn.* To walk lame, or as one having corns.
Old Norse *herpast*, to be contracted as with cramp. If not another form of *hurkle*, Old Norse *hörkla*, to hobble.

HESP. *sb.* A latch, clasp, or fastening.
Ang.-Sax. *hæps*, Old Norse *hespa*, Dan. *hasp*, a latch or bolt.

HEUGH. *sb.* A dry dell, a ravine without water.—*Dick.* Lonsd., a rocky hill. *Jam.* gives both the above meanings, and connects the word with Ang.-Sax. *hou*, hill. I am rather inclined to think that there may be two different words, one of which, containing the sense of a dell or ravine, may be allied to *howk*, Suio-Goth. *holka*, to excavate.

HIGHT. *va.* To promise.
Ang.-Sax. *hátan*, Old Norse *heita*, to promise.

HIKE. *va.* To throw up in the arms, as nurses do children.
Old Norse *hæcka*, elevare.

HINE-BERRY. *sb.* A raspberry.
Dan. *hindbær*, Dial. Swed. *hinbär*, Germ. *himbeere*, raspberry.

HIND. *sb.* An upper farm-servant.
Ang.-Sax. *hína*, a servant. "The word properly signifies member of a family, in which sense the Swed. *hjun* is used at the present day."—*Wedg.* And throughout the North the farm-servants used formerly, as is still the case to a considerable extent, to live as members of the family.

HIPPINS. *sb.* Napkins or under-clothes for infants.
Jamieson's explanation is, "for wrapping about the *hips*," which, as Atkinson observes, would be more satisfactory if *hip* were the word generally used in the dialect. It seems to me to be most probably connected with Old Norse *hypja*, which seems to have had very much of the same meaning as our word.

G

HISK. *vn.* To catch the breath, as one does on first going into the water. Old Norse *hixta*, to gasp or sob.

HITCH. *vn.* To hop.
From the same origin as *hotch*. Bav. *hutschen*, to rock, to wriggle forward, Swiss *hotzen*, to shake, to jog. The idea is that of progression by a series of jerks.

HOBBLE. *sb.* A difficulty, a fix.
The idea is that of fettering or confining, as in *hobble*, to tie the hind feet of a horse, to prevent him from straying. The original idea is that of impeded action, as in Sco. *habble*, to stammer, Eng. *hobble*, to limp, Dut. *hobbelen*, to stammer, to jolt, Bav. *hoppelen*, to jog up and down, as a bad rider on a trotting horse.— *Wedg.*

HODDEN-GREY. *sb.* Cloth made from the natural black and white wool. Properly, I take it, *holden-grey*, from the durability of its colour. Old Norse *haldinn*, holding, enduring, *hald-gôdr*, durable, (applied to clothes,) Dan. *holden*, whole, entire. Jamieson's derivation from Old Eng. *hoiden*, rustic, clownish, is not, I think, suitable—to those who gave the name the thing would not seem rustic or clownish.

HOFE THICK. *adj.* Simple, foolish.
Perhaps not from *half*, but from *awf*, an elf, Ang.-Sax. *ælf*, Old Norse *alfr*. *Thick* in our dialect means intimate ; hence *hofe-thick* may mean intimate with elves, those who were supposed to have relations with another world being, as regards this, "not all there." Comp. Lonsd. *hoafen*, a half-witted person, Clev. *awfish*, half-witted.

HOG. *sb.* A lamb for twelve months after weaning.
I think that the origin of this word may be found in Welsh *hogiau*, *hogyn*, stripling, lad, *hogen*, a young girl—*hog* meaning simply a young animal. The Teutonic idioms have *hag*, perhaps a parallel word, as in Ang.-Sax. *hægsteald*, Dut. *hagestolt*, bachelor, virgin, novice.

HOGGERS. *sb.* Upper stockings without feet.
Probably, like *hough*, and *hock* (of a horse), from Ang.-Sax. *hoh*, the ham.

HOKKER. *vn.* To scramble in an awkward manner.
Also *Lonsd.*, to crouch over the fire. The idea in both cases is the same—that of crookedness. Old Norse *hokra*, to go bent, to crouch.

HOLM. *sb.* An island. Also alluvial land by a river side, "which in time of flood may become more or less insular.

and which, at an earlier time, may have been complelely so."—*Atk.* Ang.-Sax. *holm*, Old Norse *holmr*, Dan. *holm*, a small island.

Hoo. *intj.* Well!
Icel. *hu*, seems to be used very much in the same way, ho! well!

HOOD. *sb.* The hob or corner of the fire place.
I am rather inclined to take the word to be the same as the Icel. *hlôd*, which appears to have the same meaning. It is a derivative of *hlada*, to pile, to heap, in reference to its use for setting things upon. So *hob* seems to be from *heap*.

HOOP. *sb.* A six-quart measure, "formerly made of a broad wooden hoop."—*Dick.* Or, bound with hoops like a barrel.

HOOSE. *sb.* A cough.
Clev. *hooze*, to wheeze or breathe with difficulty and noise. Lonsd. *hooze*, difficult breathing or half-cough, peculiar to cattle. "Hoose, or cowghe (host or hoost),—*Pr. Prv.* Old Norse *hâs*, Ang.-Sax. *has*, hoarse. Ang.-Sax. *hweosan*, Old Norse, *hvæsa*, Norw. *hæsa*, to wheeze, pant, have difficulty in breathing, Old Norse *hosti*, Dut. *host*, Dan. *hoste*, cough, Lonsd. and Sco. *host*, a cough, Crav. *hoste*, hoarseness.

HOPPLE. *va.* To fetter, fasten the legs of a horse, to prevent him from straying. See *hobble*.

HOPPY. *sb.* A horse, in nursery language.
Fris. *hoppe*, a horse, "now only in the language of children," *(Outzen)*, Dan. *hoppe*, horse.

HOTCH. *vn.* To shake as with laughter. See *hitch*.

HOTS. *sb.* Panniers to carry manure, &c., on horseback in the field. Dut. *hotte*, basket, pannier, Fr. *hotte*, a basket carried on the back, Prov. Germ. *hotte*, a pannier carried on the back by vintagers. *Hot* seems the same word as *hod* (of a bricklayer).

HOTTER. *vn.* To totter.
Swiss *hottern*, to shake, Dial. Swed. *huttra*, to tremble or shiver.

HOWDY. *sb.* A midwife.
Old Norse *jôd*. a baby, *jôdmodir*, a midwife.

How. *adj.* Hollow.
Probably the same as Clev. *holl*. Old Norse *holr*, Ang.-Sax. *hol*, Germ. *hohl*, hollow.

How! *intj.* A word used in driving cattle, to quicken their speed. Fris., Icel., Dan. *hou!* used in the same manner.

How. *sb.* A sepulchral mound or barrow. A natural hill.
Old Norse *haugr*, a mound, especially a grave mound. "In Clev. the word, with about two exceptions, denotes the grave-hills on the moors."—*Atk.* In our district many of them are natural hills, and of considerable elevation, as Silver How, near Grasmere, but it is possible that an artificial mound may, in some cases, have been raised, in accordance with the ancient desire for a burial-place in a conspicuous situation, upon the summit of the natural one. In North., *how* changes into *haugh*.

Howk. *va.* To excavate, to scoop out.
Suio-Goth. *holka*, to excavate. Hence *hulk*, that which is hollowed, has the inside scooped out.

Hoyse. *va.* To hoist.
Dan. *heise*, Swed. *hissa*, Fr. *hisser*, to hoist.

Hubble. *sb.* A crowd, a confused gathering.
Swed. *hop*, Dut. *hoop*, Germ. *haufe*, a heap, crowd of people, Dut. *hobbelen*, to collect into a heap.

Hulet. *sb.* The owl.
Fr. *hulotte*, a young owl.

Hull. *sb.* A small shed for calves, pigs, &c.
Ang.-Sax. *hul*, hull, shell, from *helan*, to cover. The idea is that of a light and simple structure, as we speak of a building being "only a shell."

Hullert. *adj.* Coagulated, applied to blood.
Seems allied to Bret. *kaouled*, Welsh *ceulaidd*, coagulated, Welsh *ceulo*, to coagulate.

Hummel or Humlin. *sb.* A sheep with both testicles in its loins.—*Dick.* Ang.-Sax. *hâmelan*, the testicles, Germ. *hammeln*, to castrate, Swed. *hammel*, a castrated ram.

Hunsup. *sb.* A turbulent outcry.
Originally a tune played on the horn under the windows of sportsmen very early in the morning, to awaken them. "Hence the term was applied to any noise of an awakening or alarming nature." - *Hall.*

HURSLE. *va.* To shrug the shoulders.
"Then Tyelor he began to chow,
An' *hursied* up his shoulder."—Upshot, *Lonsdale.*
Probably another form of *hurkle.* Dut. *hurken,* to crouch, to shrug. Old Norse *hörëla,* to hobble.

HUSH. *sb.* A sudden gush.
Prov. Germ. *husch,* a sudden shower of rain.

HUZZIF, HOUSEWIFE. *sb.* A woman's case for needles, &c. Old Norse *húsi,* a case, *skæris-húsi,* a scissors case. Hence *housewife* seems to be simply a woman's case, A.S. *wif,* woman.

I.

I. *prep.* In.
Old Norse, Dan., Swed. *i,* in.

ICE-SHOCKLE, ICE-SHOGGLE. *sb.* An icicle.
Fris. *is-jokel,* Norw. *is-jukel.*

ILL. *adj.* Evil, wicked.
Old Norse *illr,* Suio-Goth. *ill,* Norw. *ill,* wicked.

ILK. *pron.* Each.
"Ilke or eche."—*Pr. Prv.* Ang.-Sax. *ælc,* Dut. *elc.*

ILL-GIEN. *adj.* Ill-tempered.
Possibly from Old Norse *illgiarn, malignus,* if not simply *ill-given.*

IME, IMIN. *sb.* Scum, thin covering, hoar-frost.
Sco. *oam.* Old Norse *hem,* a thin film of ice, *eimr,* thin vapour.

IMP. *sb.* A ring or circle added to a bee-hive from beneath. Ang.-Sax. *impian,* Germ. *impfen,* Dan. *ympe,* to engraft. Welsh *imp,* a scion, *impio,* to graft. Hail. gives *imp,* an addition, insertion, *North.*

INCOME. *sb.* A sore or swelling not caused by external injury. See *ancome.*

ING. *sb.* Meadow land, in a low situation.
Old Norse *engi,* Suio-Goth. *æng,* Dan. *eng.* According to Ihre, *æng* properly denotes level land by the sea-shore. From the root-meaning of the word, which seems to be found in Old Norse *engr,* Ang.-Sax. *enge,* Germ. *eng,* Welsh *ing,* narrow, Sansc. *ac,* to bend or contract, I should suppose that the original meaning has been, as Ihre says, strips of pasture land by the sea-shore ; or still more commonly, in the bed of a river, formed by the shifting of its channel.

INGLE. *sb.* Fire, flame.
"An *ingle* of sticks is a common expression in Cumb."—*West. and Cum. Dial.* Gael. *aingeal*, fire, light.

INKLE. *sb.* Coarse narrow tape, as used for shoe-ties, &c. Derived by Wedg. from Fr. *lignol*, strong thread used by shoemakers, &c., whence Eng. *lingel*, thread, and then, by the loss of the initial *l*, *ingle*. It does not seem to me, however, altogether certain that *inkle*, narrow tape, may not be directly from *ing*, which (see *ing*) both in Celtic and Teutonic signifies narrow.

INSENSE. *va.* To make one to understand a thing.
A good old Shakesperian word.

IZELS. *sb.* Embers, hot ashes, flakes from burning straw, &c. "Isyl of fyre."—*Pr. Prv.* Ang.-Sax. *ysela*, embers, hot ashes, Old Norse *eysa*, cinis ignitus.

J.

JAB. *vn.* To slop over, or against the sides, (as of liquids in a vessel). Clev. *jaup.* Old Norse *gialpa*, to dash against, as waves upon the shore.

JABBER. *sb.* Garrulity, chattering.
Clev. *javver.* "Javeryn, jaberyn, garrulo."—*Pr. Prv.* Fr. *japper*, to yelp, *javioler*, to gabble.

JACKALEGS. *sb.* A pocket clasp-knife.
From Jacques de Liege, a famous Flemish cutler.—*Jam.*

JAGS. *sb.* Rags, splinters.
"Jagge or dagge of a garment, fractillus."—*Pr. Prv.* (referring to the prevailing fashion of fancifully *jagging* or cutting the edges of a garment). Old Norse *jacka*, to cut with a blunt instrument, Dan. *jask*, rag, tatter.

JAM. *va.* To squeeze, compress, wedge.
"To press in between something that confines the space on either side like the *jambs* of a door."—*Wedg.* This definition, I own, strikes me as somewhat narrow, and I rather suspect a connection with Wel., Corn., Bret. *gen*, Ir. *gein*, Gael. *geinn*, a wedge, allied to Lat. *cuneus*.

JAMMERS, JIMMERS. *sb.* Small cupboard hinges.
Properly *jimmels*, from Fr. *jumelles*, Lat. *gemelli*, twins, in reference to the hinges as working in pairs.

JAMP. *vb.* Jumped, pret. of jump.

JANGLE. *vn.* To wrangle, squabble.
"Jangelyn or iaveryn, oggario."—*Pr. Prv.* Dut. *jangelen*, to yelp, Old Fr. *jangler*, to prattle, jest, lie, Old Norse *jagg*, squabbling.

JANNOCK. *adj.* Just, proper, right, straight, or even.
Old Norse *jafn*, Old Swed. *jæmn*, even or straight, Old Swed. *jæmka*, Dial. Swed. *janka*, to make even or straight. Comp., also, Welsh, *iawn*, right, equitable, just.

JARBLE. *vn.* To bespatter.
Probably for *jabble*. See *jab*.

JAYLS. *sb.* Cracks and fissures in timber.
See *geals*.

JAYFEL. *vn.* To stagger, walk unsteadily.
Seeing the close connection that exists between different kinds of imperfect action, as between limping or walking lame and stammering, (see *hakker*, *hobble*, *stotter*), I am inclined to think that the origin of the present word may be found in Old Norse *geifla*, to mumble.

JEDDER. *vn.* To jar.
Dan. *jaddre*, to babble, prattle.

JEEST. *sb.* A joist.
"Gyste, that gothe over the flore."—*Palsg.* in *Way.* Fr. *giste*, a bed, place to lie on, from *gesir*, Lat. *jacere*, to lie. "The term *sleeper*, with which railways have made us so familiar, is a repetition of the same idea."—*Wedg.*

JERT. *vn.* To jerk.
Jert and *jerk* seem to be different forms of the same word, *t* and *k* interchanging as in various other instances. The root may perhaps be traced to Wel. *gyr*, impetus, impulse.

JEYK. *vn.* To creak.
Sco. *jeeg*, *geig*. Jam. refers to Germ. *geigen*, to play on the fiddle, which is related to *jig*, a rapid movement, Welsh *gogi*, to shake. It refers, therefore, to the action of playing on the fiddle rather than to the sound produced. In any case, I think the Welsh *gwicio*, to creak, offers a more probable derivation. The Bav. *gigken*, to utter broken sounds, may also be allied.

JILLET. *sb.* A jilt.
Clev. *giglet* shows the original form, whence comes first our *jillet*, and then Eng. *jilt*. The origin may be Celtic—Pryce having *giglot* as a Corn. word, signifying a wanton, lascivious girl. The root is the same as that of *geggles*, Welsh *gogi*, to move, stir.

JIMP. *adj.* "Tight, too little, tucked up in the flank as greyhounds are."—*Dick.* The most general sense, however, is that of elegance derived from slenderness, as in Sco. *jimp*, neat and slender. Welsh *gwymp*, smart, neat.

JOGGLE. *sb.* To jog, to shake.
A frequentative from *jog*, Welsh *gogi*, to shake.

JOME. *sb.* The jaumb or side-stone of a door or window.
Fr. *jambe*, leg, also side of a door or window.

JOOK. *vn.* To stoop or bend to avoid a blow or a missile.
Germ. *zucken*, to shrink. Jam. also refers to Suio-Goth. *duka*, Dut. *duycken*, to duck or stoop, as radically allied.

JOOK. *sb.* A long and tiresome journey on foot.—*Dick.*
Germ. *zug*, pull, tug, expedition.

JORAM. *sb.* A large mess, abundance.
Welsh *gorm*, full, *goramlu*, to superabound, from *gor*, much, excessive.

JOWL. *vb.* To jumble.
"Relates more particularly to the disturbing of a vessel containing fluid."—*Dick.* This might make us think of Old Norse *giögl*, water, fluid. But perhaps only a contraction of *joggle*.

K

KALE, (pron. *keall*). *sb.* Broth, oatmeal porridge, greens,
Old Norse *kâl*, Dan. *kaal*, Ang.-Sax. *cawl*, Germ. *kohl*, Welsh *cawl*, Gael., Ir. *câl*, Corn. *caul*, Bret. *caol*, Lat. *caulis*, Eng. *cole*. The original meaning, then, is first cabbage, then greens in general, and finally broth, as made from greens of all sorts.

KANJY. *adj.* Cross-grained, ill-tempered.
Comp. Old Norse *kangin-yrdi*, jeering words, Icel. *kank*, jibes.

KAYK. *vn.* To poke out the neck and stare.
"An' Peat lass, wud her yallow muffs,
Stuid *kaikin* leyke a gezzlin."—Upshot. *Lonsdale.*
Old Norse *kaga*, to bend forward and peep, pry (*Cleasby*) exactly represents our word, which seems to be the same word as *keek*, with a little difference of application.

KAY-BITTIT. *adj.* Marked by having a piece cut out of the ear, applied to sheep. The former part of the word seems to be connected with Old Norse *kjagg*, a blunt hatchet, Dial. Swed. *kage*, a stump. *Bittit* may be from O.N. *bildôttr*, marked on the cheek, (applied to sheep) perhaps in the sense of marked by cutting, from *bildr*, a hatchet.

KAYK. *sb.* A twist in the neck.
Clev. *keek*, to throw back the head and neck. Crav. *keak*, a distortion of the spine. Old Norse *keikr*, having the back-bone bent back, Norw. *kjeika*, to bend back or to one side.

KAYMT. *adj.* Crooked, contradictious.
Welsh, Gael., Ir. *cam*, crooked.

KAVE, (pron. *keav*). *va.* and *n.* To move restlessly, paw, as a horse, also to rake straw, &c. Old Norse *kafa*, to spread or turn over hay, &c., Norw. *kava*, to use a rake, turn over hay, &c., move things fidgettingly, Dut. *kaven*, eventilare paleas, (*Kil.*)

KEBBY-STICK. *sb.* A hooked stick.
Lonsd. *kibble*, a thick, strong stick. Old Norse *képpr*, Dan. *kiep*, stick, staff, Lat. *cippus*, pole.

KEEK. *vn.* To peep.
Suio-Goth. *kika*, Dut. *kijken*, Fris. *kiecke*, to gaze, stare.

KEENS. *sb.* Cracks or chaps in the hands from frost.
Clev. *kins*. Ang.-Sax. *cine*, chink, cleft.

KEEN. *adj.* Eager, sharp, earnest.
Ang.-Sax. *cêne*, Jutl. *kön*, Germ. *kühn*, vigorous, energetic.

KELD, KELL. *sb.* A spring.
Old Norse *kelda*, Suio-Goth. *kælla*, Dan. *kilde*, spring, fountain.

KELK. *va.* To beat or thump.
  "Why, man! she *kelk'd* thee leyke a log,
  An' chess'd thee leyke a cwoly dog."—*Stagg*,

Atk. suggests that *kelk* is a transposed form of *click*, in the sense (which I have taken to be the original one) of striking.

KELTER. *sb.* Condition, circumstances.
To be in high *kelter* = to be in good condition. *Wedg.* approves of Skinner's suggestion that the origin is to be found in Dial. Swed. *hiltra sig*, signifying to gird oneself up, as in readiness for work.

KEMPS. *sb.* Hairs among wool.
: Seems most probably connected with *kemb*, comb, *kempster*, a woman who cleans wool.—*Hall.*

KEN. *va.* To know, be acquainted with.
: Ang.-Sax. *cennan*, Old Norse *kenna*, Germ. *kennen*.

KENSPECT, KENSPECKLED. *adj.* Conspicuous, easily distinguished. Clev. *kenspect.* Suio-Goth. *kænnespak*, Norw. *kjennespak*, sharp or quick in finding out. Our word contains an inversion of the sense, probably arising out of the idea that *spak* (Old Norse *spakr*, wise, knowing), is from *speck* in the sense of a distinguishing mark.

KEP. *va.* To catch, as a ball.
: Ang.-Sax. *cêpan*, to catch, Old Norse *kippa*, to snatch.

KERN-WINNIN. *sb.* Harvest-home.
: Ang.-Sax. *winnan*, to strive, labour, hence to acquire by toil. *Kern* (Ang.-Sax. *cyrn*, churn) has reference to the ancient custom, referred to by Brand, of producing cream in a churn as part of the entertainment.

KESH. *sb.* The cow-parsnip.
: Lonsd. *kesh*, white weed, a kind of hemlock. *Kecks, cashes,* the dry, hollow stalks of umbelliferous plants.—*Prior.* "Kyx or bunne, or drye weed."—*Pr. Prv.* Prior's objection to what seems the most natural derivation, from Welsh *cecys*, hollow stalks, hemlock, on the ground that "our ancestors borrowed nothing (in the way of agricultural terms, I apprehend to be his meaning) from that language but proper names of localities," does not seem at any rate to be borne out in our district, where it is in such terms more especially that the vestiges of the Celt are to be traced.

KESLOP. *sb.* The cured stomach of a calf used for making rennet. Dut. *kaeslibbe*, cheese rennet, Ang.-Sax. *ceselib*, Germ. *käslab*, curded milk.

KETT. *sb.* Carrion, hence filth of any kind.
: Old Norse *köt, ket*, flesh, meat, Dut. *kaet*, filth.

KEVVEL. *vn.* To sprawl, kick, or leap awkwardly.
: "Lang sair they *kevveled*, danced, and sang."—*Stagg.*
: A frequentative of *kave*, q.v.

KICK. *sb.* The top of the fashion.
: Perhaps from Old Norse *skick*, Dan. *skik*, custom, usage, fashion.

KILP. *sb.* A bend, a crook.
Lonsd. also a pot-hook. Old Norse *kilpr*, flexura, ansula, quâ manubrium mulctri annectitur, Dial. Swed. *kjelp*, handle of a bucket.

KILT UP. *va.* To tuck up a dress.
Dan. *kilte op*, Suio-Goth. *upkilta*, to fasten or tuck up a dress.

KINK. *sb.* A twist in a rope or cord, which prevents it running freely. Also, a convulsive fit of coughing, as in the hooping cough. Old Norse *keingr*, a crook or bending, Swed. *kink*, a twist in a chain, such as to prevent its running. Ang.-Sax. *cincung*, a paroxysm of laughter. Atk. connects these two last together, "the transition of idea from the twist which prevents the free passage of the chain, rope, or string, to the effects of the paroxysm which interferes with the free passage of the breath, being both simple and natural."

KING-COUGH. *sb.* The hooping-cough.
Properly *kink-cough*. North. *kink-haust.—Hall.* Dut. *kink-hoest*, hooping-cough (*hoest*, cough), Swed. *kik*, cough. See *kink*.

KIPPER. *sb.* A term applied to salmon when out of season or spawning. Dut. *kippen*, excludere ova. Old Norse *kæpa*, parturire, (referring to the seal.) "A *kipper* is thus a spawner."—*Jam.*

KIPPERT. *adj.* Partly cured (applied to fish.)
"As salmon, in the foul state, are unfit for use while fresh, they are usually cured and hung up. Hence the word, properly denoting a spawning fish, has been transferred to one that is salted and dried. Indeed, through Scotland, the greatest part of those formerly *kippered*, by the vulgar at least, were foul fish." *Jam.*

KIRROCK. *sb.* A circle of stones, of the sort generally called druidical. I take the word to be the same as Lat. *circus*, Welsh, *cwrc*, curvature, from the root *car* or *cir*, to bend or turn. The subject is more fully discussed in another place.

KIST. *sb.* A chest.
Old Norse, Suio-Goth, *kista*, Ang.-Sax. *cyst*, Dan. *kiste*, Dut. *kist*, chest.

KIT. *sb.* A small tub or pail.
Dut. *kit, kitte*, a small tub or pail, Welsh *cydan*, a small bag, *cydu*, to pouch.

KIT. *sb.* Lot or company, used contemptuously.
Germ. *kitte*, flock, covey. The origin, I take it, is to be found in Welsh *cydio*, to join, couple.

KITE. *sb.* The belly.
   Old Norse *kvidr*, Ang.-Sax. *cwith*, Suio-Goth. *qwed*, stomach; belly.

KITLIN. *sb.* A kitten.
   Old Norse *ketlingr*, a kitten, Norw. *kjetla*, to kitten.

KITTLE. *va.* To tickle.
   Ang.-Sax. *citelian*, Old Norse *kitla*, Dut. *kittelen*, to tickle.

KITTLE. *adj.* Ticklish, excitable, easily acted on.
   Norw. *ketall*, Swed. *kittlig*, Dial. Swed. *ketall*, excitable.

KIZZENT. *adj.* Parched or shrivelled.
   Crav. *kizzened.* I think the author of the Crav. Gloss. is right in taking the word to be the same as *guizened*, which Ray gives as applied to tubs or barrels that leak through drought. The origin, then, is evidently to be found in Old Norse *gisinn*, leaky (of tubs and vessels.)

KNACK. *vn.* To speak affectedly.
   I take *knack* to be another form of *knap*, q.v.

KNAP. *va.* To tap, strike gently and quickly, to crack or break. Suio-Goth. *knæppa*, Belg. *knappen*, to strike, to crack or break, Welsh *cnipws*, fillup.

KNAP. *vn.* To talk in an affected manner, to ape fine speaking, a common way of doing which is to give a close sound to the broad open vowels.

> "She talk'd a' vast, but *knapp't* sae sair,
> At nin cud understand her."—*Lonsdale.*

   Clev. *knapper.* Sco. *knap,* "to speak after the English manner, to *knap* Suddrone, to speak like the Southerners."—*Jam.* Old Norse *hneppa*, to cut short, curtail, Old Norse *knappr*, Dan. *knap*, tight, contracted.

KNEP. *va.* To bite in play, as horses do.—*Dick.*
   Clev. *knep*, to crop the herbage in small bits, to bite or crop short herbage. Suio-Goth. *knappra*, to bite gently, Dan. *knibe*, to nip.

KNEUDD. *va.* To butt with the head, as a calf or lamb does when sucking.—*Dick.* Old Norse *knoda*, to knead, Dan. *gnide*, to rub.

KNIDGEL. *va.* To castrate by ligature.
   Ang.-Sax. *cnytan*, Suio-Goth. *knyta*, to bind, tie, fasten.

KNOP. *sb.* A small tub.
   Seems allied to Old Norse *knappr*, Dan. *knap*, Dut. *knoppe*, knob, in the sense of rotundity.

KNOPPY. *adj.* Lumpy, knotty.
Ang.-Sax. *cnæp*, Fris. *knob*, Dut. *knop*, Germ. *knopf*, Welsh *cnwb*, a knob or knot.

KNOW. *sb.* A rounded hill.
Properly *knoll*. Ang.-Sax. *cnoll*, hill, summit.

KNURR'T. *adj.* Stunted in growth.
Lonsd. *knorr*, a dwarfish fellow, Sco. *knurl*, a dwarf. Jam. refers to Dut. *knorre*, a knot in timber. Comp. also Swed. *knorla*, to curl or twist up, and Prov. Germ. *knorz*, a knot, and, figuratively, a little stumpy, fellow.

KYE. *sb.* Cows.
Ang.-Sax. *cy*, Old Norse *kŷr*, cows.

KYPE. *vn.* To insinuate to the disadvantage of any one.
Perhaps allied to Old Norse *kifa*, Dut. *kijven*, to quarrel, to wrangle.

KYPE. *vn.* To die.
Seems to be used somewhat as a cant phrase—"'t' ould horse is gaan to *kype*."—*Dick.* I am rather inclined to take it to be an oblique form of *coup*, to overturn, corresponding with Germ. *kippen*, to tip over, to upset.

KISTY. *adj.* Ill-tempered.—*Dick.* "Dainty, nice in eating."—*West. and Cumb. Dial.* The latter sense, which is also that of *Lonsd.* and *Crav.*, must at all events have been the original one. Belg. *zeisetig*, Dut. *kiesch*, nice, fastidious, from *kiezen*, to choose. Ang.-Sax. *cis*, nice in eating, *cisnes*, daintiness, fastidiousness.

L.

LAAL, LYLE. *adj.* Little.
Comp. Dan. *lille*, small, similarly contracted from Old Norse *litill*.

LABBER. *vn.* To splash or dabble.
North. *labber*, to splash, to dirty, *lape*, to walk about in the mud. Clev. *labber*, to splash, make wet. Prov. Germ. *läppern*, to make wet, sprinkle, Dut. *lobberen*, to tramp through wet and mire. The sense seems to vary between that of wet and dirt, and we may think of Gael. *laib*, mud, mire, and of the root as Sansc. *li*, Gael. *leagh*, Old Norse *hla*, liquescere.

LAGHTER. *sb.* A brood of chickens, &c. Also a setting of eggs. The latter sense, which is that of various other dialects, is, I apprehend, the correct one, from Ang.-Sax. *leegan*, Dut. *leggen*, to lay (eggs).

LAGGIN. *sb.* The end of the stave outside a cask.
Lonsd. *lag*. Old Norse *lögg*, Suio-Goth. *lagg*, Swed. *lagg*, border of a cask.

LAIK. *vn.* To play, to amuse oneself.
Ang.-Sax. *lâcan*, Old Norse *leika*, to play. The original meaning, as found in Goth. *laikan*, would seem to be to jump about, to dance.

LAIT. *va.* To seek, search for.
Old Norse *leyta*, Old Swed. *laita*, Dan. *lede*, to seek.

LAITIN. *sb.* The circuit of neighbours invited to a funeral, &c. See *lait*.

LALL, LALLUP. *vn.* To loll out the tongue.
Chesh., Somers. *lolliker*, the tongue. Comp. Sansc. *lallana*, Swiss *lalli*, Bav. *leller*, the tongue, Swiss *lallen*, to put out the tongue, the general origin being probably onomatopœic.

LAM. *va.* To beat.
Old Norse *lemja*, to beat, *lama*, to bruise.

LAND-LOUPER. *sb.* One who decamps without paying debts, a vagabond. Old Norse *land-hlaupari*, a vagabond.

LANE. *vb.* To connive at, or hide a fault.
Old Norse *leyna*, to cover, to conceal.

LANGEL, LANKET. *sb.* A fetter for sheep.
Lonsd. *langled*, having the legs tied. Suio-Goth. *laenka*, to fasten. Dan. *lænke*, to fetter. *Lang(el)* and *lank(et)* seem only different forms of the same word *lang* or *lank*.

LANGSEN. *adv.* Long since.
Swed. *längesedan*, Dial Swed. *lang-san*.

LANGSOME. *adj.* Tedious, wearisome.
Old Norse *langsâmr*, Dan. *langsom*, tedious.

LANT, LANTER. *sb.* The game of loo.
Rather seems to have some connection with *lonter*, to loiter, either in the sense of an idle way of passing time, or in that of "the flapping or shaking of loose things," (as cards), Swiss

lottern, to joggle, &c., which, according to *Wedg.*, is the original idea in many of the words signifying idleness.

LAP. Leap't, pret. of leap.

LAPSTAN. *sb.* The stone on which the shoemaker beats his leather. Not, as might be supposed, from his having it in his lap, but from Dut. *lappen*, Dan. *lappe*, to botch, to mend, Dut. *schoen-lapper*, a cobbler.

LARRAP. *va.* To beat.
Dut. *larp*, lash, *larpen*, to thrash in a particular manner, all the flails being lifted from the ground at once.— *Wedg.* Comp. also Welsh *llarpio*, to rend, tear to rags.

LASH. *sb.* The diarrhœa.
Crav. *lask*, Clev. *lax*. Germ. *laxiren*, to purge, Lat. *laxus*.

LATHE. *sb.* A barn.
Old Norse *hlada*, Dan. *lade*, barn, Old Norse *hlada*, to load, lay up.

LAVE. *sb.* The rest.
Ang.-Sax. *lâv*, Old Norse *leifar*, remainder.

LAV-LUG'T. *adj.* Having the ears hanging instead of being erect. Old Norse *laf-eyrdr*, having hanging ears, from *lafa*, to hang.

LAVRICK. *sb.* The lark.
Ang.-Sax. *lawerc*, *laferc*, whence, by contraction, Eng. *lark*.

LEAH. *sb.* A scythe.
Old Norse *ljâr*, Old Swed. *lee*, Dan. *le*, Fris. *lee*, Low Germ, *lehe*, scythe. Comp. Sansc. *lava*, sickle, from *lu*, to cut, reap.

LEEVE-TALE. *adj.* Easy to sell or dispose of.
Would rather seem to be properly *leef-telt*, easily reckoned, from *leef*, willingly, readily, and Ang.-Sax. *tellan*, to reckon.

LEISTER. *sb.* A pronged spear for catching eels, &c.
Old Norse *liôstr*, a fish-spear, from *liôsta*, to transfix, the root of which is perhaps to be found in Sansc. *lu*, to cut.

LERT. *vn.* To jerk, to pitch a light article out of hand. Would rather seem to be formed on Welsh *llaw*, the hand, *llawio*, to handle. I am unable to suggest anything more precise.

LESSIL. *sb.* A wanton woman.—*Hall.*
Prob. from Ang.-Sax. *leas*, empty, false, Norw. *leos*, lascivious.

LET-WIT. *vn.* To make known, let out.
Dut. *laeten weten*, to make known.

LIB. *va.* To castrate.
Dut. *lubben*, Dial. Dan. *live*, to castrate, the root of which may perhaps be Sansc. *lu*, to cut,

LIBBIE. A contraction of Elizabeth.
Libb is similarly used for Elizabeth in Dial. Swed., according to Rietz.

LICK. *va.* To beat.
Welsh *llachio*, to beat, cudgel, Suio-Goth, *laegga*, to strike.

LIG. *vn.* To lie.
Ang.-Sax. *liegan*, Old Norse *liggja*, Germ. *liegen*.

LIG ON. *vn.* A thing is said to *lig on* or *lie on*, when it is of importance that it should be done. The same expression is used in the Scand. tongues, Old Norse, Icel. *liggja á*, to lie on, to be of importance. So also the Germans say *es liegt mir daran*, it lies upon me, is of consequence to me.

LILT. *vn.* To sing without using words.
Suio-Goth. *lulla*, to sing, Dut. *lollen, lullen*, to sing without words. Probably formed by onomatopœia, like Dan. *lalle*, Dut. *lillen*, to prattle. See *lall, lallop*.

LIM. *sb.* A mischievous person.
Sco. *limmer*. Dut. *slim*, bad, Old Norse *slæmr*, vilis, abjectus, properly deficiens, *sleima*, homuncio. These seem to be formed by the prefix of *s*, on the form found in Welsh *llymio*, to make bare, whence *llyman*, sorry fellow—the sense being, first, that of deficiency, as in Old Norse *slæmr*, deficiens, and in Eng. *slim*, and then, that of vileness or wickedness. I have some doubt whether to ascribe our word to a Celtic or a Teutonic origin.

LIMBER. *adj.* Supple, pliant.
Old Norse *limpiaz*, to become relaxed or slack, Swiss *lampig*, loose, flabby, Welsh *lleipr* flaccid, drooping.

LIMMERS. *sb.* The shafts of a cart.
Old Norse *lim, limi*, bough, branch of a tree, of which it is probable the first rude shafts were made.

LIN.. *sb.* A precipice.
Sco. *lin* means both a cataract, and also the pool at the bottom of the fall. "It seems uncertain which of these is the primary sense. For Ang.-Sax. *hlynna* denotes a torrent, Icel. *lind* a cascade, and Welsh *llyn*, Arm. *len*, Ir. *lin*, a pool."—*Jam.*

LING. *sb.* Heather, *calluna vulgaris.*
"Lynge or hethe."—*Pr. Prv.* Old Norse *ling*, Dan. *lyng*, heather, any small shrub of like growth.

LING-COW. *sb.* A stem of heather.
Welsh *myncog*, heath. Our *cow* would rather seem to be related to *cog* in above *myncog*. Perhaps to Welsh *cawn*, reeds, stalks.

LIRK. *sb.* A fold, crease, or wrinkle.
Old Norse *lerka*, to plait or fold, *lerkad-fat*, a rumpled dress.

LISH. *adj.* Nimble, active, sprightly.
Perhaps from *lisk*, the groin, as the seat of activity.

LISK. *sb.* The groin.
Old Norse *ljoski*, Dan. *lyske*, Dut. *liesch.*

LISTIN. *sb.* Woollen selvidge.
Old Norse *listi*, Dan. *liste*, selvidge, Dut. *lijst*, edge, border.

LISTY. *adj.* Strong, active.
"Lusty or listy."—*Pr. Prv.* Derived, like *lusty*, of which it is another form, from Ang.-Sax. *lystan*, Dan. *lyste*, to take pleasure in, Dan. *lystig*, merry, jovial. The change of sense has taken place from alacrity of will to that of physical energy. Hence the converse *listless*, in which the older sense is retained. The Icel. *lystugr* is now used in the sense of a hearty appetite for food.—*Cleasby.*

LITE. *vn.* To rely, trust, depend upon.
"Aal *lite* on tha to pay't."—*Dick.* Old Norse *hlita*, Swed. *lita*, Dan. *lide*, to trust, rely on.

LOB. *va.* and *n.* To run or leap in a heavy or lazy manner. To pitch, throw under hand, and necessarily gently. The root may probably be found in Welsh *llob*, an unwieldy lump, whence Old Norse *lubbaz*, to loiter about, Eng. *lubber*, and other words indicative of slackness or indolence.

LOCK. *sb.* A small quantity of anything that can be taken in the hand, as a *lock* of meal, &c. Dial. Dan. *løge*, a handful, a small wisp or bundle.

LOFE. *sb.* A chance, opportunity.
　Old Norse *lofa*, Dan. *love*, to permit, to promise.

LOFT. *sb.* A garret.
　Old Norse *lopt*, a garret or top room, from *lopta*, elevare, Dan. *loft*. It is also found in Celtic, as Welsh *lloft*, Gael. *lobht*. See *cock-loft*.

LOG. *adj.* Still, quiet.
　"Log watter," calm water.—*Dick.* Old Norse *logn*, calmness or stillness of the atmosphere, *lygna*, to become calm, Dut. *luw*, sheltered from the wind, Fris. *logh*, *loy*, dull, lazy.

LONNIN. *sb.* A country lane.
　Clev. *lone.* Sco. *lonnin* or *loaning.* Fris. *lona*, *laan*, a lane or narrow passage. Perhaps from Old Norse *leyna*, to hide.

LONTER. *vn.* To loiter.
　Dut. *lunderen*, to dawdle.

LOOF (pron. *leeuf.*) *sb.* The palm of the hand.
　Goth. *lofa*, Old Norse *lóft*, Welsh *llawf*, palm of the hand.

LOOK, LOWK. *va.* To weed corn.
　Ang.-Sax. *lyccan*, to pluck up, Dan. *luge*, to weed, Fris. *luke*, Swiss *leuchen*, to pull up out of the ground.

LOOM. *sb.* A chimney.
　"Sibb. conjectures that this may be from Ang.-Sax. *leom*, light, scarcely any other light being admitted than through this hole in the roof."—*Jam.* One might also think of Swed. *ljumma*, Dial. Swed. *lumma*, to warm. But I rather suspect that the origin is to be found in Old Norse *hlemmr*, an opening in a floor, a trap-door (*Cleasby*).

LOOM. *sb.* A scamp.
　Old Norse *lauma*, to sneak, *lómr*, meanness, Dan. *lumsk*, deceitful.

LOOM. *sb.* The slow movement of water in a deep pool.
　Probably allied to Old Dut. *lome*, slow, lazy.

LOOVER. *sb.* An opening in a roof to let out the smoke, &c. "Old Norse *liôri*, (pron. *liowri* or *liovri*,) Norw. *liore*, West Goth. *luira*, described in the statistical accounts of those countries as a sort of cupola with a trap door, serving the two-fold purpose of a chimney and a sky-light."—*Garn.* Davies, however, refers in preference to Welsh *lwfer*, a chimney (*Lewis*).

LOPPEN. Leapt. The past part. of *loup*.

LOPPERT. *adj.* Curdled, coagulated.
Old High Germ. *leberen*, Old Norse *hlaupa*, Germ. *laben*, to, curdle, Dut. *lobberig*, gelatinous, Dial. Dan. *lubber*, anything coagulated. Gael. *lamban*, curdled milk, seems also allied.

LOUNDER. *va.* To beat severely.
North. *loun*. Clev., Sco. *lounder*. Gael. *lundraig*, to cudgel, from *lunn*, stick, cudgel. Comp. also Old Norse *hlunnr*, Norw. *lunn*, stick, staff, (whence *Atk.* derives our word.)

LOUP. *vn.* To leap, to jump.
Old Norse *hlaupa*, Ang.-Sax. *hleápan*, Germ. *laufen*, to run, to leap.

LOWDER. *sb.* The foundation supporting mill-stones.
Occurring in the muniments of Greystoke Castle. Old Norse *hlad*, platea, stratum.

LOWE. *sb.* Flame, blaze.
"Low of fyyr."—*Pr. Prv.* Old Norse *log*, Dan. *lue*, flame, blaze, Welsh *llug*, gleam, *llwg*, what is bright.

LOWN, LOUND. *adj.* Calm, still, quiet.
" There cannot be anudder spot so private an' so sweet,
As Billy Watson lonnin of a *lound* summer neet."—*Gibson*.
Old Norse *logn*, calmness, stillness of the atmosphere, *lygna*, to cease to blow, become calm, Dan. *luun*, North Fris. *lowen*, calm, still. Our *log*, calm, still, represents the adj. on which the above are formed.

LOWSE. *adj.* Loose, free from engagement.
Old Norse *laus*, free, released.

LUG. *sb.* The ear, handle of a jug, &c.
" The origin is seen in Swiss *lugg*, *luck*, loose, slack, *luggen*, to be slack. Hence *lug* is applied to what flaps or hangs loosely." — *Wedg*. *Atk.*, however, prefers Suio-Goth. *lagg*. See *laggin*.

LURRY. *va.* To hound eagerly, hurry, persecute.—*Dick*.
Old Norse *lûra*, coercere. Or Gael. *lorg*, to track, pursue by footsteps.

LYERY. *adj.* Tough-fleshed.
Sco. *lire*, muscle and flesh as distinct from bone. Ang.-Sax. *lira*, muscle, flesh.

LYPE. *sb.* A large slice.
: Probably for *slipe*. Ang.-Sax, *slifan*, to slice. *Slive*, a large piece (*Mrs. Baker*).

LYTHE. *vn.* To listen, hearken.
: Old Norse *hlýda*, Dan. *lytte*, to listen.

LYTHY. *adj.* Thick, applied to fluids.
: Clev. *lithe*, to thicken, broth especially, with meal, &c. Welsh *llith*, meal soaked in water.

M.

MADDLE. *vn.* To ramble, talk incoherently.
: Swiss *madeln*, to chatter. A frequentative of *mad*, used in Old Eng. as a verb, to be beside oneself.

MAFFLE. *vn.* To blunder, act incoherently.
: The original idea is to speak imperfectly, to stammer. Dut. *maffelen*, to stammer, Bav. *muffeln*, to mumble.

MAFF, MAFFLIN. *sb.* A simpleton. See *maffle*.

MAILIN. *sb.* A farm.
: The meaning is "that which is rented," from *mail*, Ang.-Sax. *mal*, Old Norse *máli*, Gael. Ir. *mal*, Welsh *mael*, rent, tribute.

MAN. *sb.* A pile of stones on the top of a mountain,
: as "Skiddaw man," &c. The general idea has been that the name has been given on account of the resemblance of the object from below to a man on the top of the mountain. Then Welsh *maen*, a stone, has been proposed by Peacock and others. The true origin of the word I take to be found in Old Norse *mæna*, cacuminare, to come to a point, whence *mænir*, fastigium domus. (In Old Norse and Ang.-Sax. *æ* is pronounced as the *a* in man.) Found in Celtic, as allied words, are Welsh *main*, Corn. *moin*, fine, slender. Skiddaw man, then, like the Swiss Righi-kulm, would simply mean the culminating point of the mountain.

MAN. *sb.* Husband.
: "A set o' dow-for-noughts, to draw
    Fwok's *men* away to th' public-houses,
    An' here to haud yer midnight bouses."—*Stagg.*

Dan. *mand*, husband, man.

MANDER. *vn.* To talk confusedly.
A nasalised form of *madder*, formed, like *maddle*, on *mad*, used in Old Eng. as a verb. See *maddle*.

MANT. *vn.* To stammer.
Gael. *manntach*, lisping, stammering, Welsh *mantach*, toothless, *mantai*, mumbler, Ir. *manntac*, one that stutters, or has lost the front teeth.

MARROW. *sb.* An equal, a match, one of the same sort.
"A word the derivation of which seems very obscure."—*Ath.* On the whole, Jamieson's derivation from Suio-Goth. *mager, magher*, affinis, a relation, seems as probable as any. Dut. and Fris. *marren*, ligare, alligare (*Kil.*), may also present a possible origin.

MASK. *va.* To infuse, applied more particularly to making tea. Dan. *mæske*, Swed. *mäska*, to steep in hot water, Germ. *meischen*, to mash, Gael. *masg*, to infuse, Sansc. *masj, marj*, to wet. The root does not seem to be the same as *mix*, Lat. *misceo*, Welsh *mysgu*, to which some have placed it; the Lat. relative is rather, I take it, *mergo*.

MASTEL. *sb.* Part of an arable field never ploughed.
Ang.-Sax. *mæst-lond*, pasture land, from *mæstan*, to feed, fatten.

MATTIE. *sb.* The mark at quoits or any such game.
Dut. *maat*, measure, in reference to the *mattie*, as the point from which the distance of each competitive cast is measured.

MAWK-MIDGE. *sb.* The flesh-fly or bluebottle.
Mawk is from Old Norse *madkr*, Norw. *makk*, maggot. And *midge* from Ang.-Sax. *mycg*, Low Germ. *mügg*, Germ. *mücke*, a gnat or fly, comprising nearly all two-winged insects. The Scandinavian words, Suio-Goth. *mygga*, Dan. *myg*, seem restricted to the sense of gnat, an insect that bites, and so not so suitable for the present word *mawk-midge*, a "maggot-fly."

MAZED. *adj.* Bewildered, stupified.
Swiss *mausen*, to speak unintelligibly, Old Norse *masa*, to jabber, Norw. *masast*, to drop asleep.—*Wedg.*

MAZLIN. *sb.* A simpleton, one in a state of stupor or confusion. See *mazed*. Comp. also Dial. Dan. *maasle*, to do a thing in a disorderly manner.

MEAL OF MILK. *sb.* The quantity of milk that a cow gives at one milking. Old Norse *mâl*, Dan. *maal*, measure.

MEEN. *vn.* To moan.
Ang.-Sax. *mǽnan*, to moan, lament.

MEERISH. *adj.* Effeminate.
Old Norse *mær*, a modest virgin, Ang.-Sax. *mearo*, tender, soft, delicate. Our word, from its ending (*ish*, as in childish), would rather seem to be formed from the noun.

MEG-O'-MANY-FEET. *sb.* A kind of small centipede.
Meg in the above seems to be from Old Norse *madkr*, Norw. *makk*, maggot.

MEER-STAN. *sb.* A boundary-stone.
Old Norse *mæri*, Ang.-Sax. *mǽre*, a boundary.

MEKKIN. *sb.* The yellow-flag.
Would seem to be from Ang.-Sax. *mece*, a small sword, its other Cumb. name, *seggin*, being also from a similar origin, Ang.-Sax. *sæcg, seax*, a small sword, (*Prior*), in reference to its sharp-pointed leaves. Peacock, however, refers to Gael. *meacan*, plant, bulb, applied to various plants.

MELL. *vn.* To meddle.
Old Fr. *mesler, medler, meiller*, to mix, meddle.

MELL. *sb.* A conical hill, as Mell Fell, Mell Break.
Welsh *moel*, Gael. *mul*, a conical hill, Welsh *moel*, bare, bald. Comp., also, Old Norse *múli*, frons montis, promontorium.

MELL. *sb.* "The jockey who is last in the race is called the *mell*. It has been said that he is so called from it having been the custom to give a *mell* (mallet) to the owner of the last horse; the presumed custom, however, lacks proof."—*West. and Cumb. Dial.* Dick. also explains *mel* as "the last cut of corn in the harvest field." We may perhaps think of a connection with Gael. *mall*, slow, lazy, *maille*, delay.

MELDER. *sb.* The quantity of meal ground at one time.
Old Norse *meldr, mælder*, the corn in the mill, Gael. *meildreach, meiltir*, a quantity of corn sent to be ground.

MENG. *va.* To renew.—*Dick.*
Properly, I think, to mix. Clev. *mang*, to mix up.

"Here, lanleady, sum mair shwort keaks,
An' *meng* us up thar glasses."—*Stagg.*

Ang.-Sax. *mengean*, Old Norse *menga*, Germ. *mengen*, to mingle. The word might be used for renew in the sense of mixing up old with new.

MENSE. *sb.* Propriety, politeness, decorum, with also a sense of carefulness and proper management. Sansc. *manusas*, humanus, Old Norse *mennskr*, humanus, capax moralitatis, Ang.-Sax. *mennisc*. The idea of *mense*, then, would be that which becomes a man. Unless, indeed, we can remount at once to the ancient root from which *man*, as the thinking animal, is perhaps derived, viz., Sansc. *man*, to think, whence *manas*, sense, judgment, corresponding with our *mense*. The parallel word *nous*, sense, mother-wit, Sansc. *nayas*, intelligence, from *nay*, to direct, might seem to warrant us in supposing a noun-form directly corresponding with the Sanscrit. But the form *menske*, in which the word occurs in *P. Pl.*, seems to indicate that it is formed from the Ang.-Sax. and Old Norse *mennisc*, *mennskr*.

MERTH. *sb.* Greatness, extent.—*Hall.*
Old Norse *mergd*, multitude, from *margr*, much, Ang.-Sax. *mǣrth*, greatness.

MESS! *intj.* Truly, indeed, "by the mass."

MESSAN. *sb.* A small dog of indefinite breed.—*Gibson.*
Sco. *messan* is defined by *Jam.* as properly a lap-dog, and as "applied more laxly to denote such curs as are kept about country houses." The derivations which he suggests are not to the purpose. The word is no doubt from the Gael. *measan*, a lap-dog, *meas*, fancy, conceit. Comp., also, Old Norse *myshyndi*, a mongrel, the change of which first into *missen*, and then into *messan*, is natural and easy. It seems by no means improbable that there may be a concurrence of these two words, in the senses respectively of a mongrel and of a lap or fancy dog, but now confused together.

METHY. A difficult respiration, as occasioned by the thinness of the atmosphere. An obsolete word, found in Hutchinson's Hist. Cumb. Probably allied to Ang.-Sax. *mēthe*, weariness, fatigue.

MEWTLE. *vn.* "The cow or ewe *mewtles* when she yearns over her newly-dropped young, and utters a low sound of fondness."—*Dick.* Bav. *mutilon*, to mutter or speak low.—*Gl. in Schm.*

MICKLE, MUCKLE. *adj.* Much, great.
Goth. *mikils*, Ang.-Sax. *mycel*, Old Norse *mikill*.

MIDDIN. *sb.* A dunghill.
Old Norse *moddyngia*, Dan. *mödding*, from Old Norse *mod*, refuse, and *dyngia*, a heap.

MIDDIN-PANT. *sb.* The pool which receives the drainage of the dunghill. Welsh *pant*, hollow place, depression.

MIDDIN-SUMP. *sb.* Same as middin-pant.
Old Norse *subb*, sordida colluvies, Dan., Swed. *sump*, mire, bog. Low Germ. *swamp, swamm,* Germ. *schwamm,* a sponge, that which sucks up water, Eng. *swamp.*

MIDGE. *sb.* A gnat. See *mawk-midge.*

MIMP. *vn.* To talk mincingly.
Seems, along with Sco. *mump*, to speak indistinctly, to be allied to Eng. *mumble*, Dut. *mompelen*, Bav. *mumpfen, memmelen*, the narrow vowel being employed to convey the sense of affectation of fine speaking, a main feature of which is the contraction of the broad open sounds.

MIN. Vocative of *man*, used only in familiarity, and most commonly with something of a contemptuous sense.

MIRK. *adj.* Dark, gloomy.
Ang.-Sax. *mirc*, Old Norse *myrkr*, dark.

MISCANTER. *vn.* To miscarry.
Sco. *mishanter*, misfortune, shows the proper form, (*anter* for *adventure*). See *anter.*

MISLEERT. *adj.* Led astray.
Ang.-Sax. *misléran*, to teach wrongly.

MISLIKKEN. *vn.* To neglect or forget.
Dut. *misselick*, ambiguus, dubius, in quo errare, aut de quo dubitare potest.—*Kil.*

MISMAY. *vb.* "This word is used negatively, to express absence of fear. Our cowt met soldiers, and niver mismay't hissel."—*Dick.* *Mis*may and *dis*may are parallel words, formed (probably) from the Goth. *magan*, to have power, to be able, with the respective negatives *mis* and *dis.* *Dis*may comes to us through the Romance languages, Span. *desmayer* to despond, Prov. *esmagar, esmaier,* to trouble, frighten, Fr. *s'esmaier,* to be sad or astonished, which Diez refers to Goth. *magan,* as above. Our word *mismay* may probably be altogether of Teutonic origin. *Wedg.* collates with *dis*may, Dan. *af*magt, swoon. Our "mismay't *hissel*" is the parallel of Fr. "*se* esmaier." This is an interesting word, which I have never met with elsewhere, unless the Crav. *mismeave*, to perplex, be, as seems rather probable, the same.

MISNARE. *va.* To incommode, to put out of the way.
—*West. and Cumb. Dial.* Perhaps from Old Norse *næra*, fovere, recreare, with the negative termination *dis.*

MISTALL. *sb.* A cow-house.
Probably cow-stall, from Ang.-Sax. *mes*, a cow.

MISTETCH. *va.* To teach improperly. A *mistetched* horse signifies a horse that has some peculiar vice.—*West. and Cumb. Dial.* Ang.-Sax. *mistǽcan*, to instruct amiss.

MITTENS. *sb.* Woollen gloves.
Fr. *mitaine*, a winter glove, Gael *mutan*, a muff, thick glove.

MIZZLE. *sb.* Small rain.
Dut. *mieselen*, to rain gently.

MOAM. *adj.* Mellow, soft.
The radical meaning is a degree of ripeness approaching to dissolution.—*Wedg.* Dut. *molmen*, to moulder away, Germ. *malm*, dust, powder, Manx *mholm*, to moulder, Welsh *mallu*, to rot, *moam*, a crumbly stone found in Oxfordshire, Ang.-Sax. *mealm-stân*, sand-stone, Prov. Germ. *molsch*, mellow, applied to apples and pears.

MOOR-TIDY. *sb.* The ground-lark.
Clev. *moor-titling.* Old Norse *tita, titlingr*, both applied to small birds, Dut. *tijt, tita*, a chick or small bird. Hence our *tidy* seems to be the same as *tit* in titmouse, titlark, &c.

MOWDY-WARP. *sb.* The mole.
Old Norse *moldvarpa* (*mold*, earth, and *varpa*, to throw), Dan. *muldvarp*, Germ. *maulwurf.*

MOYDERT. *adj.* Confused, bewildered, overworked.
Atkinson's derivation from Suio-Goth. *mōda*, trouble, applied as well to mental anxiety as to bodily fatigue, Dut. *moeite*, trouble, Old Norse *môdr*, defatigatus, Germ. *müde*, tired, seems to me to be well-founded.

MUCK. *sb.* Dirt generally, especially manure.
Old Norse *myki*, Norw. *mok*, fimus, manure.

MORT. *sb.* A large quantity.
From the same origin as *merth.*

MOTE-HEARTED. *adj.* Timid, faint-hearted.
Dut. *moetigh*, vacuus, otiosus, Dan. *matt*, Swed. *matt*, weak, faint. See also *moydert*, which seems to be from the same origin.

MUD. *vb.* Must, pret. of *mun*.
"But he has sent ye this bit cake,
He thought that he *mud* treat ye."—*Miss Blamire*.
Perhaps for *mund*. "The pret. *munt* (of *mun*) is still used in some of our northern counties. If it exist in our southern dialect, it would no doubt take the shape of *mund*, answering to the Ang.-Sax. *ge-munde*."—(Dr. Guest, Proceedings Phil. Soc., vol. 2, p. 155.)

MUGGY. *adj.* Damp and thick, applied to the weather.
Old Norse *mugga*, damp, thick weather, Welsh *mwg*, smoke, *mwygl*, sultry, close, Gael. *muig*. cloudiness, darkness, gloom.

MUG-SHEEP. *sb.* The white-faced breed from which the improved Leicester originated.—*Dick*. Seems to be from *mug*, the face, now only applied in ridicule. Esth. *mok*, snout, mouth, Sansc. *mukhas*, mouth, Gael. *smuig*, snout.

MULL. *va.* and *n.* To crumble.
Old Norse *mylia*, Low Germ. *mullen*, to bruise, to pulverise, S. Jutl. *mulje*, a broken or crumbled piece (as of bread), Gael. *mol*, chaff, Welsh *mwl*, chaff and broken straw on a floor after thrashing.

MULL. *sb.* Dust, anything crumbled. See above.

MUN. *aux. vb.* Must.
Old Norse *mun*, Old Swed. *muna*, aux. vb. "*Mun*, there can be little doubt, is the same verb as Ang.-Sax. *ge-munan*, to think of. In the Old Eng., it often indicates mere futurity, like the Icel. *mun;* and the peculiar sense now given to it, that of obligation, appears to have been its latest derivative meaning. The phrase "we *mun* go" may have taken successively the meaning "we think of going," "we shall go," "we must go." —(Dr. Guest, Phil. Soc., 2, 153.)

MURL. *vb.* To crumble into small pieces.
Welsh *murl*, a crumbling stone, Fin. *murrella*, to break, Swed. *mör*, Germ. *morsch*, friable. Diefenbach collates *murl* with Goth. *ga-maurjan*, to reduce, to shorten.

MUSH. *sb.* Dust or powdery refuse of decay.
Old Norse *mosk*, Norw. *musk*, powder, dust.

MUSHAMER. *sb.* Mushroom.
I am rather inclined to the opinion that this is not a corruption of *mushroom*, but an independent word, and perhaps derived from Ang.-Sax. *myse*, table. Now the most striking feature in all this class of fungus is their flat shape, as compared with the

pointed forms presented by plants in general. Hence the popular idea (see *paddock-stool*) has likened them to a stool, for which the idea of a round table is just as suitable. From a similar origin I take the Fr. *mousseron*, (whence Eng. *mushroom*), viz., *mousse*, blunt, pointless, and not from *mousse*, moss, as proposed in *Notes and Queries*, and sanctioned by *Wedg*. The ending *mer* might be from Ang.-Sax. *mear*, field, Old Norse *mæri*, planities. The change of *mis* into *mush* would very naturally arise, when the origin came to be forgotten, and at the same time the Eng. word *mushroom* came into parallel use.

MUSTY. *adj.* Morose, gloomy.
Low Germ. *muulsk, mustrig*, Fris. *mutsch*, sour-looking.—*Wedg*.

MY SONG! A corruption of an ancient oath, *la sangue*, or *la sangue Dieu.*—*Atk.*

MYTER. *vn.* To crumble or decompose.
Thus soft stone exposed to the atmosphere is said to "*myter* away." Welsh *methu*, to decay, perish, *mwytho*, to make soft, *mythlu*, to canker. The root is, I take it, to be found in Sansc. *mid*, to soften.

N.

NAB. *va.* To sieze, to lay hold of.
Dan. *nappe*, to snatch, Fin. *nappata*, to sieze suddenly.

NAGGY. *adj.* Quarrelsome, contradictious.
Old Norse *nagga*, to rub, to chafe, whence, figuratively, to squabble.

NAIL. *va.* To beat, to thump.
Old Norse *hnalla*, to beat with a stick, *hnallr*, stick, cudgel.

NAPH. *sb.* Nave of a wheel.
Ang.-Sax. *nafa*, Dan. *nav*, Swed. *naf*.

NARDER. *adj.* Nearer.
Dut. *naerder, naeder*, nearer.—*Kil.*

NASH, NESH. *adj.* Brittle, tender, delicate.
Ang.-Sax. *hnesc, nesc*, tender, soft; properly moist, Goth. *natjan*, Germ. *benetzen*, to wet, Germ. *nass*, wet.—*Wedg*.

NATTLE. *vn.* To tap, to knock gently and quickly, as with the fingers on a window. Welsh *naddial,* to keep chipping, Dial. Swed. *gnaddra,* to emit a low sound as in tittering, playful screaming, *gnatta,* to nibble, "probably in reference to the sound, rather than to the nibbling action."—*Atk.*

NE. *adv.* No, used as an assent to a negation.
Mun we gan hyem to-night? Na, (negation.)
We'll nit git hyem to-night. *Ne* (assent to negation.)
Ang.-Sax. *ne,* nay, by no means.

NEDDERT. *adj.* Withered; not in a thriving state.
Ah the helthe was *neothered*
For lurre of his monnen.—*Layamon.*
King Ælfric had recovered from his wounds, but his health was *nithered* for the loss of his men.
Ang.-Sax. *nitherian,* to put down, *niered* (contraction of *nithered?*) afflicted, straightened, Dan., Swed. *nedrig,* low, abject.

NEED-FIRE. *sb.* Fire produced by the friction of wood and carried from house to house for the purpose of passing cattle through the smoke, as a preventive of murrain and other epidemics. In use so late as about 1841.—*Dick.* Swed. *gnida,* Dan. *gnide,* to rub.

NEEZE. *vn.* To sneeze.
Ang.-Sax. *niesan,* Old Norse *hnjosa,* Dan. *nyse,* Dut. *niezen,* to sneeze.

NEIF. *sb.* The fist, clenched hand.
Old Norse *hnefi,* Dan. *næve,* fist.

NIEVEL. *va.* To strike with the fist. See *neif.*

NEIVY-NACK. *sb.* A game which consists in guessing in which of the closed hands any article is to be found.
"Burgh lass laik't at *neivy-nack.*"—*Lonsdale.*
From *neif,* as above, and *knack,* a trick of doing anything with the fingers, Ir. *cnog,* a knock, crack. "In the same way, from Dut. *knappen,* to snap, *knap,* alacer, *knap-handig,* dexter, manu expeditus."—*Wedg.*

NEUK. *sb.* Nook, corner.
Fin. *nokka,* the beak of a bird, nose, point, *maan nokka,* a nook of land, Esth. *nukka,* tip, corner, nook, Wall. *nouk,* knot, ex-

crescence. — *Wedg.* *Atk.* also collates Dial. Dan. *nogg*, an angle or corner made by the winding of a river or beck, " a sense exactly coincident with ours in one application of the word."

NEWDELT. *adj.* Bewildered, stupified.
Dut. *neutelen*, frivola agere, *neuteler*, homuncio frivolus.—*Kil.* Comp., also, Welsh *nwydwyllt*, whimsical, freakish, from *nwyd*, whim.

NICKER. *vn.* To neigh, also to laugh.
Old Norse *gnaka*, Low Germ. *nicken*, Fris. *nöggre*, to neigh.

NICKT I' T' HEAD. *adj.* Having extravagant fancies, not quite sane. Perhaps to be connected with Dan. *nykke*, Swed. *nyck*, Dut. *nuk*, whim, caprice, foolish fancy, Low Germ. *nücksch*, fanciful, capricious.

NIGGARTS, NEEGARS. *sb.* Iron plates used for contracting a fire-place to save coals. Welsh *nigio*, to contract, to straighten. See also *nigler*.

NIGLER. *sb.* A careful and industrious person.
Probably from the same origin as *niggard*. Norw. *nyggja*, Swed. *njugga*, to rub, to scrape, Swed. *njugg*, niggardly, sparing.—*Wedg.*

NIM. *vn.* To walk or run with short, quick steps, Clev. also to catch up quickly. The latter seems to be the original sense, as in Ang.-Sax. *numol*, capable, quick at grasping a thing, (whence Eng. *nimble*,) Goth. *niman*, Ang.-Sax. *niman*, to sieze, snatch.

NIP UP. *va.* To snatch up a thing hastily, often with a sense of thieving. Old Norse *hnefa*, to snatch, Germ. *knippen*, to snap, Dan. *nappe*, to twitch, pluck.

NOBBUT. *conj.* Nothing but, only.
Old Eng. *nought but*, *not but*, for which we now use elliptically *but*.

NOG. *sb.* A handle for the shaft of a scythe.
I take the sense to be that of joint. Dan. *nokke*, to joint, Dut. *knoke*, ankle. In Craven, cattle are said to be well *nogged* when they have strong legs or joints. Comp. also Old Norse *hnöggr*, flail.

NOGGIN. *sb.* A quarter-pint measure.
Gael. *noigean*, a wooden cup.

NOGGY. *sb.* Coarse thread.
Would seem to be immediately from *nogs*, hemp (*Salop.*) But comp. Welsh, Corn. *noden*, Bret. *neuden*, thread. Also Old High Germ. *nagan*, Mod. Germ. *nähen*, Dut. *naeden, naeyen*, to sew. And Esth. *noggel*, Fin. *negla*, Bret. *nados*, Welsh *nodwydd*, needle. It may be a question whether our *noggy* does not belong to the same group, the root of which is probably to be found in Sansc. *nah*, to join, and through which, it will be seen, runs the interchange of *d* and *g*.

NOP. *va.* To crop, to nip the ends off gooseberries, &c.
Old Norse *nappa*, to pluck, Lap. *nappet*, to cut off the extremities, to crop, Dut. *nopen*, rem breviter tangere (*Kil.*)

NOPE. *va.* To strike on the head.
Lonsd. *nope*, a small blow. Dut. *nopen*, to touch lightly. If not from Old Norse *nöp*, head, Eng. *nob*.

NOUS. *sb.* Intelligence, sense, mother-wit.
Sansc. *nayas*, intelligence, from *nay*, to direct, Gr. *νους*, sense, sagacity, from *νοεω*, mente agito, cogito. Though corresponding both in sense and in form so much more nearly with the Sanscrit and the Greek, the more immediate connection of our word is probably with Ang.-Sax. *neòsian*, Old Norse *hnÿsa*, to search out, investigate.

NOWT. *sb.* Cattle.
Old Norse *naut*, Ang.-Sax. *neât*, Swed. *nöt*, horned cattle, oxen.

NOWTHER. *conj.* Neither.
Ang.-Sax. *nauther, nâther*.

NUDGE. *va.* To jog or touch lightly, generally for the purpose of calling attention to something. Old Norse *nudda*, frequenter fricare, Norw. *nugga*, to rub, scrape.

NUNTY. *adj.* Formal, old-fashioned, verging on shabbiness (of female dress). Perhaps, taking the nasal, from Dut. *nuttig*, utilis, *nutten*, sobrie sumere ad necessitatem et utilitatem (*Kil.*)

NYFLE. *va.* To pilfer, make away with small things.
Old Norse *hnefa*, arripere, from *hnefi*, the fist or closed hand.

O.

OAD-FARRANT. *adj.* Wise with the sagacity derived from experience. As applied to children, old-fashioned, sagacious beyond their years. Old Norse *fara*, Old High Germ. *faran*, to gain experience, become used to, or experienced in Dan. *erfaren*, Dut. *ervaren*, experienced. Or from Gael. *farranta*, brave, stout, which in our *farrantly* seems to have acquired the sense rather of judgment and propriety. I can hardly agree in Cleasby's suggestion that *oad* in *oad-farrant* is not *auld*, but the Old Norse *aud*, Ang.-Sax. *eáthe*, easy ; *oad-farrant* certainly has not with us the sense he suggests of "easy-going."

OAF. *sb.* A simpleton, an idiot.
Ang.-Sax. *ælf*, Old Norse *alfr*, Dan. *alfe*, elf, fairy. The word originates in the superstitious belief that idiot children are changelings, the originals having been carried away by fairies.

OAST. *sb.* Curd for cheese.—*West. and Cumb. Dial.*
Dan. *oste*, to curdle, *ost*, cheese, Fris. *aast*, cheese. Ang.-Sax. *ost* signifies a knot, and the idea in the above seems to be that of hardening.

OD WITE. A profane oath. God's punishment.
Ang.-Sax. *wite*, punishment, affliction.

ON. *prep.* Of, used before a vowel.
Seems to be only a phonetic substitution.

OO. *sb.* Wool.
Old Norse *ull*, Ang.-Sax. *wúll*. While, as in above, our dialect sometimes follows the Scandinavian form in omitting an initial *w ;* in other cases, as in *worchit* for *orchard*, we have instances of the opposite tendency.

ONDERMER. *adj.* The lower of two things.
A favourite pleonastic form, as in *bettermer*, for better.

OOMER. *sb.* Shade, shelter. Also used as a verb.
Fr. *ombre*, Lat. *umbra*, shade.

OOT-RAKE. *sb.* A free way or outlet for sheep from the inclosures to the common. See *rake*.

OOTRAY. *va.* To outrage.
Fr. *outrager*, from *outre*, Old Fr. *oultre*, Lat. *ultra*, beyond.

ORNDINNER, HORNDORN. *sb.* A luncheon, forenoon
repast. Seems to be a corruption of *aandorn* or *undern*. Ang.-
Sax. *undern*, Old Norse *undorn*, afternoon, Welsh *anterth*,
forenoon, S. Jutl. *onden* or *undern*, mid-day meal. "The word
is sagaciously referred by Schmeller to the proposition *unter*,
anciently denoting *between*, q.d., the intervening period; which
accounts for its sometimes denoting a part of the afternoon, or
a meal taken at that time—and sometimes a period between
noon and sunset."—*Garnett.*

Oss. *vn.* To try, to essay, to set about a thing.
Garnett refers it to Welsh *osio*, to offer to do, to essay. Doubt
has been thrown upon this as a genuine Celtic word. Gluck,
however, treats it as such, deriving from it the name of the Celtic
tribe Osismi, in the sense of *audaces*. It may be cognate with
Lat. *audeo*. The derivation from the Welsh is rendered all the
more probable by the use of the word in Shropshire, near the
Welsh border (*Athenæum*, April 20, 1872).

Owe. *vn.* To own. See *awe*.

Owsen. *sb.* Oxen.
A Low Germ. form, as in Dut. *os*, Holst. *os*, ox.

Oxter. *sb.* The arm-pit.
Ang.-Sax. *oxta*, the arm-pit.

P.

Pace-eggs. *sb.* Eggs boiled hard and stained or
ornamented as playthings for children at Easter. The custom,
which prevails over a great part of Christendom, has probably
reference to the Resurrection, of which the egg is a type. Dan.
paaske-æg, an egg boiled hard, stained with various colours, and
eaten commonly on Easter eve.

Packs. *sb.* Dense heavy clouds collected in the sky.
Germ., Dut. *pack*, a bundle, Fin. *pakkata*, to stuff, to cram.

Paddock. *sb.* The toad or frog.
Sco. *pade*. Ang.-Sax. *pade*, Old Norse *padda*, Dut. *padde*,
Dan. *padde*, Swed. *padda*, Prov. Germ. *padde*, toad or frog.

Paddock-rud. *sb.* The spawn of frogs and toads.
Old Norse *ruda*, rejectaneum.

Paddock-stool. *sb.* A toad-stool, applied to most
sorts of non-esculent fungi. North. *pad-stool*. Dut. *padde-
stoel*, Germ. *paddenstuhl*.

PAICKS. *sb.* A thrashing.

"O thou's a menseless urlin, ista,
Weel thou deserves thy *paicks*, at dista."—*Stagg.*

Old Norse *piaka*, pungere, tundere, Dial. Swed. *pakka*, to beat, Germ. *peitschen*, to whip, to flog.

PAN. *vn.* To pair, to fit, agree, work together.

Clev. *pan*, to fit in, to correspond. Comparing Welsh *panan*, what involves or works together, *pannas*, plaited straw, *panelu*, to plait, one might presume a Celtic word *pan*, with the meaning of combination, and probably allied to Sansc. *panktis*, cohesion. Again, in the Ang.-Sax. *pan*, piece, plate, hem, *pan-hose*, pieced or patched hose, and in the Dial. Dan. *paaniværk*, patchwork, we seem to have a trace of a similar word in the Teutonic idiom. Then, in the Rom. we have Prov. *pan*, rag, clout, lap, piece, Fr. *pan*, pane, piece, or pannel of a wall, the *pane* of a hose or cloak.—*Cot.* In the Sclavonic branch we have Lith. *paine*, entangling, *pinnu*, I plait. Coming to the English dialects, Forby has *paned* curtains, curtains made of long narrow stripes joined together, also *pan*, the hard earth below that which is stirred by the plough, the sense being, we may presume, probably that of something compact or adhering together. The general root I am inclined to take to be found in Sansc. *pac*, to join, to fasten, which takes the nasal in *panktis*, cohesion. A parallel formation to that of *pan* from *pac* is seen in Welsh *gwyn*, from the root *cvid* = Germ. *hwit* (Glück, Kelt. Nam.) It first takes the nasal, as in Old Celt. *vind*, and then drops the *d*, as in Wel. *gwyn*. Similarly *pac* would become *panc*, and then, dropping the *c*, *pan*. According to Grimm's Law, however, which replaces Sansc. *p* by Germ. *f*, we should have to presume that the Teutonic words in the above group were not indigenous. Or that they are in some way exceptional.

PANG. *vn.* To stuff, to cram.

"An' some there were could scarcely speak,
Their thropples were sae *pang'd.*—Bridewain, by *Stagg.*

Sco. *pang.* *Jam.* refers to Old Dut. *banghen*, to force into small compass, which, according to Kilian, is for *be-anghen*, from *ang*, implying constriction. This seems doubtful, comparing Lat. *pangere*, to drive in, to fasten, Fin. *pakkata*, to stuff, to cram, and I rather think of the general root as the same as that of the last word *pan.*

PANT. *sb.* Pool, swamp. See *middin-pant.*

PARLISH. *adj.* Remarkable, noteworthy.

"An' *parlish* pranks, on Silloth banks,
They hed as they were comin."—*Stagg.*

I

This has been supposed by Peacock and others to be a corruption of *perilous*, which seems doubtful, at least so far as regards the sense in question. I am rather inclined to think of a connection with Fr. *parler*, in the sense of something worth talking about.

PARTLES. *sb.* **The globular droppings of sheep, &c.**
Perhaps from Welsh *pardduo*, to smut—though if so, the sense has become somewhat divergent.

PASH. *va.* **To force or throw violently down.**
"Deeth cam dryvynge after,
And al to duste *passhed*
Kynges and knyghtes.—*P. Pl.*

"Barn! I *pash't* them down,"—said by a noted Cumberland wrestler to a neighbour's daughter on his first victory.—*Gibson.* Probably another form of *bash*, Clev. *pash*, to strike hard. See *bash.*

PASH. *sb.* **A heavy and sudden shower.**
There is a distinction between a *pash* and a *splash*. "It may be a bit of a *splash*, but it willent be a girt *pash*."—*Dick.* Germ. *patsche*, puddle, Dan. *piaske*, Dial. Swed. *paska*, to splash.

PATTLE. *sb.* **A plough-scraper.**
Probably the same as Eng. *spattle*, a trowel, Germ. *spattel*, Ital. *spatella*, diminutives of Eng. *spade*, Germ. *spaten*, Lat. *spatha.*

PAW. *sb.* **The hand, used familiarly or contemptuously.**
Bret. *pav*, *pao*, Welsh *pawen*, hand, paw.

PAWKY. *adj.* **Sly, impudent, too familiar.**
Jamieson connects the above with Ang.-Sax. *pæcan*, to deceive, *pæca*, a deceiver. It seems to me, however, to be rather allied to Gael. *pocanach*, impudent, *pocan*, an impudent little fellow. One might think of the origin as found in Gael. *puc*, to push, jostle, Welsh *pwg*, thrust, shove, in the sense of forwardness. The Swed. *poka*, to presume, demand with insolence, may also be referred to.

PAWT, POAT. *vn.* **To push or stir with the hand or foot. Also to walk heavily.** Atkinson refers to Dial. Dan. *pote*, to stamp or pound the earth, as, for instance, round something newly planted, Suio-Goth. *potta*, digito vel baculo explorare. Compare also Corn. *poot*, to kick like a horse, Welsh *pwtio*, to butt, push, poke.

PAY. *va.* **To beat.**
"It seems uncertain whether it be an oblique sense of Fr. *payer*, or from Welsh *pwyo*, to beat."—*Jam.*

PAZE. *va.* To force or lift with a lever.
: Perhaps, as suggested by *Atk.*, only another form of *prize*, which is referred by *Wedg.* to Fr. *priser*. I do not feel at all sure, however, that it is not a separate word, and to be referred, as *Brockett* has it, to Fr. *peser*, to weigh. *Peise*, to weigh, occurs in *P. Pl.*

PEANN (or PAN?) *sb.* A state of matting or entanglement. Lith. *paine*, entangling, *pinnu*, I plait. I take the origin to be the same as that of *pan*, q.v.

PEAN. *va.* To strike, to beat.—*Hall.*
: Dan. *pine*, Dut. *pijnen*, Ang.-Sax. *pinan*, to punish, torment, torture.

PEDDER. *sb.* A pedlar.
: "Pedder, revolus, negociator."—*Cath. Ang.* A *ped* in Norfolk is a pannier or wicket basket; a *pedder*, or *pedlar*, a packman, one who carries on his back goods in a *ped* for sale.—*Wedg.*

PEE. *vn.* To spy with one eye. To shut one eye in taking aim.—*Dick.* Probably the same as Eng. *peer.* Low Germ. *plira*, *pira*, to look with half-shut eyes, look closely.

PEEK. *vn.* To pry into other people's affairs.
: *Peek* was in use in Old Eng. in the sense of *peep*, of which it is no doubt another form, *k* and *p* interchanging as in *dank* and *damp*.

PEENGING. *adj.* Puling, sickly. Starving with cold.—*Dick.*
: Properly the same as *peaking*. taking the nasal. Swed. *pjāka*, *pjunka*, to pule, *pjunkig*, puling, sickly, delicate.—*Wedg.*

PEET or PEED. *adj.* Blind of one eye. See *pee*.

PEAT. *sb.* Sods of turf cut and dried for fuel.
: From *bete*, to mend or kindle a fire, whence *beetin*, *peetin*, or *peat*, fuel.

PEAT-COOM. *sb.* The dust of peat.
: *Coom* is perhaps the same as *culm*, applied to loose powdery coal. The proper meaning of *culm*, according to *Wedg.*, is smut, and he connects it with Icel. *kāla*, *quola*, to smut or dirty. The Germans have *kumm* for dust, in *kumm-karren*, a dust-cart, which, unless it has undergone the same change, throws some doubt upon the above derivation.

PEG. *sb.* A tooth, used only with reference to children.
: Welsh *pig*, Fr. *pic*, point.

PEG. *va.* To beat, to thump.
Dan. *pukke*, to stamp, to pound, Dut. *picken*, Welsh *pigo*, Fr. *piquer*, to prick.

PEGH, PECH. *vn.* To pant, breathe hard.
Clev. *pech*, to cough in a subdued way. *Jam.* considers *pech* to be radically the same as Swed. *picka*, to palpitate, to give out a low sound, as a repeater watch, Dan. *pikke*, to palpitate, Germ. *pochen*, to beat, throb. A more certain connection, it seems to me, is with Welsh *pucio*, Fin. *puhkia*, to pant, blow, Boh. *puch*, a breathing.

PELK. *va.* To beat.
Perhaps another form of *pelt*, *t* and *k* interchanging as in *jert* and *jerk*. Or perhaps from Old Norse *piaka*, tundere, taking a phonetic *l*.

PELTER. *sb.* Anything very large.
"Theer a Whillimer cheese abuin t' bed heed,
An' dall! but it's a *pelter*."—*Lonsdale*.
One might perhaps think of a connection with Gael. *pailt*, plentiful, abundant, Bret. *pulder*, abundance. Or perhaps *pelter* may only be like *bumper*, *thumper*, and other words in which the sense of something large is derived from that of a heavy blow.

PENNIES-A-PIECE. For a penny-a-piece.
"An' dancers pat i' Brammery's hat,
Pennies-a-piece for the fiddler."—*Lonsdale*.
A Cumbrian, if asked the price of anything, as, for instance, eggs, invariably uses this plural form. A further instance of this tendency occurs in the following, relating to a game at cards—
"For Jen was always *winners*."—*Lonsdale*.
I am unable to say how far the same may prevail in other dialects, never having seen it noticed in any glossary.

PENNY-STONE. *sb.* A stone used in pitching in place of a quoit. One might possibly think of *penny-stone* as a corruption of Gael. *peilisteir*, a quoit, or a flat stone used instead of a quoit, provided that the word, which seems to be the same as the Lat. *palæstra*, was ever in popular use among the Gael. Jamieson, and, following him, the author of the Craven Glossary, refer it to Swed. *pena*, to flatten, flat stones only being adapted for the purpose. I should rather, however, failing the former suggestion, be disposed to look on *penny-stone* as a corruption of *spenny-stone*, Norw. *spenna*, to project. See *spang*.

PENSY. *adj.* Of delicate appetite. Applied to one who trifles with his food. Perhaps to be connected with Fr. *penser*, Ang.-Sax. *pinsian*, Dut. *peinzen*, to meditate, ponder. Or with Fr. *panse*, paunch, belly, Prov. Fr. *panser*, to live daintily. Or again, we might think of Fris. *pän*, nice and affected in eating and in other things.

PENTAS. *sb.* A sloping roof built against a wall.
Not a corruption of *penthouse*, but, according to *Wedg.*, from Fr. *appentis*, Ital. *pendice*, anything bending or down-hanging, Lat. *pendere*, to hang.

PEPPER-CAKE. *sb.* A cake of ginger-bread.
Dan. *peber-kage*, ginger-bread.

PETTLE. *vn.* To occupy time with trifles.
The same as Eng. *piddle*, the fundamental idea of which "seems to be to pick, to use the tips of the fingers in doing."—*Wedg.* Prov. Germ. *pötteln*, to work at anything by small touches, Norw. *pitta*, to pluck, pick, sip. The root may probably be found in Welsh *pid*, a point, *pitw*, small.

PEYL. *va.* To beat.—*West. and Cumb. Dial.*
Dan. *pille*, Dut. *pellen*, Welsh *pilio*, to strip, skin, peel, whence, metaphorically, to flog or beat.

PICK. *va.* To pitch, lift or throw with a fork.
Hence to let fall prematurely, of a cow, &c., in reference to her young. The original idea is that of something pointed, Old Norse *pikka*, Welsh *pigo*, to prick, Welsh *picio*, to dart, cast.

PICKLE. *sb.* A grain of corn.
Jam. gives the more extended definition of "any minute particle, as a grain of sand." The original idea is that of a point. See *pick*.

PICKS. *sb.* The diamond at cards.
"Furst deal aboot he gat spead yace,
An' crew an' yammer't sair than.
But *picks* was trump, and he tuik grump,
An' sed he wad laik nae mair than."—*Lonsdale.*

"Probably from their two sharp points resembling a limestone pick."—*Peacock.* But the term seems to apply so much more naturally to the spade, that one would almost be inclined to think that it had originally been, as in Germany *pieke*, and in France *picque* now are, applied to it.

PIGGIN. *sb.* A small tub with an upright handle.
Gael. *pigean*, Welsh *picyn*, a little jar, a pipkin.

PIKE. *sb.* A peak, the name of many mountains in the district. Dan. *pig*, Welsh *pig*, point.

PILE. *sb.* A blade of grass, &c.
Welsh *pil*, stem, Old Norse *pila*, Dan., Swed. *pil*, shaft, arrow.

PILEY. *sb.* A white game fowl with some black feathers,—*Dick.* Probably from the Fr. *piolé*, specked, spotted.

PINNERT. *adj.* Shrivelled, starved, sickly.
Lonsd. *pinder*, to shrivel. Clev. *pine*, to shrink, contract, under the influence of cold, drought, sickness. *Pinner* seems to be a frequentative from Ang.-Sax. *pînan*, to pine, languish.

PIPE-STOPPLE. *sb.* A broken piece of the shank of a clay pipe. *Stopple* is no doubt a diminutive of Old Norse *stôlpi*, Dan. *stolpe*, a post, pillar. Halliwell's explanation of North. *pipe-stopple* as a tobacco-stopper must, I think, be a mistake ; the word must be the same as ours.

PISSIMER. *sb.* An ant, pismire.
Old Norse *maur*, Ang.-Sax. *mire*, Dan., Swed. *myre*, ant. The prefix has reference to the sharp, urinous smell of an ant-hill, Dut. *pismiere*, pismire. The same idea, see *Wedg.*, runs through other languages.

PLACK. *sb.* A small copper coin, formerly in currency.
The word is now used in the sense of a thing of no value. Dut. *placke*, Fr. *plaque*, a small coin of various value in different countries.

PLASH. *va.* To trim a hedge.
"To lower and narrow a broad-spread hedge by partially cutting off the branches and entwining them with those left upright."—*Hall.* Old Fr. *plesser*, "to plash, to bow, fould, or plait young branches one within another ; also to thicken a hedge, or cover a walk by plashing."—*Cotg.* Mod. Fr. *plisser*, to plait.

PLASH. *va.* To splash.
Dan. *pladse*, to pour, as rain, *pladske*, to splash, Swed. *plaska*, Dut. *plasschen*, to paddle, splash, Dut. *plasch*, a plash or puddle left by rain.—*Atk.*

PLAT. *vn.* To walk heavily.
Gael. *pluit*, a clumsy foot.

PLAT. *sb.* A broad ridge of land.
Germ. *platz*, a broad even surface, Dut. *plat*, flat.

PLEEN. *vn.* To complain.
Fr. *plaindre.*

PLENNETS. *sb.* Abundance.—*Dick.*
" Down in *plennets* teems the rain."—*Stagg.*
If the above explanation be correct, we may think of Fr. *plenté,* abundance, plenty. But there seems a doubt about this, for I do not remember ever to have met with the word except, as above, in connection with rain, and it seems rather probable that it may be the same word as *planets,* used in Craven and also in Northumberland, where to fall " in planets" is to rain fitfully and in sudden showers. So in East Anglia " by planets" means irregularly or by fits and starts. Craven has also to " fall in *plats*" with a similar meaning. This seems to be derived from the Gael. *plath,* gust, and suggests that *planet* or *plennet* may be a corruption of *plathaid* as a diminutive of *plath,* a gust.

PLOAT. *va.* To pluck, as a fowl.
Flem. *ploten.* decipere lanam, membranam sive corium exuere.—*Kil.*

PLOAT. *vn.* To wade laboriously through wet and dirt·
Crav. *pload.* Gael. *plod, plodach,* a puddle, Dan. *pladder,* mire, Germ. *pladdern,* to dabble. The above *ploat* or *ploud* is the same word as Eng. *plod,* of which the original sense, according to *Wedg.,* was to tramp through the wet.

PLODGE. *vn.* To wade through water.
See *ploat.*

PLOOK. *sb.* A pimple, especially on the face.
Gael. *pluc,* a pimple.

PLOY. *sb.* Employment, occupation.
For *employ,* from Fr. *employer,* from Lat. *plicare,* to fold or bend, " as Germ. *anwenden,* to employ, make use of, from *wenden,* to turn."—*Wedg.* Unless we can suppose *ploy* to be, as seems possibly the case with the next word *ply,* directly from the Welsh *plygu,* to fold, in a similarly derived sense to the French, which seems, however, scarcely likely. Sco. *ploy* is explained by *Jam.* as "a harmless frolic, a piece of entertainment," and is referred to Ang.-Sax. *plegan,* to play. It seems probably, however, to be the same word as ours with a little variation of the sense.

PLY. *sb.* A fold of cloth.
Welsh *plyg,* Bret. *pleg,* a fold, Welsh *plygu,* to fold, to double, Fr. *pli,* a fold, *plier,* to fold, from Lat. *plicare.* It seems uncertain whether our word is from the Celtic or the French.

POCK-ARR. *sb.* The mark left by the smallpox.
Ang.-Sax. *pocc*, Germ. *pocke*, Dut. *pok*, a pock, pustule, Dan. *koparret*, marked with the smallpox. (In Dan. *kop*, Swed. *koppa*, a pock, the consonants are transposed.—*Wedg.*) See *arr.*

POD. *va.* To poke.
Probably the same as *prod.*

PODDISH. *sb.* Porridge of oatmeal, in common use throughout the agricultural districts, especially for breakfast, and though irreverently compared by Dickens to "diluted pincushions without the covers," a very wholesome article of diet. Welsh *potes*, Manx *poddash.*

POIK. *vn.* To steal when playing at marbles.—*Dick.*
Perhaps the same as Eng. *poach.* From Gael. *poc*, to pocket. Or from Fr. *pocher*, to thrust or dig out with the fingers.

POKE. *sb.* A small sack.
Pooke (or poket or walette).—*Pr. Prv.* Old Norse *poki*, a sack, Ang.-Sax. *pocca*, a bag, poke.

POLLY. *sb.* A cow without horns.
Dut. *polle, pol*, head. "To *poll* is to cut off the head of a tree, to shave the head, to clip."—*Wedg.* Other names are *doddy* and *cowt cow.*

POPE, POAP. *vn.* To walk about vaguely, or as one in the dark. Seems to be from Fr. *palper*, Lat. *palpare*, to touch lightly, in reference to groping or feeling with the hands.

PORR. *sb.* Poker.
Dut. *porren*, to stir up, Dan. *purre*, to rouse, excite, Low Germ. *purren*, to stir, to poke.

POSS. *va.* To work clothes in washing, either with the feet or with a heavy stick. Probably from Gael. *post*, to tread with the feet, which, we may presume, was the original system, and which is still the general way in Scotland.

POTTER, POTTLE. *vn.* To work in a trifling or ineffectual way. Prov. Germ. *pöttelen*, to work at anything by small touches.

POW. *sb.* A swamp.
Probably for *pool.* Old Norse *pollr*, standing water, Dut. *poel*, marsh, lake, Welsh *pwl*, Gael. *poll*, hole, pool.

POWSODDY. *sb.* An ale-posset.
  Sco. *powsowdy*, sheep's-head broth, also milk and meal boiled together. The Eng. *posset* is from the Fr. *posset*, for *posquet*, Old Fr. *posquè*, Lat. *posca*. But the Sco. *powsowdy*, sheep's-head broth, seems to be a different word, from *pow*, head, and Swed. *saad*, broth,—*Jam.* To which of the two our word belongs seems uncertain.

PREEN. *va.* To comb and dress the hair.
  The origin is Old Norse *prion*. Sco. *preen*, a pin or knitting-needle, from the notion of picking or arranging nicely with a pointed implement.—*Wedg.* Hence Eng. *prune*, to dress or trim trees.

PRESS. *sb.* A cupboard, especially for clothes or linen.
  Bret. *pres*, armoire, (dialect of Léon), Gael. *preas*, a wooden case, armarium. In the Dict. of the Highland Society, the word is taken to be derived from the English, but the coincidence of the Bret. word suggests whether in this particular sense the word may not be of Celtic origin.

PRIG. *va.* and *n.* To beat down in bargaining.
  Dick. gives the above sense, as well as the ordinary one to pilfer. The Swed. *preja*, to use extortion in dealing, coincides with the former, which may be the original sense.

PRIZE. *va.* To raise or lift with a lever.
  From Fr. *prise*, a taking, seizing, any advantage.

PROD. *sb.* A thorn, sharp point.
  Old Norse *broddr*, Suio-Goth. and Swed. *prodd*, point, spike.

PROD, PRODDLE. *vn.* To poke, to prick.
  Ang.-Sax. *bryrdan*, to goad, Old Norse *brydda*, to form a point. *Proddle* is a frequentative of *prod*.

PRY. *sb.* A kind of short coarse grass.
  Seeing that *bent*, another kind of coarse grass, is in all probability derived from *bant*, high, whence, in a secondary sense, bleak, I think that *pry* may in like manner derive its origin from Welsh *brig*, top, summit, the interchange of *b* and *p* being of common occurrence in Celtic as in Teutonic. Comp., however, Dial. Swed. *pärr*, star-grass, a kind of carex.

PUBBLE. *adj.* Plump, as a "pubble goose."
  Gael. *plub*, a soft unwieldy lump, the original idea in which (see *bleb*) is the sound of some soft body falling into water.

PULT. *sb.* A fat and lazy cat or woman.—*Dick.*
Perhaps connected with Old Norse *pŏlti*, globulus. But comp. *polt*, a thump or blow.—*Hall.* Hence *polt-foot*, a club-foot, "the notion of a blow and of massiveness being frequently connected."—*Wedg.* Swed. *bulta*, to knock or beat, Manx *polt*, a blow, thump.

PUM. *va.* To beat, to pummel.
Welsh *pwmpio*, to beat, thump, Corn. *bom*, blow.

PUMMER. *sb.* Anything very large.
Like *banger*, *thumper*, *slapper*, &c., similarly derived from the idea of a blow.

PUNCH. *va.* To strike with the foot, to kick.
Bunchynge, tundo.—*Pr. Prv.* Dut. *bonsen*, Low Germ. *bunsen*, to knock, Prov. Dan. *pundse*, to butt as a ram, Dut. *ponssen*, to punch.

PURDY. *sb.* A short and thick-set person.
Perhaps, assuming the *r* as phonetic, to be connected with Low Germ. *puddig*, stout, thick.—*Brem. Wt. B.*

PUTT. *vn.* To butt, strike with the head or horns.
Welsh *pwtio*, to poke, thrust. Hence "*putting* the stone" in Highland games.

PUTTY-COW. *sb.* A cow given to striking.
See *putt*.

Q.

QUERN. *sb.* A hand-mill for grinding corn.
Ang.-Sax. *cwĕorn*, Old Norse *qvŏrn*, a hand-mill.

QUILT. *va.* To beat.
Probably from Ang.-Sax. *cwellan*, Old Norse *quelia*, to kill, Ang.-Sax. *cwild*, slaughter, destruction. Formed like *rift*, to belch, from the noun as a secondary verb.

QUIT. *adj.* Free, released, rid of.
Old Norse *quittr*, free, Dut. *kwijt*, rid of.

R.

RACKLE. *adj.* Rough, unmanageable.
Wedg. connects *rackle* with *rack* (in the expression *rack* and ruin). Sco. *rak*, crash, uproar, Boh. *rochati*, to make a crash. Comp. also Swed. *raka*, to riot about, *rakande*, rioting, disturbance.

RAFF. *sb.* An idle and disorderly person.
Lonsd. *raff*, idle, dissolute. "To *raff* was formerly used in the sense of scraping or raking. Hence *raff*, *riff-raff*, scrapings, scum, refuse, the refuse of society; *raff*, (like *rake*), a debauched, unprincipled person."—*Wedg*. Fr. *rafler*, to scrape or scratch, Old Norse *hrafla*, to scrape together.

RAFT. *sb.* A concourse or crowd.
Old Eng. *raff*, a confused heap, from *raff*, to scrape or gather together. See *raff*. So we speak of a *hubble* of people, in a similar sense of heap.

RAG. *va.* To scold, reproach.
The sense seems to be derived from that of a harsh, unpleasant tone of voice. Swiss *räggen*, to speak in a harsh, disagreeable manner, Ital. *ragghiare*, to make a harsh, broken sound.
" My voice is ragged, I know I cannot please you."
As You Like It.

RAGGELT. *sb.* An idle, abandoned person.
Clev. *ragel*. Atkinson's reference to Old Swed. *rækel*, homo nihili, Swed. *räkel*, a worthless fellow, Dan *rækel*, a word of contempt for a mean or upstart fellow, is probably the right one.

RAISE. *sb.* A cairn of stones, generally of a sepulchral origin. Dunmail *Raise* is said to mark the spot where the last British king of Cumberland is buried. Dan. *rös*, a pile of stones, Old Norse *reisa*, to raise.

RAKE. *sb.* A journey, most frequently used in connection with a horse and cart. Also a track or mountain path. Thus the place whence the Countess of Derwentwater made her escape by clambering up one of the clefts of Walabarrow Crag, is still called "the Lady's *rake*." Old Norse *reika*, vagari, *reik*, vagatus, ambulatio, Swed. *raka*, to rove about, Lap. *raeket*, vagari.

RAKE-STEEL. *sb.* The handle of a rake.
Low Germ. *steel*, Germ. *stiel*, handle.

RAM. *adj.* Having a strong or fetid smell.
Old Norse *rammr*, Dan. *ram*, rank, fetid.

RAM. *vn.* To rush violently.
Dut. *rammelen*, tumultuare, (*Kil.*), Germ. *rammelen*, to rout about, sport in an excited manner.

RAMMEL-SLATE. *sb.* A coarse kind of slate.—*Dick.*
Rammel is properly rubbish or debris. Swed. *ramla*, to rattle, fall with a clash. "In like manner, from Dut. *rabbelen*, to rattle, is formed Eng. *rubble*, what comes rumbling down, the ruins of old walls. And from Fr. *rabascher*, to rattle, comes Eng. *rubbish.*"—*Wedg.* Comp. also Dut. *rommelen*, to rumble, *rommelerij*, rubbish.

RAMP. *sb.* A sprain. See *wramp*.

RANDIT. *adj.* Streaked.
"This term is chiefly applied to butter, when of two colours." —*Dick.* Norw. *randut*, striped, marked in strokes, from *rand*, a stripe.

RANDY. *sb.* A termagant, a noisy and riotous person. See *ranty*.

RANK. *adj.* Close or thick together.
"Ranke, crassus."—*Pr. Prv.* Ang.-Sax. *ranc*, rank, fruitful.

RANNEL-TREE, RANNEL-BAWK. *sb.* A cross beam in the chimney, on which hang the pot-hooks. Clev. *randle-balk.* "In a collection of words from Vend-syssel, *rane* is explained as a pole or bawk, fixed at some height in the chimney, to hang meat to smoke on. Elsewhere in Sweden, *rander*, *rände*, and *rände-stänger.*"—*Atk.*

RANNIGAL. *sb.* A wild or riotous person.
Clev. *rannack*, a wild, unsteady person. Norw. *rangla*, to revel, riot, wander about, Germ. *ranken*, *ränkelen*, to run wildly about.

RANTY. *adj.* Wild, riotous, frisky.
Germ. *ranten*, *ranzen*, to make a noise, move noisily about, Bav. *ranten*, to play tricks, Dut. *randen*, *randten*, delirare, ineptere, insanire, (*Kil.*), Swab. junger *rande*, a young sportive person, (*Wedg.*)

RAPPACK. *sb.* A pet name for an unruly child.—*Dick.*
Perhaps from Gael. *rapach*, noisy, boisterous.

RAP OUT. *va.* To speak rapidly, as to "rap out" oaths.
Old Norse *hrapa*, to rush, to do a thing in a hasty manner, *hrapordr*, speaking with precipitation, Dan. *rap*, quick, nimble.

RAPT. *adj.* Ragged, dishevelled.
Old Norse *hraufa*, divellere, Germ. *raufen*, to pluck, Old Norse *rifa*, to tear asunder, *ræfill*, res lacera, Dut. *ravelen*, to ravel out.

RASH. *adj.* Brisk, active.
Old Norse *röskr*, Dan. *rask*, Germ. *rasch*, quick, impetuous, spirited.

RATCH. *vn.* To roam about, with some sense of roughness.
Old Norse *reika*, vagari, *racki*, canis plautus, Ang.-Sax. *ræcc*, Old. Eng. *rache*, a hound that runs by scent.

RATE. *va.* To whiten by bleaching on the grass.—*Dick.*
Hall. gives *rate* as a Cumb. word, "to become rotten." These are probably only different senses of the same word, as the effect of continued bleaching is to rot. In Lonsd. and Clev. the term is applied to hay, &c., the fibre of which has been partially destroyed by exposure. *Atk.* refers to Dan. *röde*, to lay flax or hemp in steep, "the intention being to induce partial decay of the stalk," Norw. *röyta*, "as nearly as possible coincident with *rate* in all respects."

RATTAN. *sb.* A rat.
Ratun.—*Pr. Prv.* and *P. Pl.*

RAVEL. *vn.* To speak in a confused and rapid manner.
Dut. *rabbelen*, to rattle, gabble, precipitare sive confundere verba, (*Kil.*), is precisely the equivalent of our word. Comp. also Low Germ. *räbeln*, Dut. *ravelen*, to rave, Gael. *rabhd*, idle talk.

REAN. *sb.* A bawk or strip of land left for a boundary in a common field. Old Norse *rein*, a boundary, Dan. *agerreen*, a boundary between two fields, Welsh *rhan*, Gael., Ir., Bret. *rann*, Corn. *ran*, Manx *ranney*, a division.

RECKLIN. See *wrecklin.*

REE. *va.* To shake corn in a sieve.
Old Norse *rida*, Dut. *rüderen, rijeren*, to tremble, Germ. *rüttoln*, to shake, sift, winnow corn. Hence Ang.-Sax. *hriddel*, Eng. *riddle*.

REEDENT. *adj.* Passionate, excitable.
Sco. *reth*, fierce, unruly. Ang.-Sax. *hrêthian*, to rage, to excite.

REEK. *sb.* Smoke.
Ang.-Sax. *rêc*, Old Norse *reykr*, Dut. *rook*, smoke.

REEP *(of corn). sb.* A handful of corn in the straw, used as a bait to catch a horse with.—*Dick.* Ang.-Sax. *ripe, ripa*, a handful of corn in the ear.

REEP UP. *va.* To refer back to some unpleasant subject.
Old Norse *rippa upp*, Dan. *opprippe*, to rip up an old sore or grievance.

REEST, REESTY. *adj.* Stupid or obstinate.
Fr. *restif*, stubborn.

REESTY, REESTIT. *adj.* Rancid.
" Reest, as flesche (resty) rancidus."—*Pr. Prv.* " The radical meaning seems to be stale or over-kept bacon, as *chars restez*, remnants, broken meat, is glossed in Bibelesworth by *resty* flees, (reesty flesh), and *resty* or *restive*, from Fr. *rester*, is pronounced *reesty* in the North of England. 'Bure assez reste,' stale or rancid butter, (*Reliq. Ant.*) * * * On the other hand, the word may be the equivalent of Germ. *räsch, räss, ressig*, sharp-tasting, harsh, Swab. *räs*, over-salted, sharp, biting, harsh in taste, Fr. *rêche*, rough to touch."—*Wedg.*

RENDER. *va.* To melt tallow.
Sco. *rind.* Old Norse *renna*, to flow, to be made liquid, to be melted. Dan. *rende*, to run.

RENKY. *adj.* Lengthy, extended.
Dut. *recken*, Ang.-Sax. *râcan*, to stretch, to reach, Wesh *rhenc*, Bret. *renk*, line, rank, that which is stretched.

RESH. *sb.* The rush.
Ang.-Sax. *risc*, Low Germ. *risch*, rush, from Ang.-Sax. *hriscian*, to rustle, shake, vibrate.

RESTLES. *sb.* The stakes to which cattle are fastened in the stalls. Other words are *rid-stakes, rest-stakes, rud-stowers.* In all these words the prefix seems to be *rid*, which may be the same as the Ang.-Sax. *rith* in *rith-fald*, a pasture where cattle are bred and fattened, and which is probably from *hrither*, cattle. Hence *restle* would be *rith-stel*, cattle-stake, from *stela*, stalk, stake ; and *rud-stower* similarly from *stower*,

Old Norse *staurr*, a stake, the word *rest-stake* being probably only a corruption of the other form *rid-stake*. One might think, for *restle*, of Welsh *rhestl*, rack, grate, but for the coincidence of the other words, all seemingly from a similar prefix.

REUTLE. *vn.* To grub in the ground, as a swine with its snout. A frequentative from Ang.-Sax. *wrotan*, Dut. *wroeten*, Dan. *rode*, to grub as a pig or a mole.

RIFT. *vn.* To belch.
Fris. *rebe*, Dan. *ræbe*, to belch. This, like *quilt*, seems to be one of the cases in which our word is formed, not directly from the corresponding verb, but from a noun formed from the verb.

RIG. *sb.* A ridge, a long narrow hill.
" Rygge, of a lond. Porca (agger)."—*Pr. Prv.* Ang.-Sax. *hricg*, Old Norse *hryggr*, the back, Swed. *rygg*, Dan. *ryg*, the back, the highest portion of a field, of land, of a house-roof.

RIGGELT. *sb.* An animal imperfectly castrated.
Wedg. refers to Manx *riggan*, to rut, *reagh*, wanton, lecherous, *riggelt* being an animal imperfectly castrated, and consequently liable to sexual excitation.

RINGE, (*g* soft). *va.* To rinse.
Not, I think, a different pronunciation of *rinse*, but same as Dut. *reingen*, Fris. *reinigje*, Germ. *reinigen*, to cleanse, rinse. The Eng. *rinse* may be taken to be from the Old Norse *hreinsa*, either directly or through the Fr. *rincer*, Old Fr. *reinser*. In any case, the general origin of all is the same, viz., Goth. *reins*. Old Norse *hrein*, Germ. *rein*, clean, pure. Another Northern form is *rench*, corresponding with Low Germ. *renschen*.

RIP. *sb.* A reprobate. Also a worthless or worn-out horse. Low Germ. *rif*, *rift*, a skeleton. " Applied metaphorically to a morally ill-conditioned person."—*Wedg.*

RISE. *sb.* Branches used for hedging or weiring.
Ang.-Sax. *hris*. Old Norse *hris*, Dan. *riis*, branch or twig. The origin may probably be found in Sansc. *ris*, to cut, the word being used only in reference to branches when cut.

RISMS. *sb.* Straws left on the stubble.
Dial. Swed. *ressma*, Dial. Dan. *rusme*, a spike or ear of corn.

RIT. *va.* To mark out the line of a trench or drain with a spade. Ang.-Sax. *writan*, to cut, engrave, write, Swed. *rita*, to trace, Low Germ. *riten*, to draw, make strokes.

RIVE. *va.* To rend or tear asunder, to pull or tug violently. Old Norse *rifa*, lacerare, Dan. *rive*, to rend, to tear, to pull.

ROAN-TREE. *sb.* The mountain ash.
Old Norse *reynir*, Suio-Goth. *runn*, Dan. *ronne*. Ihre supposes that the Scand. name of the tree is derived from *runa*, incantation, magic, in referece to the supposed efficacy of its wood as a charm, which seems probable.

ROCK. *sb.* A distaff.
Old Norse *rockr*, Old High Germ. *rocco*, Dut. *spinrock*, Dan. *rokkehoved*. "The origin of the term seems preserved in Fin. and Lap. *ruoko*, a reed, from the distaff having been made of that material."—*Wedg.* Rather, it seems to me, from the sense of rocking, shaking, or moving, common to both the distaff and the reed.

ROKE. *vn.* To scratch glass, &c., with a sharp point.
Probably formed, like *rook*, from the imitation of a harsh grating sound. Gael. *róc*, a harsh sound or cry, Lat. *raucus*. So Germ. *ratsch*, sound imitative of scraping, scratching.

ROOL, (pron. *reeul.*) *sb.* An unruly person or animal.
West. *raul*, to pull about roughly.—*Hall.* Clev. *roil*, to romp or play boisterously. Crav. *rool*, to rumple. Lonsd. *roggle*, to shake. Old Norse *rugla*, confundere, turbare, Swab. *rollen*, to be noisily merry.

ROOVE, (pron. *reeuv.*) *va.* "To unroof. T' wind *reuv't* our hay-stack."—*Dick.* I do not feel sure, however, that the word is really from *roof*, tectum, and not from Dut. *rooven*, Germ. *raufen*, Old Norse *hraufa*, to pluck, tear asunder.

ROUGHNESS. *sb.* Grass left for winter eating.—*Dick.*
Hall. has *rough*, luxuriant, as grass, *North*. One might possibly think of Sansc. *ruh*, to grow, whence *rauhas*, plant. Or from *rough* in the sense of coarse and rank, as Germ. *rauch-hafer*, wild oats.

ROUSE. *sb.* A drunken debauch, a carouse.
Old Norse *rúss*, Swed. *rus*, Dut. *roes*, Germ. *rausch*, drunkenness, Swed. *rusa*, to fuddle.

ROWK. *sb.* The mist of the valleys.
Clev. *roke*. Dut. *roock*, vapour, Dial. Dan. *rag*, fog or mist, Old Norse *rakr*, madidus.

ROWT. *vn.* To roar or bellow, as cattle when uneasy
or excited. Ang.-Sax. *hrutan,* Old Norse *hriôta,* to snort,
snore, Norw. *rjota, rauta,* to roar, Sansc. *rud,* to roar.

ROWTH. *sb.* Plenty, abundance.
Clev. *rowty,* rank or thick-growing, coarsely luxuriant. Garnett
refers to Welsh and Corn. *ruth,* a heap, while in the Dict. of
the Highland Sco. it is referred to Gael. *rath,* prosperity, increase, profit, collating Welsh *rhad,* gratia, and Germ. *rat,*
salus, prosperitus, et copia rerum parata *(Wacht.)* This seems
to be the more probable origin, the root being probably in either
case to be found in Sansc. *ruh,* to grow, to increase.

ROYSTER. *vn.* To bully, to be noisy or turbulent.
Swed. *rusta,* to make a riot or disturbance, Fr. *rustre,* a roister,
hackster, squabbler, *(Cotg.).* Gael. *riastair,* become turbulent
or disorderly.

ROZZLE. *sb.* Rosin.
Ang.-Sax. *hrysel,* rosin.

RUCKLE. *sb.* A disorderly crowd.
Old Norse *rugla,* confundere, turbare, Dut. *rukken,* to pull,
tug, Norw. *rugla,* to shake, waggle about.

RUCKSHIN. *sb.* A riot, disturbance. See *ruckle.*

RUFT. *sb.* The plot of lea ground to be ploughed in
the year. Probably from Old Norse *hraufa,* Dut. *rooven,* to
pluck, tear asunder, in the sense of opening out the ground.

RUG. *vn.* To pull roughly.
Clev. *row,* to use vigorous exertions. Old Eng. *rugg, rogg,* to
tug. Old Norse *roga,* moliri, niti, *rugga,* to rock, Dut. *rukken,*
to tug.

RUMBUSTICAL. *adj.* Boisterous, noisy, overbearing.
See *rumpus.*

RUMPUS. *sb.* A disturbance.
Sco. *rummys,* to roar, bellow. Ital. *rombazzo,* a clatter, Swiss
rumpusen, to pull one another about. The general origin is to
be found in Old Norse *rumr, rymr,* clash, noise.— *Wedg.*

RUMPLEMENT. *sb.* Coarse materials. Also disorder.–*Dick.*
The first idea is that of broken sounds, Germ. *rummein, rumpeln,* to rumble, rattle. Then that of confusion, disorder, Bav.
rummel, a disturbance, uproar. Then that of rubbish. Germ.
rummel, lumber, old things — *Wedg.* Hence the origin is
similar to that of *rammel-slate.* q.v. The ending in *ment* is a
favourite one in the dialect.

Runch. *sb.* A thick-set person or animal.
I think that *runch* may he the same as *rump*, *nk* or *nch* and *mp* interchanging as in dank and damp. Fris. *romp*, Dut. *romp*, Germ. *rumpf*, trunk, carcass. "We are led from analogous forms to suppose that the primitive meaning is projection."—*Wedg.*

Rung. *sb.* A staff, step of a ladder or gate.
Old Norse *raung*, rib of a boat, Goth. *rugga*, staff, rod, Gael. *rong*, staff, rib of a boat, any piece of wood by which others are joined.

Runner. *sb.* A small stream.
Ang.-Sax. *rynele*, Old Norse *renna*, *rensl*, a stream, channel, from *renna*, to flow.

Runrig. *sb.* In some undivided common lands, the ownership of the parcels changes annually in succession.—*Dick.* Respecting this custom in Scotland, see *Jam.*, who supposes it to be a relic of the custom of the ancient Germans, to hold their cultivated lands in common, and thinks that it was introduced from Germany or Scandinavia first into Orkney and Shetland, where it is most prevalent, and whence it has gradually found its way from North to South.

Runt. *sb.* An aged ox.
Dut. *rund*, an ox, bullock, Germ. *rinde*.

Runt. *sb.* A short and thick-set man.
Fin. *runto*, truncus corporis major, *runtewa*, corpulent, robust.

Ruttle. *vn.* To breathe with a broken or rattling noise, as one suffering from asthma. Dut. *rotelen*, murmillare, *rotel*, murmur, quale moribundi edunt, murmur raucum.—*Kil.* Another form is *ruckle*.

Ryle. *va.* To teaze, to vex.
Lonsd. *royle*, to bluster. To *roil*, to disturb, trouble, vex.—*Hall.* Fris. *rule*, Jutl. *role*, South Dan. *ryle*, to cry in a harsh voice. The above are probably contracted forms, the word from which they are formed being *rok*, in the sense of a harsh noise.

Ryner. *sb.* An augur.
Seems to be the same word as Lonsd. *rimer*, a tool used for enlarging screw-holes in metal or wood, probably from Ang.-Sax. *rȳman*, to enlarge.

Rysel. *sb.* A turbulent child.
Perhaps to be connected with Old Norse *risialldr*, homo varius et violentus, Ang.-Sax. *rese*, violence.

S.

SACKLESS. *adj.* Simple, innocent, inoffensive.
" The parson swears a bonny stick
Amang our *sackless* asses."—*Anderson.*
Ang.-Sax. *sacleas*, Old Norse *saklaus*, peaceable, innocent, from *sac* or *sak*, contention, and the privative termination *less*.

SAD. *adj.* Heavy, applied to bread or pastry.
Welsh *sad*, firm, steady, Dan. *sat*, solid, sedate, Swab. *satt*, firm, fast. The above is the original meaning of *sad*, whence, metaphorically, comes the sense of mental heaviness or sorrow.

SAF-TREE, SAUGH-TREE. *sb.* The willow.
Clev. *sap-tree*. *Atk.* thinks of a connection with *service* or *sorb*. I am inclined to think, however, that the word is simply the Ang.-Sax. *salig, salg*, willow, our dialect, as in many other cases (comp. *faugh, faff*, fallow, from Ang.-Sax. *fealg*) suppressing the *l*, and changing *g* into *f*, while the Clev., again, hardens the *f* into *p*.

SAGGY. *sb.* The name of a game at marbles.

SAIM. *sb.* Lard.
Welsh *saim*, grease.

SAIMED. *vn.* Overcome with heat.
Perhaps from above *saim*, in the sense of melting.

SAIRY. *adj.* Poor, pitiable, generally used as a term of pity.
" Fie, Roger, fie ! a *sairy* lass to wrang."—*Relph.*
Ang.-Sax. *sârig*, miserable, afflicted, pitiable.

SAM-CAST. *sb.* Two or more ridges ploughed in one.
See *ham-sam.*

SANK. *sb.* A quantity, collection of things, as a *sank* of potatoes.—*West and Cumb. Dial.* Dut. *sanghe*, manipulus spicarum (*Kil.*), Swab. *sange*, a bundle of hemp, Dan. *sanke*, Swed. *samka*, to gather, collect, from *sam*, signifying combination. See *ham-sam.*

SAP, SAPPY. *adj.* Wet, moist.
Ang.-Sax. *sæpp*, Low Germ. *sapp*, juice, moisture, Low Germ. *sappig*, wet, juicy.

SAP-HEAD, SAP-SKULL. *sb.* A simpleton.
As in *sumph*, the idea of folly is derived from that of softness and wetness.

SARK. *sb.* A shirt.
: Ang.-Sax. *serc*, Old Norse *serkr*, toga, tunica, indusium, Fris. *sêrc*, a shirt, Dan. *særk*, a garment formerly worn under the armour, Flem. *sarck*, telæ genus subsericum.—*Kil.* I am inclined to take the original meaning to have been a shirt of mail, or possibly a garment worn under it, and the word to be formed on Ang.-Sax. *searo*, Old High Germ. *saro*, armour, equipment, (cognate with Lat. *sero*, I join, connect, fasten ?) In which case it would seem probable that Welsh *seirch*, equipage, harness, trappings, is the same word as our *sark*. Unless, indeed, we can suppose the *r* in *sark* to be intrusive, and the word properly *sak*, in the sense of a loose garment. Comp. Sansc. *sagga*, surtout.—*Eich.*.

SARRA. *va.* To serve.
: In other cases, as in *div* for *dee* (do), our dialect assumes the sound here rejected.

SATTLE. *sb.* A wooden seat or sofa.
: Ang.-Sax. *setl*, Germ. *sessel*.

SCALD-HEAD. *sb.* The ringworm in the head.
: Lonsd. *scald*, scabby, particularly in the head. Dan. *scaldet*, bald, *skaldehoved*, bald-head, Swed. *skallot*, bald, Old Norse *skållda*, to be bald, Gael. *sgall*, baldness, scab. The above seem to be formed, by the prefix of *s*, upon the form found in Ang.-Sax. *calo*, Germ. *kahl*, Eng. *callow*, Lat. *calvus*, bald.

SCALE. *va.* To spread, as manure over a field.
: Dan. *skille*, Swed. *skilja*, to separate persons or things from one another, Old Norse *skilja*, discriminare.

SCANTED. *part.* Kept short, insufficiently supplied.
: " They wadn't see him *scanted*."—*Miss Blamire.*
Old Norse *skamta*, dividere, dimetiri, *skammr*, brevis, accisus, Norw. *skanta*, to measure off, to cut off a little so as to make a thing exact, to give sparingly.

SCAR. *adj.* Shy, wild, frightened.
: Old Norse *skiârr*, timid, shy, Norw. *skjerra*, to scare, frighten.

SCAR. *sb.* A precipice, a steep,rock.
: Old Norse *skor*, Norw. *skar*, breach, cleft in a rock, Old High Germ. *scorro*, præruptum montis, scopulus, Old Dut. *schaere*, scopulus, rupes, Dan. *skier*, rocks, cliffs. The origin seems to be Old Norse *skera*, to cut, a *scar* being that which is cleft *sheer* down.

SCAR. *sb.* A bed of rough gravel.
Dan. *skare*, fragment, shard. The connection seems to be with Old Norse *skara*, to rake, scrape.

SCARN. *sb.* Cow-dung.
Ang.-Sax. *scærn*, Old Norse *skarn*, dung.

SCODER. *va.* To scald.
Dan. *skolde*, to scald. It may possibly be a question whether, in some of these verbs, as *scoder*, Dan. *skolde;* *snifter*, Dan. *snöfte;* *skiander*, Dan. *skiende*, our form in *er* does not simply represent the Scandinavian ending in *e* or *a*, as from the mute sound of *r* final no difference can be distinguished between them. But if so, the participle form, as in *scodered*, must have been a later formation.

SCODER. *sb.* The skin when frayed by heat and friction during violent exercise. Clev. to be *scaldered*, to be in such a state that the surface peels off in scales. "The more immediate connection of this word is with Eng. *scald-head.*"—*Atk.* Comp. also Gael. *sgiolta*, unhusked, hulled, having the skin peeled off, Lith. *skelti*, to split, burst.

SCOGGERS. *sb.* Stockings with the feet cut off worn on the arms. Probably from Old Norse *skockr*, sheath, envelope.

SCONCE. *sb.* A stone bench or shelf.—*Dick.* A screen capable of being drawn across the front of the fire.—*West. and Cumb. Dial.* Lonsd. *sconce* has both these two meanings. Old Norse, Suio-Goth. *skans*, munimentum, Germ. *schanze*, fort, shelter, *schanzkleid*, a canvass screen drawn round a ship during an engagement.

SCON. *sb.* A barley cake.
Probably from Old Norse *skân*, crusta, cortex, Fris. *skân*, rind, skin.

SCOODER. *va.* "To take great effect upon, bring down quickly. Ned went a-shutting. and he *scoodered* them down."—*Dick.* Probably from the same origin as Eng. *scud*, Dut. *schudden*, to shake, toss, jog. "As the figure of shaking expresses the exertion of superior power over an object, Eng. *scud* is used to signify the movement of a body under the influence of overpowering force. To *scud* before the wind is to drive before it without attempt at resistance."—*Wedg.* Very much of the same idea runs through the word *scooder* as described by *Dick*.

SCRAFFLE. *vn.* To scramble, to struggle hard for a living. Old Norse *skreflaz*, to keep one's feet with difficulty, *skriflaz*, to scramble through difficult places. The Dut. *schraeffelen*, again, to scrape together, a frequentative of *schraeffen*, to scrape, coincides more with the second of the above meanings.

SCRAFFLES. *sb.* An empty boaster.

" Peer *scraffles!* thy lan' grows nae girse."—*Anderson.*

Suio-Goth. *skrafla*, boaster, prater, Old Norse *skræfa*, homuncio, meticulosus jactator, *skrapr*, futilis jactator, *skrapa*, crepere, Swed. *skräfta*, to rant, to rave, to rattle. In the dialect of Holstein *schraffel* is similarly used as a term of contempt, signifying a good-for-nothing person.

SCRAPPLE. *sb.* An iron scraper.

A diminutive of Swed. *skrapa*, Dan. *skrabe*, a scraper.

SCRAT. *va.* and *n.* To scratch. Metaphorically to strive hard for a living, "Scrattyn, or scratchyn."—*Pr. Prv.* Suio-Goth. *krat.a*, Dan. *kratte*, Dut. *kratsen*, to scratch.

SCREE. *sb.* The debris of loose stones running down the side of a mountain from the decomposition of its surface. Hence the name of the Screes upon Wast-water. Perhaps from Old Norse *skrida*, ruina montium, Old Norse *skrida*, Gael. *sgiorr*, to slip or slide.

SCREEN. *sb.* A wooden sofa.

Similarly, in the case of *sconce*, the idea of *screen* is extended to that of something to sit down or rest upon; the connection of thought is not very obvious.

SCRIBE. *sb.* A line, stroke, most frequently used in the expression "*scribe* of a pen." Clev. *screeve*, "to mark metal or wood with an instrument that scratches or cuts some of the material away." Gael. *sgriob*, to scrape, Welsh *ysgrifo*, to notch, to write, Dut. *schreef*, line, stroke. This is a collateral word with Lat. *scribo*, but not, I think, derived from it.

SCRIMPY. *adj.* Scanty, pinched, given grudgingly.

Dan. *skrumpe*, to shrivel, contract, Norw. *skrumpet*, shrunk, emaciated, Dial. Dan. *skrimpe*, a miserable half-starved creature, Dan. *krympe*, Welsh *crimpio*, to contract.

SCROBY. *adj.* Mean, niggardly.

Perhaps from Dan. *skrubbe*, Swed. *skrubba*, Dut. *schrobben*, to scrub, scrape, Gael. *sgriob*, to scrape, scratch, make bare by rubbing. Or we might think of Old Norse *scrûfa*, Dut. *schroeven*, to screw, the connection of which with the idea of meanness is obvious.

SCROGS. *sb.* Stunted bushes, low brushwood.
"Comp. Dan. *skrog*, a shrivelled, dried-up carcase, Dial. Dan. *skrav*, *skrag*, a twisted, stunted branch, Gael. *sgrog*, to shrivel, wither up, *sgrogag*, anything shrivelled, a stunted tree, useless old timber."—*Atk.*

SCROW. *sb.* Confusion, disturbance, untidiness.
Clev. *scow*, Lonsd. *scrow*. The Clev. is probably the correct form, our dialect, as in some other cases, taking a phonetic *r*. *Atk.* refers to Dial. Swed. *sköj*, disturbance, uproar, *sköja*, to bustle, make a noise.

SCRUDGE. *va.* To squeeze.
Lonsd. *scrouge*. Wedg. refers to Fr. *escrager*, to squeeze, to crush.—*Cotg.*

SCRUFFINS. *sb.* Scrapings from a pan in which sowens have been boiled.—*Dick.* West. *scrawf*, refuse.—*Hall.* Clev. *scruff*, anything that rises from the surface and may be removed as an impurity. Old Norse *skroppa*, scum.

SCRUNTY. *adj.* Low, short, stunted.
Dan. *skrante*, to be weakly.

SCUFF. *sb.* The back part or nape of the neck.
"The loose skin hanging about the neck of a dog like the collar of a coat or cuff of a sleeve. Dut. *schoef*, collar of a cloak, replicatio, reflexio togæ."—*Wedg.*

SCUFTER. *vn.* To bustle, hurry, scramble.
Swed. *skuffa*, to nudge, jog, shove, *skuffas*, to hustle, scramble.

SCUGG. *adj.* Lurking or lying hid in a corner.—*West. and Cumb. Dial.* Old Norse *skuggi*, shade, shelter.

SCUMFISH. *va.* To suffocate, to stifle.
Sco. *scomfis*. Most frequently used in the passive. Jamieson's suggestion of Suio-Goth. *kufwa*, to suffocate, seems to me on the whole more probable than his alternative suggestion of *discomfit*. Indeed, the word might almost be taken to be a remnant of a Scandinavian passive ending in *st*.

SCURRAN-TOP. *sb.* A peculiar kind of top, formerly used at a game called *Scurran-meggy*, which was much in vogue in Cumberland during the last century.—*Hall.* Perhaps from Dan. *skurre*, Swed. *skorra*, to make a harsh or grating sound. Or else from *scur* in the sense of rapid motion.

SCUT. *sb.* A short tail, as that of a hare or rabbit.
Old Norse *skuts*, a tail, from *skúta*, to project. Or perhaps rather like *scutty*, short, from Wel. *cwta*, short, *cwt*, tail.

SCUTTY. *adj.* Short.
: The same as *cutty*, on which it is formed by the prefix of *s*.

SEAG. *sb.* The *Iris pseudacorus*.
: "*Sedge, segg,* or *segs*, originally the same word, Ang.-Sax. *secg*, which is identical with *sæcg* and *seax*, a small sword, and was applied indiscriminately to all sharp-pointed plants growing in fens."—*Prior.* Its other Cumb. name *mekkin*, may be from a similar origin, Ang.-Sax. *mece*, a small sword.

SEED. Saw, pret. of see.

SEETER. *sb.* A worn or frayed place on a garment.
: Clev. *sieter*, a sieve or riddle. "As thin as a *seatre*, worn into transparency or holes, as cloth when it grows thin."—*Wh. Gl.* Old Norse *sigti*, Dan. *sigte*, Germ. *sichter*, a sieve.

SEEVE. *sb.* The rush.
: Old Norse *sef*, Dan. *siv*, rush. The origin seems to be Sansc. *si, siv*, to join, Eng. *sew*, in reference to the use of the rush for plaiting or weaving.

SEG. *sb.* A callous place on the hand or foot.
: Old Norse *sigg*, callus, hard and thick skin.

SEG. *sb.* A castrated bull.
: Clev. *segg*, a bull castrated after it has grown to maturity. Dial. Swed. *sigg*. a castrated boar or ram, Dial. Dan. *seeg*, a boar castrated after having come to maturity. The origin is probably to be found in Old Norse *seigr*, lentus, quiet, gentle, *seigaz*, lentescere, cognate with Lat. *segnis*, in reference to the effect produced upon the animal's disposition. So *riggelt*, an animal imperfectly castrated, is probably derived from a word of opposite signification.

SEGGIN. *sb.* The *Iris pseudacorus*.
: See *seag* and *meckin*.

SELT. Sold, pret. of sell.

SEN. SYNE. *adv.* Since.
: Ang.-Sax. *sithen*, (*sith-than*, after then), Old Norse *sidan*, contracted *syne*.

SET. *va.* To nauseate.
: The idea seems to be that of settling the appetite for food. Ang.-Sax. *settan*, to settle, appease.

SETTEN. Past part. of set.

SETTLE. *sb.* A wooden sofa. See *sattle.*

SHACKLE. *sb.* The ring which slides upon the cow's restle.
In Clev. and Lonsd. also the wrist. Ang.-Sax. *sceacul*, shackle, Dut. *schakel*, link of a chain, Dial. Swed. *skak*, a link, a chain.

SHAFF! *intj.* An expression of contempt. Stuff!
I am inclined to take it to be properly *shraff*, and to connect it with Old Norse *skraf*, babbling, *skrapr*, futilis jactator. Swed. *skrap*, trash, lumber. See *scraffles*.

SHAFFLE. *vn.* To be undecided, to vacillate.
Atk. refers to Low Germ. *schüfeln*, to shuffle or act in an underhand way. If not from the same origin as *shaff* above.

SHAGRAG. *sb.* A mean, beggarly person.
"*Guerselet*, somewhat like our *shagrag*, a by-word for a beggarlie souldier."—*Cotg.* Perhaps a corruption of Gael. *sgrogag*, anything shrivelled and contemptible, a little old woman, from *sgrog*, to shrivel. Hence also, perhaps, *shragges*, rags, patches.—*Hall.*

SHARPS. *sb.* Flour, with the bran in it.
Crav. *sharps*, flour with a portion of bran, *shaps*, "oats without the grain, retaining nothing but the *shape.*" Sco. *shaup*, hull, husk. I am inclined to think that *sharps* is the same word as the Sco. *shaup*, from the Suio-Goth *skalp*, vagina, Dan. *skulpe*, hull, husk, in reference to *sharps* as having the flour and bran ground up together. From the way in which *r* is slurred in English pronunciation, hardly any difference can be discerned between the two. The Crav. *shaps*, which the Editor mistakenly explains as "oats retaining nothing but the shape," is also no doubt from the same origin, meaning simply husks.

SHAWL. *vn.* To walk crookedly.
Lonsd. *shool*, *shewl.* Clev. *shelder.* "Schaylyn or scheylyn. Disgredior."—*Pr. Prv.* "I shayle, as a man or horse dothe that gothe croked with his legges."—*Palg.* in *Way.* Dial. Swed. *skjäla*, to walk crookedly, Old Norse *skiâlgr*, obliquus, from *skâ*, crookedness, Cumb. *skew;* Sansc. *skahl*, to deviate, (whence Lat. *scelus*, wickedness, deviation from the right way, as Eng. *wrong*, that which is *wrung* or twisted out of truth.)

SHEAR. *va.* To reap.
"Scheryn or repe corn. Meto."—*Pr. Prv.* Ang.-Sax. *scêran*, Old Norse *skêra*, Dut. *scheren*, Germ. *scheren*, to cut. Ignorance of this Northern term once brought a London illustrated paper to grief, when, on the occasion of the late Prince Consort having been reported as present at a *shearing* in Scotland, it

forthwith presented its readers with a graphic representation of a *sheep*-shearing scene, with all the accessories, at a season when such an operation is never, under any circumstances, permitted. The Northern word for shearing sheep is *clipping*.

SHILL. *va.* To shell, or hull peas, &c.
Old Norse *skilja*, Dan. *skille*, to separate, Low Germ. *schellen*, to peel or hull.

SHILLAPPLE. *sb.* The chaffinch.
Properly *sheldapple*, from *sheld*, spotted, Dan. *skioldet*, parti-coloured (of cattle), Norw. *skioldet*, spotted. From the same origin is *sheldrake*, a parti-coloured kind of duck.—*Wedg.*

SHILLIES. *sb.* Shingles, the loose pebbles on the sea-beach. Referred by Peacock to Manx *shillee*, an assemblage of loose stones. The origin of the Manx word may probably be found in Old Norse *skélla*, to clink, clatter, in reference to the sound produced in walking among loose pebbles.

SHINDY. *sb.* A disturbance, a row.
Clev. *shine*, a row or disturbance. Perhaps connected with Dan. *skiende*, to scold.

SHIPPEN. *sb.* A cow-house.
Ang.-Sax. *scypen*, a stall, stable, Germ. *schuppen*, a cart-house, shed.

SHIVE. *sb.* A slice, of bread, &c.
Old Norse *skífa*, Dan. *skive*, Dut. *schijf*, Germ. *scheibe*, a slice, Old Norse *skífa*, Dan. *skive*, Dut. *schiften*, to divide.

SHOG. *vn.* To shake.
Dut. *schokken*, Swiss *schauggen*, to jog, Welsh *ysgogi*, to stir, to shake.

SHOO ! *intj.* An exclamation used in driving away fowls and the like. Grimm (Deutsch. Gramm.) refers to *schu* as an interjection expressive of a sense of cold—"*Schu, schu !* how cold it is !" Hence Wedg., through the sense of shuddering, suggests an origin for *shy*, Germ. *scheu*, Dut. *schouw*, timid, shunning, Old High Germ. *sciuhan*, to fear, be timid or alarmed, and other cognate words. It will be seen that our use of the word *shoo* is more distinctly connected with the sense of shyness or timidity than the German.

SHOON. *sb.* Plural of shoe.

SHOOP. *sb.* The fruit of the dog-rose. See *choop*.

SHOT. *sb.* A half-grown swine.
Chesh. *shoat*, a young pig. Old Norse *skôd*, a young pig.

SHOT. *sb.* The reckoning at an inn, &c.
Ang.-Sax. *scot*, Low Germ. *schott*, Germ. *schoss*, tribute, payment.

SHOT-ICE. *sb.* Ice frozen in sheets on the surface of the ground. Swed. *skot*, sheet.

SHOT-SHEEP, SHOT-CATTLE. *sb.* The refuse of a herd or flock. Low Germ. *schott-ossen*, oxen left unsold out of a sale.—*Hamb. Idiot.*

SHUDDER. *vn.* To *shudder* down is to fall suddenly. *Shudder* as a noun is used in the sense of a sudden fall of prices at a market.—*Dick.* Dut. *schudden.* to shake, to totter.

SIDE UP. *va.* To put things into their places. To put things to a-side.

SILLY. *adj.* Innocent, as applied to children. As applied to grown persons, hapless. "He's nobbut hed peer luck, silly man!" (*Dick.*), the Eng. equivalent of which is "poor fellow!" Ang.-Sax. *sælig*, Germ. *selig*, happy, fortunate, of which our word has come to signify the reverse.

SIN, SIND. *va.* To rinse.
Swed. *sina*, to dry.

SKAIF. *adj.* Wild, fearful.
Old Norse *skiâlfa*, *skelfaz*, tremere, *skêlfa*, terrere.

SKAITCH. *va.* To beat with a stick.
Clev. *scouce*, to inflict punishment on a child by boxing the ears, or nipping the neck, shaking him, &c. *Atk.* refers to Dial. Dan. *skussa*, to take hold of a person and shake him. Similarly, our word, which has probably originally had the same meaning as the Clev., may probably be referred to Old Norse *skakka*, Swed. *skaka*, to shake, our word retaining the hard sound of the first *k*, and softening the second.

SKEEL. *sb.* A large water-kit.
Old Norse *skiola*, Dial. Swed. *skjula*, a milk-pail.

SKEER. *va.* To skim.
Ang.-Sax. *scêran*, Old Norse *skera*, to cut, shave.

SKEERY. *adj.* Timid, fearful. See *scar*.

SKELLED. *adj.* Distorted, awry.
Old Norse *skæla*, detorquere, *skældr*, twisted, awry.

SKELLY. *sb.* The chub.
Comp. Dan. *skalle*, roach, Ang.-Sax. *scealga*, rock-fish.

SKELP. *va.* and *n.* To smack, strike with the open hand. Also to run fast, move rapidly. Old Norse *skelfa*, to strike with the hand, also to go fast. Comp. also Gael. *sgeilp*, stroke.

SKEMMEL. *sb.* A form or long seat.
Ang.-Sax. *scamel*, Dan. *skammel*, a form or bench. The word is also found, *b* or *v* exchanging with *m*, in the Celtic idiom, as Corn. *scavel*, Bret. *scabel*, Wel. *ysgavell*, Ir. *sgabhal*. Lat. *scabellum*.

SKEN. *vn.* To squint.
Clev. *skelly*. Our form seems to stand alone, the Clev. corresponding both with the Germ. and Scand. forms, as Dan. *skele*, Swed. *skela*, Germ. *schielen*, to squint, Ang.-Sax. *sceol-éage*, squint-eyed. Both are, no doubt, however, from the same root, Old Norse *ská*, obliquitas, Ang.-Sax. *sceoch*, crooked.

SKEP. *sb.* A basket of straw or rush.
Ang.-Sax. *scep*, basket, Old Norse *skeppa*, modius.

SKEYBEL. *sb.* A worthless person.
Sco. *skybald*. Dan. *skabhals*, a scamp. Probably, along with Eng. *shabby*, from *skab*, the itch, as a term expressive of contempt, "from the itching skin and scratching habits of a neglected, dirty person."—*Wedg*.

SKEW. *sb.* Something crooked.
Old Norse *ská*, obliquitas, Ang.-Sax. *sceoch*, crooked. *A-skew* = Old Norse *á-ská*, (á = on), awry.

SKIANDER. *va.* To scold, to blow up.
Dan. *skiende*, to scold. It seems possible, see *scoder*, that the ending *er* in *skiander*, may simply represent the Scand. ending in *e*.

SKIDY. *adj.* Thin, slender.
Shide, a thin board.—*P. Pl.* Old Norse *skid*, a thin piece of wood, Ang.-Sax. *scádan*, Germ. *scheiden*, to divide. Sansc. *chid*, to cut.

SKIFT. *va.* and *n.* To shift, remove.
Old Norse *skipta*, Dan. *skifte*, to shift, remove from one place to another.

SKILL. *sb.* Knowledge.
Old Norse *skil*, discrimen, *skilja*, to understand, discriminate.

SKIT. *vn.* To cast reflections on.
Probably a derived sense from Ang.-Sax. *scitan*, to dart, shoot forth.

SKIRL. *vn.* To screech.
Old Norse *skralla*, Suio-Goth. *skräla*, to screech.

SKIRL. *vn.* To slide on the ice.
Gael. *sgior*, to slide.

SKIVER, SHIVER. *sb.* A scale, fragment.
Dut. *scheveren*, to shiver, break to pieces. Old Norse *skîfa*, to split.

SKLATE. *sb.* Slate.
"Sklat or slat stone."—*Pr. Prv.* Old Eng. *sclate*. From Fr. *esclat*, a shiver, splinter.—*Wedg.*

SKOLLICK. *sb.* A thing of no value.
Perhaps connected with Old Norse *skol*, nugæ. If not another form of *scurrick*.

SKRIKE. *vn.* To screech.
Suio-Goth. *skrika*, Dan. *skrige*, to shriek.

SKURRICK or SKUDDICK. *sb.* A thing of the smallest value. Lonsd. *scurrick*, a small piece. Peacock refers to Manx *skirrag*, a splinter, which is probably from Gael. *sgar*, Welsh *ysgaru* ; or Ang.-Sax. *sceran*, Old Norse *skêra*, to divide. *Skuddick* is probably only another form, the tendency of our dialect being to change *r* in the middle of a word into *d*.

SLACK. *sb.* A hollow or depression in the ground.
Dan. *slag*, hollows in a road or track, Ang.-Sax. *slog*, hollow place, slough. "*Slack*, a depression in the ground, may be explained by Norw. *slakkje*, slackness, a slack place in a tissue."
—*Wedg.*

SLACK. *sb.* The small coal left after screening.
Perhaps the same as *slag*, the dross of metals, Germ. *schlacke*, Swed. *slag*. Or perhaps more directly connected with Swed. *slagg*, slush, Low Germ. *slakk*, so much of a slabby material as one takes up at once in a shovel, the idea being that of something soft as compared with the round coal.

SLAGGER. *vn.* To loiter, to be slovenly.
Old Norse *slôfga*, hebetare, Suio-Goth. *sloka*, vagari, otiose errare.

SLAGGER. *vn.* To scatter.
Norw. *slagga*, to spill or flow over the sides of a vessel.

SLAIN. *adj.* Blighted.
Crav. *slaiu corn*, smutted or mildewed corn. Clev. *slain*, the smut of wheat. *Atk.* refers to Dial. Dan. *slöi*, shrunken, withered, S. Jutl. *slög*, poor, having no vigour. The origin may be Old Norse *slagna*, to become soft or moist.

SLAIRY. *adj.* Nasty, wet, miry.
Formed from Old Norse *leir*, mud, mire, by the prefix of *s*.

SLAKE. *va.* To lick. To rub or clean slightly and imperfectly. Old Norse *sleikja*, Fris. *slacke*, to lick, Dan. *slikke*, to lick, to rub.

SLAM. *va.* To win all the tricks at cards.
Sco. *slam*, a share, or the possession of anything implying the idea of some degree of violence or trick in the acquisition. *Jam.* refers to Suio-Goth. *slama*, to gather or heap together, Dut. *slemmen*, to feast luxuriously. (Ihre's definition of S. G. *slama*, "per fas et nefas corradere," accords more closely with Sco. *slam* than *Jam.* renders it.) The Germans use *schlemm* at cards in like manner to our *slam ;* the connection seems to be with *schlemmen*, to carouse, feast luxuriously, so far corroborating Jamieson's view.

SLAPE. *adj.* Slippery.
Old Norse *sleipr*, slippery.

SLAPE-FINGERED. *adj.* Dishonest, thievish.
"Left-handed Sim, *slape-fingered* Sam,
Nae law cud iver teame them."—*Anderson*.
Clev. *slape-fingered*, is defined by *Atk.* as letting slip, or apt to let slip, through or from one's fingers, and he connects it with Old Norse *sleppifengr*, in acquirendo vel attigendo infelix. The connection of our word might rather be with *slope*, to cheat, Dut. *sluip*, underhand, (comp. also Corn. *slev*, cunning, skilful), but on the whole I think it is only an application of the sense of slipperiness.

SLARE. *vn.* To saunter, to be slovenly.
Probably a contracted form of *slagger*.

SLASHY. *adj.* Wet and dirty.
Dan. *slaske*, to dabble, paddle, Swed. *slaska*, to paddle, to be sloppy, *slask*, puddle, wet, *slaskig*, wet, dirty.

SLAT. *vb.* Pret. of slit.

SLATTER. *vn.* To slop, to spill.
Swab. *schlettern*, to slatter, or spill liquids, Bav. *schlottern*, to dabble in the mud.

SLAVER. *vn.* To let the saliva run from the mouth.
Old Norse *slafra*, to lick, Norw. *sleve*, slaver, Lat. *saliva*. *Slaver* comes from the form found in Lat. *lambo*, by the prefix of *s*, as Welsh *glafoerio*, to slaver, by the prefix of *g*.

SLECK. *va.* To quench, to extinguish.
Old Norse *slöekva*, Suio-Goth. *släcka*, to extinguish, Dan. *slukke*, to extinguish, to quench thirst.

SLED. *sb.* A sledge.
Old Norse *sledi*, Dan. *slæde*, Dut. *slede*, sledge, probably allied to Old Norse *sletta*, æquare, planare, Suio-Goth. *slæt wæg*, a level road.

SLEDDER. *vn.* To saunter, to walk in a lazy or slouching manner. Old Norse *slæda*, incertus vagari, *slidra*, laziness, *slödra*, ægre iter emetiri.

SLEM. *va.* and *n.* To slur over, to do in an imperfect manner. Old Norse *slæmr*, actio deficiens viribus, *slŷma*, otiosus hærere, Dan., Swed. *slem*, Dut. *slim*, Germ. *schlimm*, vile, worthless, the original idea, see *lim*, being that of deficiency.

SLEW. *va.* To turn round, whence *slewed*, partly intoxicated. "Properly, to slip. It is the same word with Eng. *slive*, to slip."—*Wedg.* The Dial. Dan. *slöfgarn*, tangled thread, Lap. *sleuwo*, confused, disordered, *sleuwahet*, in confusione sive in nullo ordine esse, convey a sense very suitable for *slewed* in the sense of partly intoxicated.

SLIP. *sb.* A child's pinafore.
The idea, like that of *slipper*, is that which is loosely or easily put on. Low Germ. *slippen*, to slip or slide into, Bav. *shlaiffen*, to slip in, slip on, Germ. *schlaff*, loose.

SLIPE. *vn.* To abscond.
Old Norse *sleppa*, to escape, to slip off, Suio-Goth. *slipa*, to steal furtively away, Ang.-Sax. *slipan*, to give the slip, Dut. *sluipen*, to slink away.

SLIPE. *va.* To strip, to unroof.
Ang.-Sax. *slifan*, to cleave, to slice, Germ. *schleifen*, to level, pull a building to pieces, Dan. *slöife*, Dut. *sloopen*, to demolish.

SLIPPEY. *adj.* Slippery.
Ang.-Sax. *slipeg*, slippery.

SLITCH. *sb.* Fine mud, silt, slake.
Dut. *slijk*, Fris. *slick*, Low Germ. *slikk*, mud, ooze, Eng. *slush*, which is another form of the same word.

SLOBBER. *vn.* To weep noisily and with many tears.
The general application of the word is to sup liquids with noise. Old Norse *slupra*, Dan. *slubre*, Low Germ. *slubbern*, to sup, Dut. *slobberen*, to sup in a noisy and vulgar way.

SLOCKEN. *va.* To extinguish, to quench thirst.
Suio-Goth. *slockna*, to be extinguished.

SLORP. *sb.* The noise which a vulgar person makes in supping or drinking. Dut. *slorpen*, to sup up. The Old Norse *slurka*, to swallow, Dan. *slurk*, draught, are parallel forms, *p* and *k* interchanging as in many other cases.

SLOT. *sb.* A fall of earth from the side of a drain.
Old Norse *slödr*, depressio rei, lacuna, *sletta*, projicere, Dut. *sloot*, ditch.

SLOTCH. *vn.* To walk heavily.
Perhaps allied to *slouch*, the idea of which is "to flag, to hang down for want of inherent stiffness."—*Wedg.* Or perhaps rather allied to Ang.-Sax. *slæge*, Old Norse *slag*, Dan. *slag*, blow, clap, Dut. *slaeghen*, Germ. *schlagen*, to strike, to thump, Old Norse *slag hamar*, a sledge hammer.

SLOWDY. *adj.* Untidy.
Clev. *slowdy*, lanky, ungainly. Dut. *slodde*, Low Germ. *slodde*, Dial. Dan. *slödder*, sloven. One of the large family of words, as *slut*, *slouch*, *sluggard*, in which the original idea is that of looseness or slackness.

SLOWMY. *adj.* Applied to soft and weak straw that has been laid in growing. Old Norse *slæmr*, deficiens, Dut. *slommer*, cumber, lumber.

SLUSH. *sb.* Wet mud, half-melted snow.
Swed. *slask*, dirty liquid, *slaska*, to slop, dabble, Bav. *schlotz*, mud, dirt. See *slitch*.

SMEETH. *adj.* Smooth.
Ang.-Sax. *smœthe*, smooth.

SMIT. *sb.* The daub or mark of ownership on sheep.
Ang.-Sax. *smitta*, Dan. *smet*, spot, smut.

SMITTLE. *adj.* Infectious.
Dan. *smitte*, Swed. *smitta*, Ang.-Sax. *smiting*, infection, contagion.

SMOOT, SMOOT-HOLE. *sb.* A hole in a fence through which hares or rabbits may pass. Dan. *smutte*, a private way of entrance or egress, *smut-hul*, a hiding-place, a smoot-hole. The origin seems to be Ang.-Sax. *smugan, smuan*, Old Norse *smiûga*, to creep, to get into a hole, Dan. *smutte*, to creep off. Hence Ang.-Sax. *smygelas*, conies. The root is the same as that of Eng. *smuggle*.

SMUG. *adj.* Spruce, neat, smart.
Germ. *schmuck*. handsome, fine, neat, Dan. *smuk*, pretty, Swed. *smycka*, to adorn.

SMUSH. *adj.* Smart, spruce.
Probably a softened form of above *smug*.

SMUTTY. *adj.* Dirty, indelicate.
Swed. *smuts*, Germ. *schmutz*, smut, dirt, whence, metaphorically, indecency.

SNAAR. *adj.* Greedy.—*West. and Cumb. Dial.*
Perhaps from Ang.-Sax. *snear*, active, nimble, through the intermediate sense of eagerness. Or perhaps formed, by the prefix of *s*, from *near*, greedy, parsimonious, Dan. *nærig*, Ang.-Sax. *hneaw*, niggardly, covetous.

SNAFLAN. *part.* Trifling, sauntering
Sco. *sniffle*, to trifle. Suio-Goth. *snafwa*, Belg. *snevelen*, to hesitate.

SNAPE. *va.* To snub, to check.
Old Norse *sneipa*, pudorem alicui suffundere, Dan. *snibbe*, to rebuke, snub.

SNAP. *sb.* A small gingerbread cake.
Old Norse *snap*, esculenta emedicata, Dut. *knupkoek*, hard gingerbread.

SNECK. *sb.* A latch.
"Snekke or latche."—*Pr. Prv.* Manx *sneg*, latch. Jamieson refers for the original idea to Dut. *snacken*, to snatch, in the sense of that which catches.

SNELL. *adj.* Keen, sharp, as a "*snell* wind."
Ang.-Sax. *snel*, Old Norse *sniallr*, quick, swift, smart.

SNERP. *vn.* To contract, tighten, as a knot or snare.
Dan. *snerpe*, to tighten, contract, Dut. *snerpen*, to nip.

SNERP. *sb.* A snare. See *above*.

SNERRILS. *sb.* The nostrils.
  Low Germ. *snurre*, Swiss *schnerre*, nose, snout. Allied words are no doubt Old Norse *snörla*, Ang.-Sax. *snora*, Eng. *snore*, the root being probably to be found in Swed. *sno*, to twist.

SNERT. *vn.* To laugh in a suppressed way.
  Nearly allied to Dut. *snorken*, Dan. *snorke*, to snore, to snort, Dut. *snerken*, to make a noise, as butter in the frying-pan, *t* and *k* interchanging as in *jert* and *jerk*.

SNEW. Pret. of snow.

SNIFTER. *vn.* To sniff, as persons do who have a cold, or who do not blow the nose properly. Dan. *snöfte* has exactly the same meaning.

SNIG. *va.* To lop the branches of fallen timber.
  Norw. *snicka*, to cut, to work with a knife, Flem. *snoecken*, to cut, lop, prune.

SNIG. *va.* To draw timber by horse and chain from the place where it has been felled. *Atk.* refers to Ang.-Sax. *snican*, to creep, Dan. *snige*, to cause to move in a gliding manner.

SNIPT, SNIP-FACED. *adj.* Having a white mark down the face. Dut. *snebbe*, Low Germ. *snibbe*, beak, Low Germ. *snepel*, a sort of fish the mouth of which becomes white at its death.—*Hamb. Idiot.* The idea, however, notwithstanding the coincidence of the last word, seems to be nothing more than that of a narrow mark.

SNITE. *va.* To wipe the nose.
  Ang.-Sax. *snytan*, Old Norse *snita*, to wipe, cleanse.

SNIZY. *adj.* Cold, cutting, (of the wind.)
  The sense seems to be that of "cutting," and the word to be allied to *snaze*, to prune trees, Old Norse *af-sneisa*, Westerwald *schnasen*, to cut off branches, prune trees. Similarly Dut. *snippen*, Dial. Dan. *sneve*, is applied to a cutting wind.

SNOCK-SNARLS. *sb.* Entanglement.
  Snarls is from *snarl*, a knot, Old Norse *snara*, Ang.-Sax. *sneâre*, knot, noose. And *snock* seems to be a word formed from the same root, Swed. *sno*, to twist.

SNOD. *adj.* Level, smooth.
  Old Norse *snoddin*, Norw. *snöydd*, smooth, bare. The origin is Ang.-Sax. *snidan*, Old Norse *snida*, to cut, the idea being that of something lopped or pruned till it is smooth.

SNOTTER. *vn.* To blubber.
The idea seems more properly to snivel, Low Germ. *snotteren*, to snifter, Bav. *schnudern*, to draw breath through the impeded nose, Swiss *schnudern*, to snivel, to snift in crying.

SNOTTY. *adj.* Mean, contemptible.
Ang.-Sax. *snote*, mucus. As from the idea of keeping the nose properly wiped is derived Ang.-Sax. *snoter*, sensible, prudent, so from the opposite idea comes the sense of contempt.

SNOWK. *vn.* To scent out, to snuff at, as a dog at a rat-hole. Suio-Goth. *snoka*, insidiose scrutari, Dial. Dan. *snökke*, to smell after, spy out, Fris. *snucke*, Dut. *snicken*, to sniff, scent out.

SOBBY. *adj.* Heavy, like a sod.
Welsh *sob*, bunch, tuft, mass, Old Norse *soppr*, a ball.

SODDY. *adj.* Heavy, fleshy.
Gael. *sodach*, clumsy, robust.

SOGGY. *adj.* Same as *soddy*.
Clev. *sodgy*. North. *soggie.—Hall*. Probably, from the frequent interchange of *d* and *g*, the same as *soddy*.

SOIL. *sb.* The fry of the coal-fish.—*Hall*.
In a list of Norfolk words communicated to the Phil. Soc. by A. Gurney is *sile*, the fry of fish, which she refers to Old Norse *sil*, *sili*, a long and small herring. Comp. also Suio-Goth. *sill*, Swed. *sill*, Fin. *silli*, herring, Lapp. *sjilah*, pisces minusculi. Also Corn. *silli*, Bret. *sili*, an eel. The general origin may, as suggested by Ihre, be found in the Gael. *sioil*, seed, spawn or fry of fish, Welsh *sil*, issue, seedling, spawn, *silio*, to spawn. But it is to be observed that we find in the Old Norse itself the word *svil*, the milt or soft roe of fish.

SONN. *vn.* To meditate, think deeply.
Sco. *sonyie.* Ang.-Sax. *sinnan*, Germ. *sinnen*, to ponder, meditate, Old Norse *sinna*, mens, attentio, Welsh *synu*, to observe steadfastly, *synio*, to consider. *Jam.* refers to Fr. *soigner*, which, however, according to Grimm, is itself of Teutonic origin.

SONSY. *adj.* Plump, voluptuous in form.
Dan. *sandselig*, sensuous, voluptuous.

SONSY. *adj.* Lucky, fortunate. *Dick.* gives also the meaning of generous. Sco. *sonce*, prosperity, felicity. *Jam.* refers to Gael. *sonas*, prosperity, good fortune.

SOUGH, SOO. *sb.* The distant sighing or surging of
the wind or sea. *Atk.* and *Jam.* both collate cognate words,
as Ang.-Sax. *swogan*, to sound, howl as the wind, but seem to
have overlooked the word most distinctly concerned, the Old
Norse *súgr*, ventus per rimas in domum penetrans, maris æstus.
The former of these two definitions is Haldorsen's; the latter is
added in my copy in the handwriting of the late Charles Konig,
of the British Museum. The Low Germ. *sukk*, Germ. *zug*, a
draught of wind, may perhaps be connected.

SOOA! *int.* Still! Be quiet!
Old Norse *svei*, fie. Ang.-Sax. *swiga*, silence?

SOOALS. *sb.* A swivel joint in a chain, commonly
termed a pair of *sooals*.—*Dick*. *Sooal* is another form of
swivel, as *soople* of *swipple*. Old Norse *sveifla*, to swing round,
to brandish, *svif*, sudden and rapid motion.

SOOP. *va.* To sweep.
Old Norse *sópa*, to sweep, *sópr*, a besom, Swed. *sopa*, to sweep.

SOOPLE. *sb.* The upper part of a flail.
Old Norse *svipa*, to brandish, move rapidly to and fro, Norw.
sviva, to turn round, Old Norse *sveifla*, to swing round, to
brandish.

SOOREN. *vn.* To become sour.
Ang.-Sax. *súrian*.

SOP. *sb.* A tuft of grass, &c. A milkmaid's cushion
for the head. The masses in which the plumbago or black-lead
is found in the famous mine at Keswick are called *sops*. Welsh
sob, *sopen*, bunch, tuft, *swp*, compressed mass. Old Norse
soppr, ball.

SOSS. *sb.* A boiled mess for a cow.
Gael. *sos*, a mixture of meal and water given to dogs, Welsh *sos*,
pulpamentum sordidulum.

SOTTER. *sb.* The noise made in boiling.
Gael. *sod*, noise of boiling water, Germ. *sod*, bubbling up of
boiling water, Low Germ. *suddern*, to boil with a gentle sound.

SOUSE. *sb.* The pickle of brine, chiefly used in the
phrase "sour as souse." *Wedg.* refers to Fr. *saulse*, sauce.
Or we may think of Old Norse *súrs*, cibaria acida.

SOWDER. *sb.* A bungled mixture in cookery.
Perhaps connected with Old Norse *sódaz*, to become nasty. Or
perhaps rather with Old Norse *súlda*, to become mouldy or
fusty.

CUMBERLAND DIALECT. 133

Sowe, Seugh. *sb.* A wide, wet ditch.
Prov. Eng. *soggy*, wet. Old Norse *söggr*, wet, *sûgr*, alluvies maris, Gael. *sûgh*, moisture, wetness, Welsh *swgio*, to soak, Sansc. *sic*, to be wet.

Sowens. *sb.* Pottage of oatmeal dust.
Gael. *sughan*, the liquid of which *sowens* is made by boiling, from *sugh*, juice, appears to give the origin of our word.

Sowt. *sb.* The joint-ill in lambs and calves.
Ang.-Sax. *sûht*, Old Norse *sût*, *sôtt*, illness, disease.

Sowpy. *adj.* Soft, watery.
Clev. *soup*, to soak, saturate. "Simply another form of *sop*." *Ath.* Norw *subba*, to dabble, *subben*, soaked, Low Germ. *sappig*, wet, sloppy.

Spane (pron. *spean*.) *va.* To wean.
Germ. *spänen*, Low Germ. *spennen*, to wean, Ang.-Sax. *spana*, Old Norse *speni*, teat.

Spang. *va.* and *n.* To leap, to spring. To shoot, fling, project with force. Old Norse *spenna*, to bend a bow, Norw. *spenna*, to move oneself with force or spring, *spenna*, to thrust or kick with the foot. Comp. also Welsh *ysponc*, a spring, jerk.

Spanghew. *va.* To pitch up suddenly.
From *spang*, as above, and perhaps Swed. *hoja*, to upraise. Or Old Norse *höggva*, Dan. *hugge*, to strike.

Span-new. *adj.* Perfectly new. See *bran new*.

Sparling. *sb.* The smelt.
Sco. *sparling*, *sperling*. Germ. *spierling*, Dut. *spiering*, the smelt. "Isl. *sperling* is perhaps the same. G. Andr. gives it as the name of a fish."—*Jam.* The Suio-Goth. name is *nors*, which Ihre takes to be from *nor*, a straight, because these fishes crowd into narrow friths. Or rather, from the same root as *nor*, in the sense of something small and fine in shape. So *sparling*, like *spear*, *spare*, *sparrow*, *sprat*, seems to be from a root signifying fineness and smallness. (While I write, Cleasby confirms me with *nôra*, a small, wee thing, *silungs nôra*, a small trout.)

Spate. (pron. *speeat*.) *sb.* A sudden and heavy shower.
Dut. *spatten*, to splash, Norw. *sputta*, to spirt, spout. *Spate* is similar to *spout* in water-spout.

Spaulder. *vn.* To sprawl, move in an awkward manner.
Probably from Dan. *sprælde*, to toss about the limbs, the *r* being dropped for the sake of euphony.

SPAVE. (pron. *speeav.*) *va.* To castrate a female animal.
Gael. *spoth,* Manx *spoiy,* to castrate, Lat. *spado,* eunuch.

SPEER. *vn.* To inquire.
Ang.-Sax. *spyrian,* Old Norse *spyria,* to investigate.

SPELK. *sb.* A long splinter or slip of wood.
Ang.-Sax. *spelc,* Old Norse *spiâlk,* a splinter, Gael. *spealg,* splinter, fragment.

SPIDDICK. *sb.* A spigot.
Manx *spyttog.* "Not to be considered as a corruption of *spigot,* but as formed in a similar manner from the parallel root *spid, spit,* signifying splinter, Bav. *speidel,* a chip, splinter."—*Wedg.*

SPILE. *sb.* The vent-peg of a cask.
It. *spillo,* a spigot or gimlet, also a hole made in a piece of wine with a gimlet or drawing-quill, Venet. *spilare,* to bore a hole for a peg in order to let in the air.—*Wedg.* Comp. also Swiss *spiggel,* splinter, Bav. *spickel,* wedge, Welsh *yspig,* spike.

SPINK. *sb.* The chaffinch.
Welsh *yspincyn,* chaffinch.

SPITTEN-PICKTER. *sb.* "Strong likeness. Yon barn's his varra *spitten-picter.*"—*Dick.* "That barn's as like his fadder as an he'd been *spit* out of his mouth."—*Crav.* The expression was used in Early Eng. "He was as like him as if he had been *spit* out of his mouth."—*Cotg.*

SPLAT. *va.* Pret. of split.

SPOLE. *va.* To partially separate the shoulders of an animal from the chest. Lonsd. *spalch,* to split. Suio-Goth. *spjäla,* Dan. *spalte,* Fris. *spjellen,* Germ. *spalten,* Gael. *spealt,* to cleave or split, Dial. Dan. *spaalde,* to split a fish without actually separating the halves. North. *spalding*-knife, a knife used for splitting fish.—*Hall.*

SPRECKELT. *adj.* Speckled.
Old Norse *sprekklöttr,* Dan. *spraglet,* speckled.

SPREED. *va.* To spread.
Dut. *spreeden,* Dan. *sprede,* Germ. *spreiten.* While, in English, *spread,* the pres., is confounded with *spread,* the pret., both being pronounced *spred,* the Northern dialects preserve the proper distinction of *spreed* and *spred.*

SPRINT, SPRENT. *vn.* To sprinkle, splutter like a pen.
Swed. *sprätta*, Bav. *spratzeln*, to splutter like a pen, Old Norse *spretta*, to sprinkle.

SPROAG. *sb.* A jaunt, pleasure excursion, spree.
Belonging to the same family of words as *spruce*, *spry*, Prov. Eng. *sprag*, *sprack*, brisk and lively, Old Norse *sprækr*, brisk, fiery, the root idea of which seems to be found in Swed. *spraka*, Dan. *sprage*, to crackle, explode.

SPUNK. *sb.* Liveliness, spirit.
Welsh *ysponc*, jerk, bound.

SPURTLE. *vn.* To sprawl, kick the legs about.
Dut. *spartelen*, to frisk, sprawl, kick, Lith. *spirti*, to kick.

SPURTLE. *sb.* An instrument used in thatching.
A corruption, I take it, of *spattle*.

SQUAB, SWAB. *sb.* A wooden sofa with a cushion.
Dial. Swed. *skvabb*, loose flabby fat, *skvabba*, a fat woman, are referred to by *Atk.* as cognate, the allusion being to the soft cushion.

STACK. Pret. of *stick*.

STAG. *sb.* A colt. Also a young game-cock.—*Dick.*
Old Norse *steggr*, the male of the fox, also of various other wild animals.—*Hald.*

STANG. *sb.* A pole.
Old Norse *staung*, Dan. *stang*, Ang.-Sax. *steng*, Dut. *stang*, stake, pole.

STANK. *vn.* To groan.
Old Norse *stianka*, Suio-Goth. *stanka*, to groan, pant.

STANK. *sb.* A pond.
Gael. *stang*, Old Fr. *estanche*, *estang*, a pool. The original idea seems to be that of stopping, Arm. *stanka*, to stop the flow of water, Swed. *stänga*, to shut.—*Wedg.* The root is probably Sansc. *stai*, to close, fasten.

STARK. *adj.* Unnaturally stiff.
Old Norse *sterkr*, Germ. *stark*, rigid, stiff, strong.

START. *sb.* The handle of a pail.
Ang.-Sax. *steort*, Old Norse *stertr*, Dan. *stjært*, tail, Germ. *pflugstert*, handle of a plough.

STARTLE. *vn.* "Cattle *startle* when they erect their heads and tails and gallop madly in hot weather through fear of the stinging flies."—*Dick.* Old Dut. *steerten*, fugere. Or possibly there may be a more direct reference to the raising the head and tail, Ang.-Sax. *steort*, tail, extremity, something which projects. So the corresponding Germ. *sturzen* is applied to a horse pricking its ears.

STAYK. *vn.* To wander vacantly, to blunder.
Norw. *stauka*, to go slowly, stump along, Gael. *stalc*, to walk with halting gait, Ir. *stailc*, stop, impediment. Hence our word seems to be from the same origin as Eng. *stalk*.

STAYVEL or STAYVER. *vn.* To wander about in a listless way. Suio-Goth. *stapla*, to reel, stagger, a frequentative of *stappa*, to walk, step.

STEAD. *sb.* The fixed or allotted place of a thing, as a *farm-stead*, *midden-stead*, &c. Ang-Sax. *stede*, a place, station.

STEADLIN. *sb.* A foundation for a corn or hay-stack. A diminutive of *stead*.

STECK. *vn.* To be obstinate, as a horse that will not draw. Lonsd. *stecked*, stubborn. Old Norse *steigr*, contumax.

STEE. *sb.* A ladder.
Old Norse *stigi*, Dan. *stige*, Swed. *stege*, ladder, Ang.-Sax. *stigan*, Old Norse *stiga*, to climb, to mount. Hence *sty*, in the sense of a mountain path, in the Lake district.

STEEK. *va.* To shut, fasten.
Clev. *steck*. "To *stick* or *steke*, to stab, to stick, to fix or fasten, and thence to close, to shut."—*Wedg.* Dut. *stecken*, figere, pangere, claudere ligneis clavis.—*Kil.* The Mid. High Germ. *stecken*, rendered by Ziemann "befestigt, festgehalten sein," seems also to have had a sense akin to our own.

STEG. *sb.* A gander.
Old Norse *steggr*, *steggi*, a gander or drake, (*Wedg.*), Norw. *steg*, the male of any bird.

STELL. *sb.* A large open drain.—*Hall.*
"There can be no doubt that this is merely the abbreviation of *water-stell*, Ang.-Sax. *water-steal*, a water-place."—*Atk.*

STEVEN. *sb.* To set the steven is to agree upon the time and place of meeting previous to some expedition.—*West. and Cumb. Dial.* Ang.-Sax. *stefnian*, to call, cite, proclaim, Old Norse *stefna*, to summons, Lapp. *stebno*, convocatio, concio.

STEW. *sb.* Dust.
Dan. *stöv*, dust, Germ. *staub*.

STEW. *sb.* Trouble, difficulty, perplexity. To be in a *stew*. Perhaps metaphorically, as *Wedg.* has it, from *stew*, dust, confusion. But comp. Old Norse *stid*, labor molestus, Dan. *stöi*, Swed. *stoj*, noise, bustle, hubbub, Lapp. *stivos*, tumultus, perturbatio.

STICKS. *sb.* Furniture.
Germ. *stück*, piece, article.

STIDDY. *sb.* An anvil.
Old Norse *stedi*, Swed. *städ*, Old Dut. *stiete*, anvil, connected with Ang.-Sax. *stith*, firm, steadfast, Lapp. *stittjo*, rigidus, and probably with Welsh *syth*, stiff, firm (as Gael. *sruam*, Eng. *stream*.)

STIFE. *adj.* Sturdy, obstinate.
Old Norse *styfr*, durus, rigidus, obstinatus, Ang.-Sax. *stif*, inflexible, stiff, Germ. *steif*.

STILT. *sb.* The handle of a plough.
Swiss *stelz*, stalk. Probably another form of Old Norse *stilkr*, Dan. *stilk*, stalk, stem, *t* and *k* interchanging as in *jert* and *jerk*.

STILT. *vn.* To walk in a stiff manner.
Swed. *stylta*, to halt, to limp, Ang.-Sax. *styltan*, to hesitate, stammer, Germ. *stilte*, a wooden leg.

STINT, STENT. *sb.* A right of pasturage for a certain number of cattle. Ang.-Sax. *stintan*, to stint.

STIRK. *sb.* A young heifer or bullock.
Styrk, neet or heefer.—*Pr. Prv.* Ang.-Sax. *styrc*, Dut. *stierik*, Germ. *stärke*, heifer.

STOB. *sb.* A stump, post.
Gael. *stob*, stump, stake, Old Norse *stubbr*, Dan. *stub*, Ang.-Sax. *styb*, a stock, stub, Sansc. *stabh*, *stubh*, to fix.

STOOK. *sb.* Twelve sheaves of corn set up in the field. Welsh *ystuc*, shock of corn, Germ. *stauch*, Low Germ. *stuke*, heap, Boh. *stoh*, heap, hay-cock.

STOON, STOUND. *sb.* The benumbing sensation arising from a blow. Ang.-Sax. *stunian*, to strike against, to stun, Germ. *staunen*, to lose the power of action, to be stupified.

STOOR. *sb.* Flying dust.
That which is stirred. Ang.-Sax. *styrian*, Dut. *stoeren*, Belg. *stooren*, to stir. The Dict. of the Highland Soc. has *stûr*, dust, as a Gaelic word.

STOOTHE. *va.* To plaster a wall by the application of battens and laths. "Stothe or post of a house."—*Pr. Prv.* Ang.-Sax. *styth*, *stuth*, pillar. Gael. *stuadh*, pillar, also the wall of a house.

STOOV'T, STUF'T. *adj.* Marked in indication of ownership by having the end of the ear cut off, applied to sheep. Old Norse *styfa*, amputare, *stufa*, a female slave whose ears have been cropped for theft, Low Germ. *stuven*, to lop or cut off the head of trees. In Iceland an animal with closely-cropped ears was called *al-styfingr;* it was forbidden by the law to mark sheep in this way unless public notice had previously been given.

STOP. *va.* To stuff, to cram.
Dut. *stoppen*, Dan. *stoppe*, Germ. *stopfen*, to stuff, fill, cram. This (see *Wedg.*) is the original sense of Eng. *stop.*

STOPE. *vn.* To walk as one does in the dark.
Low Germ. *stuppen*, to strike the ground with a stick in walking, N. Fris. *stuppin*, to strike against.

STORE. *sb.* To set *store* on a thing is to put value or place dependence upon it. We may perhaps refer to what *Wedg.* thinks may be the origin of Eng. *store*, viz., Old Norse *staurr*, Old High Germ. *stiura*, a stake, post, prop, and thence, aid, assistance, contribution.

STOW. *va.* To cram, to surfeit.
Dut. *stouen*, Germ. *stauen*, Dan. *stuve*, to push, stow or thrust together in packing.

STOT. *va.* and *n.* To bound as a sheep or deer does when jumping with all the feet together.—*Dick.* To rebound, as a ball. Germ. *stoszen*, to strike, hit, to recoil, Dut. *stuiten*, Swed. *stutta*, to stop, to rebound. The idea, as in stutter, seems to be that of an abrupt or sudden check.

STOTTER, STOWTER. *vn.* To walk clumsily.
Swed. *stutta*, to stumble, Old Norse *stauta*, Germ. *stottern*, to stutter. "The broken efforts of the voice in imperfect speech and those of the body in imperfect going are commonly represented by the same forms."—*Wedg.* See *stutter.*

STOVE. *sb.* A young shoot of wood.—*West. and Cumb. Dial.*
Properly, I apprehend, a young shoot cut or pruned from the tree. Old Norse *styfa*, amputare, Low Germ. *stuven*, to lop or prune a tree.

STOWER *sb.* A stake.
Old Norse *staurr*, Dan. *stavre*, Old High Germ. *stiura*, Lapp. *staura*, Gr. σταυρος, a stake, pole.

STRADDELT. *adj.* Stuck fast, brought to a standstill.
"I think oald P. was varra nar *straddelt* iv his sarmon."— *Gibson* (heard at the door of a chapel after service). Seeing the tendency of our dialect towards the introduction of a phonetic *r*, as in *strunt* for *stunt*, *scrow* for *scow*, &c., I think that *straddelt* may be properly *staddelt*, Ang.-Sax. *statholiod*, made fast, from *statholian*, to make fast, establish, in the sense of sticking.

STRACK. Struck, pret. of *strike.*

STREAK. *sr.* A straight edge used to level the top of a measure of corn. Old Norse *strika*, lineam ducere. Gael. *stric*, a kind of ruler to measure grain, &c., by drawing it along the brim.

STREEK. *va.* To stretch, to lay out a corpse.
Ang.-Sax. *streccan*, Dut. *strekken*, to stretch.

STREEN. *va.* To strain, sprain.
Fr. *estraindre.*

STRICKLE. *sb.* A sanded piece of wood for sharpening scythes. Swed. *stryk-stikka*, Dan. *stryge-spaan*, a strickle, from Swed. *stryka*, Dan. *stryge*, to rub, to whet, Dan. *strigle*, to curry, Swed. *strigel*, razor-strop.

STRINKLE. *vn.* To sprinkle.
Sco. *trinkle*, to trickle. Welsh *treiglo*, to trickle, Ang.-Sax. *stregan*, to sprinkle, *strycel*, the nipple.

STRINT. *sb.* A thin stream, as of milk from the cow.
Dan. *stritte*, to spirt, Ang.-Sax. *streaan*, Swab. *stritzen*, to sprinkle, to spirt.

STRIPPINS. *sb.* The last of the milk.
The idea seems to be that of squeezing or compression, as in Swed. *strypa*, to strangle, Dut. *stroppen*, stringere, premere.

STRITCH. *vn.* To strut.
N. Fris. *staurke*, to strut. The idea seems to be that of rigidity or stiffness, as in Ang.-Sax. *streccan*, Dut. *strecken*, to make tight, to stretch.

STRUNT. *sb.* A fit of obstinacy. A horse that refuses to draw is said to "tak the strunt." Sco. *strunt.* Clev. *stunt.* The Clev., I take it, shows the proper form, our dialect and the Sco., as in some other cases, taking a phonetic *r*. Dial. Swed. *stunni*—taga *stunnt*, "exactly coincident with our tak *stunt*," (*Atk.*), Ang.-Sax. *stunt*, foolish, stupid.

STRUNTY. *adj.* Stunted, dwarfish.
Clev. *stunt*, *stunty*, shows the proper form, our dialect, as in the preceding word *strunt*, taking a phonetic *r*. Suio-Goth. *stunt*, truncatus, brevis, Swed. *stunta*, to cut short, Old Norse *stuttr*, short.

STULP, STOOP. *sb.* A gate-post.
Old Norse *stôlpi*, Dan. *stolpe*, post, pillar, Germ. *stolp*, block.

STUMMER. *vn.* To stumble.
Dial. Dan. *stumre*, to stumble.

STURDY. *sb.* A disease in sheep, caused by water in the head. Gael. *stuird*, *stuirdean*, vertigo, a disease in sheep.

STUTTER. *vn.* To stammer.
Old Norse *stauta*, Germ. *stottern*, to stammer, Swed. *stutta*, to stumble.

STYME. *sb.* Not to be able to "see a *styme*" is an expression indicative of perfect inability to discern anything. "*Styme* seems properly to signify a particle, a whit. Suio-Goth. *stomm* denotes the elementary principle of anything, Welsh *ystum*, form, figure, species."—*Jam.*

STYNE, STYAN. *sb.* A swelling on the eyelid.
Norw. *stigje*, *stighöyna*, Low Germ. *stieg*, a sty, a pustule at the corner of the eye.

SUCKAM. *sb.* The drainage from a dung-heap.
Welsh *sug*, Gael. *sugh*, moisture, Welsh *sucan*, steeping, Old Norse *súgr*, alluvies maris, Germ. *sogen*, to drip.

CUMBERLAND DIALECT. 141

SULLERT. *adj.* Stuffed or choked up with a cold.
Perhaps connected with Old Norse *sullr*, a swelling. Similarly we have *soop* for *sweep*, *sooal* for *swivel*, *sump* for *swamp*.

SUMPH. *sb.* A simpleton.
Dan., Swed. *sump*, mire, fen, bog. The same idea of folly as derived from the idea of something wet and soft is found in *sap-head*.

SWAB. *sb.* A wooden sofa. See *squab*.

SWAD. *sb.* A hull or husk, of peas, &c.
Perhaps, as suggested by *Atk.*, connected with *swathe*, to wrap, to enfold. Or perhaps another form of *sward*, Ang.-Sax. *sweard*, skin, rind. Similarly, Low Germ. *swadd* for *sward* (swathe in mowing.)

SWADDER. *vn.* To dabble in water.
Suio-Goth. *squætta*, liquida effundere, Swiss *schwadern*, Bav. *schwadern*, to dabble, splash, Dut. *swadderen*, profundere, turbare aquas.

SWADDERMENT. *sb.* Drink. See *swatter*.

SWADDLER. *sb.* A methodist.

SWAGT. *adj.* Bent downwards in the centre.
Clev. *swag*, to sway to one side. Old Norse *sweigja*, inclinare, Dial. Dan. *svakke*, to lean out of the perpendicular.

SWAG-BELLIED. *adj.* Having a hanging or protuberant belly. See *swagt*.

SWAITH. *sb.* The apparition of a person seen at the moment of his death. *Waith*, (Brockett,) an apparition in the exact resemblance of a person, supposed to be seen just before or soon after death, I take to be the same word, minus the prefix of *s*. Brockett also gives the alternative form *waff*, *th* and *f* interchanging as in many other cases. We may think, then, of Suio-Goth. *wefwa*, *swefwa*, Swed. *sväfva*, Dut. *sweyven*, to hover, float (as an apparition). Or perhaps we may refer to the Clev. *swip*, personal image or representation, exact likeness, as in the phrase "He's the varra *swip* of his father." The Scotch form of this word Jamieson gives as *swap* or *swaup*. Old Norse *svipr*, look, countenance, fashion of feature, Norw. *svipa*, Dial. Swed. *svepa*, to resemble another in features. The *swaith* (or *swaif*) of a person might then, as in the phrase "*swip* of his father," (Sco. *swap*) be his exact image or counterpart. But, again, the Old Norse *svipr* has the further sense according to Haldorsen, of a sudden apparition, a spectre, which forms a still closer connection with our word. Jamieson collates with our *swaith* the Sco. *wraith*, but this would seem to be a different word, and probably derived from Old Norse *hreda*, Mod. Icel. *hræda*, boggle.—*Cleasby*.

SWANG. *sb.* A damp or boggy hollow.
Old Norse *svangr*, lacuna, Swed. *svank*, bend, hollow. Seems formed by taking the nasal on *swag*.

SWAP. *va.* To exchange.
Ang.-Sax. *swipian*, Old Norse *svipa*, to do anything smartly or quickly. "The sense of barter or truck seems to come from the notion of a sudden turn, an exchange of places in the objects that are swapped. In the same way to *chop* is to do anything suddenly, to turn suddenly round, and to swap or barter."—*Wedg.*

SWAPE. *sb.* A lever, pump-handle.
Old Norse *svipa*, to swing to and fro, *svipa*, a whip.

SWARMEL. *vn.* To creep along a pole, scramble up a tree. Old Eng. *swarf*. Dut. *swermen*, Low Germ. *schwärmen*, to wander, Bav. *schwarbeln*, to move in a confused manner. Comp. Eng. *squirm*, to wriggle.

SWARTH. *sb.* Skin, rind, of bacon, &c.
Old Norse *svardr*, Ang.-Sax. *sweard*, Dut. *swaerde*, skin of bacon, &c.

SWAT. *vn.* To sit.
The same as *squat*, of which the original idea (see *Wedg.*) is to throw anything flat against the ground.

SWATTER, SWATTLE. *vn.* To tope.
Swattle, to consume, to waste, generally fluids.—*Brock*. Sco. *swaits*, *swats*, new ale or wort. Low Germ. *swuddern*, to tope (*Danneil*), Ang.-Sax. *swatan*, ale, beer, Dut. *swadderen*, to splash, dabble, spill, Suio-Goth. *sqwætta*, liquida effundere.

SWATCH. *sb.* A bill-hook.
Perhaps connected with Dut., Fris. *swade*, sickle, scythe, Old Norse *svedia*, a large knife or dagger. Is this the word upon which, by the insertion of *r*, is formed Old Norse *sverd*, Dut. *zwaard*, Eng. *sword*?

SWATCH. *sb.* A strip of cloth cut off as sample.
Dial. Swed. *skvatt*, a small portion or quantity, "a little," as *en skvatt mjöl*, a little meal.—*Atk*. Comp. also Lapp. *swattjo*, fasciculus.

SWAYVEL. *vn.* To walk unsteadily.
Old Norse *sveifla*, to swing round, Suio-Goth. *swæfwa*, motitari, librare, Dut. *sweyven*, to vacillate, fluctuate.

SWEEL. *vn.* To burn away, as a candle in a draft.
Ang.-Sax. *swêlan*, to burn, Low Germ. *verswelen*, to burn away.

SWEEL. *sb.* Sweals of laughter, peals, bursts.
Simply, I take it, for *squeals*.

SWEEMISH. *adj.* Squeamish.
Swaymous, shy (*West. and Cumb. Dial.*) is no doubt a variation of the same word. Old Norse *sveima*, to waver, to fluctuate, Low Germ. *swiemen*, to be dizzy, Dut. *swijmen*, deficere animo.—*Kil.*

SWEER. *adj.* Averse, disinclined, lazy.
Ang.-Sax. *swâr*, heavy, slothful.

SWELTER. *vn.* To be overcome with heat.
Clev. *swelt*. Old Flem. *swelten*, deficere, languescere, Ang.-Sax. *swêlan*, to burn, *swaloth*, heat, Mid. High Germ. *swelten*, to perish through heat or hunger, Germ. *schwül*, Low Germ. *swuul*, sultry, Sansc. *jval*, to burn?

SWENT, SWINT. *adj.* Bent, twisted out of truth.
Seems to be formed by the prefix of *s* on Swed. *wind*, awry, crooked, *winda*, to squint.

SWEY. *vn.* To sway, swing.
Old Norse *sveigja*, Dan. *sveie*, to bend, Dut. *zwaayen*, to swing, turn.

SWIG-SWAG. *sb.* A pendulum.
Low Germ. *swieg-swagen*, to vibrate.

SWILL. *sb.* A large open basket made of twigs.
The Old Norse has *svigi*, a twig, (from *sveigja*, to bend), whence I suppose a word *svigul*, signifying something made of twigs, and whence, by contraction, would come our *swill*. Similarly, from Ang.-Sax. *tân*, twig, *tânel*, a basket.

SWINE-CREUH. *sb.* A pig-sty.
Welsh *craw*, Gael., Ir. *cro*, Bret. *craou*, Corn. *crow*, a hovel, hut, sty. "At the present day, in Cornwall, a pig-sty is called a pig's *crow*."—*Williams*. The word is also found in the Scand. idiom, Old Norse *kro*, a small pen or fence, "in Iceland the pen in which lambs when weaned are put during the night." —*Cleasby*.

SWINGLE-TREES. *sb.* The wooden bars by which the horses draw in ploughing or harrowing. Dial. Dan. *svingeltræer*, swingle-trees.

SWIPE. *va* To drink off hastily.
Ang.-Sax. *swipian*, Old Norse *svipa*, to move quickly, do anything with a momentary action.

SWIRL. *vn.* To whirl round.
Norw. *svirla*, to whirl, revolve, a frequentative of Dan. *svire*, Swed. *svirra*.

SWIRTLE. *vn.* To move rapidly and tortuously, as a small fish in a shallow stream.—*Dick.* I am rather inclined to take the word to be more properly *swittle*, and to connect it with Sco. *swatter*, "to move quickly in any fluid substance, generally including the idea of an undulatory motion, as that of an eel in the water."—*Jam.* Suio-Goth. *squalta*, agitari, motu inequali movere, Lapp. *swattjet*, moveri, Dut. *swadderen*, turbare aquas, fluctuare.—*Kil.*

SWUM. *vn.* To swim.
Fris. *swommen*, Dan. *svömme*, to swim.

SWYKE. *sb.* A thin-shaped animal.
Dut. *swijck*, defectus, *swijcken*, deficere, labascere, *swack*, debilis, infirmus, quod facile flectitur, (*Kil.*), Dan., Swed. *svag*, weak, frail, slender, Lapp. *swaikes*, weak, yielding, Germ. *schwach*, weak.

SWYKE. *sb.* A worthless, untrustworthy person.
Sco. *swick*, fraud, deceit. Ang.-Sax. *swíc*, Old Norse *svik*, fraud, treachery, Ang.-Sax. *swíca*, Old Norse *svikari*, impostor, traitor.

SYE. *sb.* A drop, small quantity of water oozing or percolating through. "Oal Robin sank a well, an' ther wassent a *sye* of watter in it."—*Dick.* Clev. *sie*, to drop. Old Norse *sía*, Ang.-Sax. *seon*, to filter or strain by percolation, Dan. *sie*, Germ. *seihen*, to strain, to filter.

SYKE, SIKE. *sb.* A wet ditch or drain.
Old Norse *siki*, lacuna aquosa, *sijk*, rivulus aquæ, Ang.-Sax. *sich*, Fris. *sick*, a watercourse. Sansc. *sic*, to be wet, Welsh *sicio*, to soak.

SYLE. *vn.* To strain through a sieve.
Swed., Norw. *sila*, to strain, Low Germ. *silen*, Germ. *sielen*, to draw off water. Gael. *sil*, to drop, rain, drip, Bret. *sila*, to filter. Garnett suggests (*Phil. Ess.* p. 178) a possible connec-

tion between Gael. *sil* and Lat. *stillare*, to drop, which seems probable. This word is found in many river-names, as Silis, the Scythian name of the Tanais or Don (*Pliny*), the Sihl in Switzerland, and the Silaro near Naples.

SYLE-TREES. *sb.* The timber roof-blades of a clay house.
Ang.-Sax. *sýl*, a ground-post, support, pillar, Old Norse *súla*, pillar of a house. *Tree*, as in *threep-tree*, signifies something made of wood.

SYME. *sb.* A straw rope.
Clev. *semmit*, supple, pliable. Sco. *sowm*, a rope. Ang.-Sax. *sima*, Fris. *seem*, *semm*, a band, fastening, Old Norse *simi*, ductile quid, Dan. *sime*, a cord or rope of hair or straw, Fin. *sijma*, Lapp. *seima*, a cord of horse-hair. Comp., also, Gael. *sioman*, a rope or cord usually of twisted straw or heather. The root may probably be found in Sansc. *si*, *siv*, to join, fasten.

SYNE. *vn.* To draw or strain off.
Dut. *zijghen*, to strain, to filter, Germ. *versiegen*, to drain or dry up. Here, too, perhaps, Swed. *sina*, to dry.

SYPE, SIPE. *vn.* To ooze out, soak through.
Fris. *sipe*, to ooze, drop, Dut. *zijpen*, to drop; Fris. *ut sipe*, S. Dan. *sife ud*, to ooze or *sipe* out.

SYRE. *sb.* A gutter, sewer.
From the same origin as *sye* and *syne*, in reference to the *sewer*, as that by which the water is drained or drawn off.

SYZLE. *vn.* To saunter.

"To Hudless's now off they *sizelled*,
An' there gat far mair than enough."—*Anderson*.

Low Germ. *süsseln*, to perform trifling household duties, Dan. *sysle*, to be busy, Swed. *sysla*, business, occupation. The word seems to have undergone some change.

T.

TAAS. *sb.* Wood cut thin to make baskets of.—*Hall*.
Clev. *tag*, a twist of long, freshly-cut grass. Sco. *tag*, a long and thin slice of anything. Old Norse *tæ*, *tág*, twig, Dial. Dan. *tag*, long straw, rushes, &c., used for thatching.

TAB. *sb.* The narrow end of a field. The extreme end of anything. Ang.-Sax. *tæppe*, properly tip or corner, Old Norse *tæpr*, narrow.

TAFFLE. *va.* To throw into disorder, perplex, confound.
Probably from the same origin as the Old Eng. *daff.* See *daffin, daft.*

TAG. *sb.* The end of anything.
Lonsd. *tag*, the end of a fox's tail. Swed. *tagg*, Low Germ. *takke*, point, projection. Hence comes Ang.-Sax. *tægl*, Old Norse *tagl*, Eng. *tail.*

TAGGELT. *sb.* An idle, disreputable person.
The origin, like that of *tag-rag*, seems to be *tag*, the end or extremity, whence Sco. *tag*, refuse, and hence *taggelt*, one belonging to the refuse of society.

TAGGY-BELL. *sb.* The curfew bell, "still rung at Penrith and Kirby Stephen."—*Sullivan.* Referred by *Sull.* to Dan. *tække*, to cover, Swed. *täcka*, hence equivalent to *curfew* or *couvrefeu.*

TAHMY, TAAMY. *adj.* Cohesive, like tow.
Old Norse *tálma*, cohibere.

TAISTREL. *sb.* A worthless or disorderly person.
Clev. *tastrill*, a passionate or violent person. *Atk.* refers this word, given in the Leeds Gl. *tarestrill*, to Ang.-Sax. *tĕran*, to tear. But comp. Old Norse *teistr*, austerus, which seems more probably to be the origin. The termination *rel* is a common one in the dialect.

TAK EFTER. *va.* To resemble.
Old Norse *taka eftir*, imitari.

TAK TIL HISSEL. *va.* To take as personal a remark or insinuation. Old Norse *taka till sîn*, sibi arrogare vel applicare.

TAK UP. *vn.* To cease to rain, to become fine.
Old Norse *nû tekr ofan af*, imber desævit (*Haldorsen*).

TALLY. *sb.* The squads in which voters were formerly taken to the poll were called *tallies*. "From Ital. *tagliare*, Fr. *tailler*, to cut, is formed Fr. *taille*, a tally or piece of wood on which an account was kept by notches. When complete, the wood was split in two, with corresponding notches on each piece. Hence, to *tally*, to correspond exactly."— *Wedg.* Hence the *tallies* of voters, as corresponding with the lists.

TANZY. *sb.* A public-house ball.
Fr. *dancer* (of Teutonic origin), Germ. *tanzen*, Dan. *dandse*, to dance. The original idea, according to *Wedg.*, is that of

thumping, Suio-Goth. *dunsa*, impetu et fragore procedere, Dan. *dundse*, to thump, with which the Cumberland style of dancing is perfectly in accord.

TANTRUM. *sb.* A fit of passion.
Sco. *tantrums*, high airs, stateliness. *Jam.* refers to Fr. *tantran*, a nic-nack, which, however, unless we suppose the sense to have greatly changed, would not be very suitable for our word. I have elsewhere, see *dander*, suggested Welsh *tant*, spasm, throb. The converse *doldrums*, low spirits, Gael. *doltrum*, grief, seems to support a Celtic origin. And I find that Davies (Proc. Phil. Soc. 1855, p. 239) proposes the same derivation as I have done for Lanc. *tantrum*, a fit of passionate excitement.

TARGE. *va.* To beat, to thrash.
Perhaps from Suio-Goth. *targa*, Swed. *targa*, to tear, to lacerate.

TARN. *sb.* A small lake.
Old Norse *tjörn*, Swed. *tjärn*, a small lake, a morass. The connection seems to be most probably with Old Norse *tjara*, Eng. *tar*, in the sense of stagnant water, a morass.

TARNT. *adj.* Ill-natured.
Probably connected with Sco. *tirr*, quarrelsome, crabbed, Old Eng. *tar*, to provoke. Ang.-Sax. *tyrwian*, Low Germ. *tarren*, to irritate, provoke, Dan. *tirre*, to tease.

TATH-HEAPS. *sb.* Tufts of rank grass in a pasture.
Sco. *tath*, the luxuriant grass which grows in tufts where the dung of cattle has been deposited. Sco. *tath* also signifies the dung of cattle. Old Norse *tad*, dung, manure, *tada*, the grass that grows where manure has been laid.

TATHY-GRASS. *sb.* A soft grass that grows under trees.—*Dick.* Perhaps from Ang.-Sax. *tât*, *têthre*, tender. But more probably only a different application of the last word.

TATTER. *vn.* To scold.
"Tateryn, jangelyn, chateryn, jaberyn."—*Pr. Prv.* Dial. Swed. *tattra*, to prate, Low Germ. *taotern*, to prattle, Dut. *tateren*, to sound as a trumpet.

TATTERS. *sb.* A female scold.
Norf. *tatterer*, a shrew. See *tatter*.

TATY-CRAB. *sb.* The fruit of the potato.
"From Ang.-Sax. *scrobb*, a shrub, a word connected, perhaps, with Gael. *craobh*, tree, and impiying a bush—or wild—apple."
—*Prior.*

TATE, TEAT. *sb.* A lock or small quantity of anything,
such as wool, flax, or hair. Sco. *tate.* Old Norse *tæta*, lanugo,
Swed. *totte*, Dan. *tot*, a small knot of wool or other fibrous
material, Dan. *tæt*, close, compact, Old Norse *tæta*, to tease
wool.

TATTY, TATTIT. *adj.* Matted.
Clev. *tettered.* See *tate.*

TAVE. *va.* To make restless motions with the hands,
to pick the bed-clothes as a delirious person does. *Atk.*,
assuming the sense " to rave" given in the *Linc. Gloss.* and by
Hall. as the original one, refers to Ang.-Sax. *thefian*, to rage.
This seems a little doubtful, and I am rather inclined to think
of Old Norse *tifa*, manus celeriter movere. Or Old Norse
thaufa, palpare in tenebris, which seems to accord with the idea
of the aimless movements of delirium.

TAVE. *va.* and *n.* To wade through mire. To work
up plaster. Perhaps connected with Old Norse *tefja*, morari,
hærere.

TAWPY. *sb.* A simpleton.
Dut. *tulpe*, a blockhead, *tulpisch*, stolidus, stupidus, ineptus
(*Kil.*), Germ. *tölpel*, a blockhead.

TEAM. *va.* and *n.* To pour out, to empty, of solids
as well as fluids. Old Norse *tæma*, to draw out, to empty.

TEANEL. *sb.* A basket.—*West and Cumb. Dial.*
Ang.-Sax. *tænel*, a basket, from *tân*, a twig. Similarly *swill*,
(contraction of *swigel*,) from Old Norse *svigi*, a twig.

TEARIN. *sb.* The rendering of a roof.
North. *teer*, to bedaub with clay, *teer-wall*, a clay wall.—*Hall.*
Lanc. *teer*, to plaster between rafters. Swiss *tirgen*, to daub,
work in dough. Ang.-Sax. *teor*, Old Norse *tjara*, Germ. *theer*,
tar.

TECK, TACK. *sb.* A stitch.
Dut. *tacken*, tangere, arripere, apprehendere, figere.

TE-DRAW, TEU-DRAW. *sb.* A place of resort.
A place " to draw" up to. Dut. *toe-draghen*, apportare,
adferre.

TEEN-LATHE. *sb.* A tithe-barn.
Sco. *tiends*, tithes. Dan. *tiende*, Swed. *tionde*, tithe, tenth,
Dut. *tien*, ten, *tiende*, tenth, *tienden*, tithes. See *lathe.*

TELT. Told, pret. of tell.

TEMSE. *sb.* A hair sieve.
Dut. *teems*, N. Fris. *tems*, Dial. Dan. *tems*, a sieve.

TETCH. *vn.* To be restive or obstinate.
Probably for *stetch*. Old Norse *steigr*, contumax. See *steck*.

TEUFIT. *sb.* The lapwing.
Clev. *teufit*. "It is remarkable that the Danish form, or written representation, of the cry of this bird, corresponds exactly with this Clev. name of the bird itself."—*Atk.*

TEW or TUE. *va.* and *n.* To toil, take trouble, work hard. To rumple, crease, pull about. Probably another form of *tug*. Ang.-Sax. *teogan, teohan*, Old Swed. *tjuga*, Goth. *tiuhan*, to draw, pull, drag.

TEU-FAW (To-fall.) *sb.* A lean-to shed.
"To-falle, shudde, appendicium, teges."—*Pr. Prv.* Dut. *toevallen*, adjungere se, adjungi.

THACK, THEAK. *va.* To thatch.
"Thaccyn howsys, sartatego."—*Pr. Prv.* Ang.-Sax. *thaccan*, Old Norse *thekia*, Dan. *tække*, to cover, to thatch, Sansc. *tvac*, to cover.

THACK-BOTTLE. *sb.* A bundle of thatch.
"Botelle of hey. Fenifascis."—*Pr. Prv.* Fr. *botel*, diminutive of *botte*, a bunch, Gael. *boiteal*, a bundle of hay or straw. Hence the phrase, "to look for a needle in a bottle of hay."

THACK-SPITTLE. *sb.* An implement used in thatching.
Probably for *spattle*. See *spurtle*.

THAR-CAKES or THARTH-CAKES. *sb.* Thick cakes of barley or oatmeal. Properly *tharf-cakes*. Crav. *thar-cake*, a heavy, unleavened cake, *tharfy*, stiff, unleavened bread, *tharf*, stark, stiff. Ang.-Sax. *theorf*, unleavened bread.

THARTH. *adj.* Reluctant, unwilling.
Clev. *tharf*, backward, reluctant. *Atk.* refers to Old Norse *thörf*, necessitas. But the connection seems to me to be rather with Old Norse *thrâ* (pron. *thraw* or *thrav*), obstinacy, contumacy, Ang.-Sax. *thweorh*, perverse, Eng. *thwart*.

THICK. *adj.* Friendly, intimate.
Perhaps from Old Norse *theckja*, to know, be acquainted with *theckr*, gratus, acceptus.

THINK ON. *vn.* To remember.
"Therfor *thynk on* what I you say."—*Town. Myst.*
Comp. Germ. *andenken*, remembrance, from the obsolete verb *andenken*. to think on.—*Adelung.*

THIRL. *va.* To bore.
Ang.-Sax. *thirlian*, Dut. *drillen*, to pierce, drill, perforate.

THIVEL. *sb.* A stick to stir the pot in boiling.
Ang.-Sax. *thyfel*, thorn, stick.

THOWLESS. *adj.* Soft, wanting energy.
Ang.-Sax. *theáw*, behaviour, endowment, quality, with the privative term *less*.

THOLE. *vn.* To endure, suffer.
Ang.-Sax. *tholian*, Old Norse *thola*, to suffer, bear, endure.

THRANG. *adj.* Busy, closely occupied.
Old Norse *thraungr*, Ang.-Sax. *thrang*, Dan. *trang*, tight, compressed, crowded.

THREEP. *vn.* To argue, assert a thing pertinaciously.
Ang.-Sax. *threapian*, to chide, scold, Old Norse *threfa*, sublitigare.

THREEP-TREE. *sb.* The bar to which the horses are yoked in ploughing. *Threep* may possibly be a contraction of *thil-rope*, from Ang.-Sax. *thil*, pole or shaft of a carriage or wagon, and Ang.-Sax. *ráp*, Eng. *rope*. *Tree*, as in *swingle-tree*, *har-tree*, &c., signifies wood, or something made of wood, hence *threep-tree* might be the wooden pole to which the traces are attached.

THREAVE. *sb.* Twenty-four sheaves of corn.
Ang.-Sax. *threaf*, a handful, a thrave of corn, Swed. *trafwa*, Dan. *trave*, a score of sheaves.

THREETEN. *va.* To threaten.
Ang.-Sax. *threatian*.

THRESHWOOD. *sb.* Threshold.—*West. and Cumb. Dial.*
(*Dick.* has *threshwurt*, which, I take it, is simply a corruption.) *Threshwood* is a parallel word with *threshold*, Ang.-Sax. *thresc-wald*, only substituting Ang.-Sax. *wudu* for Ang.-Sax. *weald* of the same meaning. The former part is from Ang.-Sax. *threscan*, to beat, strike, tread, the threshold being the bar on which we tread on entering the house. Our word thus, by the substitution of a parallel component, serves to confirm Wedgwood's derivation of *threshold* from *wald*, wood.

THRODDY. *adj.* Plump, well-thriven.
Clev. *throdden.* *Ath.* refers to Old Norse *thrutna*, to swell, become round or plump, Dial. Dan. *trude*, to swell, become plump, as peas soaked in water, as possible connections of our word. Comp. also Ang.-Sax. *thróhtig*, Old Norse *throttugr*, strong, vigorous, enduring, the sense of which, however, is rather that of strength in enduring toil.

THROOLY or THROUGLY. *adj.* Portly, corpulent.
Perhaps, assuming a suppressed *f*, to be connected with Fris. *trüff*, hale, fresh, thriving, Old Norse *thrif*, bonus corporis habitus, *thriflegr*, bonæ corporis constitutionis, Swed. *trejlig*, healthy, thriving.

THROPPLE. *sb.* The windpipe.
Ang.-Sax. *throt-bolla*, the throat-pipe.

THROSSEN, THRUSSEN. Past part. of thrust.

THROSSEL. *sb.* The thrush.
Ang.-Sax. *throsle, throstle*, Germ. *drossel.*

THROUGH, THRUFF, *sb.* A flat tombstone.
Ang.-Sax. *thruh*, a stone coffin, vault, grave, Old Norse *thró*, cavum excisum. The meaning seems properly a stone coffin, or sarcophagus, the word being, as Bosworth suggests, probably related to *trog*, a trough.

THROW. *va.* To turn in a lathe.
"Throwyn, or turne vessel of a tre. Torno."—*Pr. Prv.* Ang.-Sax. *thrawan*, to turn, wind, Germ. *drehen*, to turn.

THUD. *sb.* The sound of a dull, heavy blow.
Allied to Old Norse *dunr*, Dan. *dunder*, hollow sound, Old Eng. *dun*, to make a hollow sound. In the Virgil of Douglas *thud* is used for the sound of thunder. Sansc. *tud*, to thump, Lat. *tundo.*

THUR. *pr.* Those.
"*Thur* taxes! *thur* taxes! Lord help us, amen."—*Clark.*
Clev. *thor.* Old Norse *their, thær*, illi, illæ.

TICE. *va.* To entice.
"Tycyn or intycyn. Instigo, allicio."—*Pr. Prv.*

TICK. *sb.* A slight mark made in checking the items of an account. Dut. *tikken*, Low Germ. *ticken*, to touch lightly. Sansc. *tig, tag,* Lat. *tango.*

TICK-TACK. *sb.* The tick of a clock.
Low Germ. *tick-tack*, a clock or watch.—*Danneil*.

TIDY. *adj.* Neat, orderly; hence, like *canny*, a general term of approbation, applied, as in Scotland, both to personal and mental characteristics. Low Germ. *tidig*, early, timely, Suio-Goth. *tidig*, decorus, decens, conveniens.

TIFT. *vn.* To pant, fetch the breath quickly, as after violent exertion. Clev. *tift*, to squabble. "Used in several senses, all ultimately reducible to that of a whiff or draught of breath."—*Wedg.* Norw. *tev, taft*, drawing of the breath, wind or scent of a beast, *teva*, to pant, breathe hard.

TIG. *va.* To touch gently. Generally used in boyish play.
Dut. *tikken*, Low Germ. *ticken*, to touch lightly, Sansc. *tig*.

TIKE. *sb.* A dog, a cur, an unmannerly fellow.
Old Norse *tik, tijk*, a bitch, Dial. Swed. *tik*, a bitch, a foolish woman, *tyke*, a petulant, insolent person.

TIL. *prep.* To.
Old Norse *til*, Swed. *till*, Dan. *til*.

TILLER. *vn.* To spread, to send out shoots.
Clev. *telly*, a straw, a stalk of grass. Ang.-Sax. *telgor*, a twig, branch, *telgian*, to branch, to shoot, Germ. *teller*, Dut. *telg*, shoot. Sansc. *till*, to grow, shoot.

TINE. *va.* To shut up a **pasture** field till the grass grows again. Ang.-Sax. *tynan*, to inclose, to shut.

TIRLT. *vb.* Unroofed, having the thatch blown off-*Dick.*
Sco. *tirl*, to uncover, as to tirl a house. Probably a frequentative of *tirr*, used in Scotland in the same sense. Ang.-Sax. *teran*, Low Germ. *teren*, to break, tear, strip.

TITE. *adv.* Soon, quickly, willingly.
Old Norse *tidt* or *titt*, soon, quickly, readily.

TITTER. *comp. adv.* Sooner, rather, more willingly.
"Na, na! au'd *titter* hev collop er puddin any day. Mess wad ah!" was the reply of a Cumberland farmer dining with his landlord, my grandfather, on being invited by the lady of the house to take some pudding. Old Norse, Old Swed. *tidare*, Dan. *tiere*, sooner.

TITTY. *sb.* Sister.
> "My *titty* Greace an' Jenny Bell
> Are gangan bye and bye."—*Anderson.*

Sco. *titty.* Jamieson's explanation, "the diminutive of sister," is very inadequate. The word is probably allied to Dial. Swed. *tutta*, a little girl, Finn. *tytty*, girl, daughter. Perhaps connected with Old Norse *tita*, a small bird, anything small, Eng. *tit*, "anything small of its kind, a little girl, a little bird."—*Wedg.* Comp. Lonsd. *tot*, a term of endearment to a child.

TITTYVATE. *va.* To adorn, make smart, deck out.
The idea seems to be that of applying small touches.

TIV. *prep.* To, used before words beginning with a vowel or a silent *h*.

TIZZIC. *sb.* A slight distemper of a catching nature.
Gael. *teasach*, a fever, from *teas*, heat. Bret. *tizick*, consumption. The latter may be an adopted word corresponding with Eng. *tisick*, corrupted from *phthisick*. Our word may rather be from the Gael., with which it corresponds to a certain extent in meaning, though the coincidence of the two words is puzzling.

TO. *prep.* To "mak to" the door is to shut the door.
Germ. *zumachen*, to shut.

TOFT. *sb.* The site of a deserted house or building.
Ang.-Sax. *toft*, a croft, a home field, Old Norse *toft*, area domus vacua, Swed., Norw. *tomt*, place where a house once stood. *Tomt* seems the original form, Old Norse *tômr*, Dan., Swed. *tom*, void, empty, *f* and *m* interchanging, as in many other cases.

TOKKER. *sb.* Portion, dowry.
> "The breyde now on a coppy-stuol
> Sits duin i' th' fauld a whithrin,
> Wi' pewter dibler on her lap,
> On which her *tokker's* gethrin."
> Bridewain, by *Stagg*,

Sco. *tocher.* Gael., Ir. *tochar*, dowry, Gael. *toic*, wealth, fortune, property.

TOME, TOOM. *sb.* A fishing-line.
Clev. *tawm.* Old Norse *taumr*, a thong, rope, fishing-line, Swed. *tôm*, Norw. *taum*, rein, line, Dut. *toom*, bridle.

TOOMING. *sb.* An aching or dizziness of the eyes.—
West. and Cumb. Dial. Germ. *tummel*, dizziness, giddiness, from *tummeln*, to roll, tumble. Similarly, our word may be referred to Old Norse *tumba*, cadere præceps, of which *tummeln* is a frequentative form.

TOOTH-WARK. *sb.* The tooth-ache.
Ang.-Sax. *toth-wearc*, the tooth-ache.

TOOZLE. *va.* and *n.* To ruffle, to pull about rudely.
Low Germ. *tuseln*, to pull the hair about.

TOPPIN. *sb.* A roll or curl of hair standing up over the forehead ; a crest, on a bird, &c. "Top, or foretop, top of the hed."—*Pr. Prv.* Old Norse *toppr*, cirrus, villus, the forelock of a horse or man, especially the former ; Old Swed. *topper*, id., Welsh *topyn*, top, crest.

TOPPIN-PEATS. *sb.* Turf with the herbage on. See *toppin.*

TOPTIRE. *sb.* Towering passion.
Tire in the above seems to be allied to Sco. *tirr*, quarrelsome, Ang.-Sax. *tyrwian*, to vex, provoke. See *tarnt.*

TORFER, TORFEL. *vn.* To fail, die, give in, decline.
Sco. *torfel, torchel.* Suio-Goth. *torfwa*, Swed. *tarfva*, Ang.-Sax. *thearfian*, to be in want, Swed. *torftig*, poor, needy, Dan. *tarv*, need, want, Ang.-Sax. *steorfan*, to starve, die.

TORREL. *sb.* "Ane kill quhair cornes are dryed.—*Life and Miracles of Sancta Bega*. This word is probably now extinct."—*Dick.* Probably, like Gael. *torran*, a diminutive of Gael. *torr*, Welsh *twr*, a hill, mound, tower.

TOWERTLY. *adv.* Kindly, in a friendly manner.
"Why that is spoken like a toward prince."
Shaks. Hen. VI.
Similarly, the reverse, *froward.*

TOWP. *va.* and *n.* To upset, overturn. Also to fall.
Towp and *cowp*, the two words of our dialect signifying to fall, or to upset, have curious points of resemblance. In neither case do we find the word from which ours is immediately derived. But *towp* bears the same relation to *tipe* (to tip up, fall over) that *coup* bears to *chip*, to trip, Old Norse *kippa*, to trip up. Again, *towp* seems to have the same relation to *top* that *coup* has to *cop* (head, top), and perhaps that Sansc. *pat*, to fall, has to *pate*. *Towp* is the word on which, as a frequentative, is formed

Eng. *topple*, and probably, by the prefix of *s*, Swed., Norw. *stupa*, to fall, Eng. *stoop*. On the same word, again, taking a liquid, may be formed Welsh *twmpio*, Old Norse *tumba*, Fr. *tomber*, to fall, Eng. *tumble*.

TOYTLE OVER. *vn.* To topple over.
Sco. *toyt*, to totter. Dut. *touteren*, to palpitate, tremble, seesaw. Comp., also, Gael. *tuit*, to fall.

TRAAVE. *vn.* To stride along as if through long grass.—*West and Cumb. Dial.* Crav. *trave*. Perhaps the same word as *trape*, to trail along. Suio-Goth. *trafwa*, currere, Germ. *traben*, to tramp. Or, if the idea be, as Carr observes of the Craven word, that of "having the feet fettered in grass," we may think of *trave*, taking a phonetic *r*, as the same word as *tave*, to wade through mire, also to work up something adhesive, and to connect it with Old Norse *tefja*, morari, hærere.

TRAFFICK. *sb.* Lumber, rubbish.
Gael. *trabhach*, rubbish of any kind thrown on shore by the flood.

TRAILY. *adj.* Slovenly.
Old Norse *treglegr*, slow, lazy, Dut. *traag*, slothful.

TRAMP. *vn.* To travel on foot.
Old Norse *trampa*, Dan. *trampe*, Germ. *trampen*, to tread, stamp with the foot.

TRAM, TRAB. *sb.* A long, narrow field.
It would seem that, as in so many other cases, the *r* in *trab* is intrusive, and that the word is properly *tab*, qv. *Tram* is another form, *b* and *m* interchanging.

TRANTLEMENTS. *sb.* Trifling or useless articles, frippery, playthings. Sco. *trantles*. Jamieson's idea is that the word is derived from *trental*, a service of thirty masses for the dead, and that, after the Reformation, the word came to be applied, first to denote trifling or superstitious ceremonies, in which sense it is used in Cleland's poems, and then, trifles in general. I am more disposed, however, to connect the word with Dut. *trantelen*, to do everything in a slow and loitering way, Vulg. Germ. *trändeln*, to tarry, to loiter, to toy, to trifle. The *r* in the above seems to be intrusive, and the proper form to be found in Germ. *tändeln*, to lounge, toy, trifle, corresponding with Eng. *dandle*, and Lonsd. *tantle*, to attend officiously, to dawdle. "She *tantles* after him," often said of the attentions of an anxious mother.—*Peacock*. In the Germ. *tändelpuppe*, a doll, we have a sense the counterpart of one of ours. With *dandle* Wedgwood connects Sco. *dandilly* and Eng. *dandy*. "A *dandy* is probably, first a doll, and then a finely dressed person."

TRAPESING. *adj.* Wandering about idly, flaunting about. *Trape*, to trail along in an untidy manner.—*Wedg.* Low Germ. *trappsen, trappen*, Germ. *traben*, Dut. *trappen*, to tramp about. See *traave.*

TRASH. *vn.* To trudge, to weary oneself.
Swed. *traska*, to trudge.

TREAK. *sb.* An idle fellow.
Old Norse *tregr*, Dan. *træg*, lazy, slow, Old Norse *tregaz*, segnescere.

TREED. *vn.* To tread.

TRET. Treated, pret. of treat.

TRIG. *adj.* Tight, well-fitted, in good trim.
Clev. *trig*, to supply, full, stuff, of the result rather than the action, of eating heartily. "I connect this with Old Norse *tryggia*, to secure, make safe, attach, Dan. *betrygge*, Old Norse *tryggr*, Dan. *tryg*, safe, secure, fearless."—*Atk.*

TRIM. *sb.* Order, condition.
Ang.-Sax. *trymman*, to establish, prepare, dispose.

TRIVET. *sb.* Something supported on three legs.
Old Norse *thrifættr*, tripes, Welsh *tribedh*, Corn. *tribet*, (derived by Williams, though, it seems to me, rather doubtfully, from Lat. *tripes*.)

TROD. *sb.* A footpath.
Old Norse *tröd*, a road or path to a farm-stead, Ang.-Sax. *trod*, a path, track.

TROLLYBAGS. *sb.* Tripe.
Swed. *trilla*, Dan. *trille*, Swiss *trällen*, to roll, "the idea being that of a convoluted bag-like receptacle."—*Atk.*

TROOAN. *sb.* A truant.
Welsh *truan*, poor, miserable, wretched, Gael. *truaghan*, a wretched creature. The primary meaning, then, of *truant* is a vagabond or wandering beggar.

TRUG. *sb.* A wooden coal-box.
Old Norse, Ang.-Sax. *trog*, Dan. *trug*,'trough.

TRUNCHER. *sb.* A trencher or wooden platter.
Fr. *tranchoir*, a wooden plate on which the meat was cut up, from *trancher*, to cut.

TURN-DEAL. *sb.* "In some undivided common fields the ownership of the pareels changes annually in succession."— *Dick.* See *run-rig.*

TUSHIE-PEGS. *sb.* A childish name for the teeth.
Ang.-Sax. *tusc,* Fris. *tosk,* tooth. See *peg.*

TUTE. *vn.* To wait upon, to hang about a person or a place. "He *tutes* about his laal wife as if she was a barn."— *Dick.* Lonsd. *tout,* to pry inquisitively. *Toot,* a verb used for the action of prying into any thing a little more curiously than the person observed likes.—*Hunter.* Old Eng. *tote,* to peep. "To *tote,* in Somerset, is to bulge out, and probably the radical meaning of the word may be to stick out. Old Norse *tota,* a snout, *tuta,* anything sticking out, having prominent eyes." —*Wedg.*

TWILL. *sb.* A quill.
"It is scarcely necessary to do more than simply advert to the very frequent interchange of *tw* and *qu* in the Northern dialects and tongues. Rietz remarks that in certain districts *tv* is sounded as *kw* or *ku,* as, for instance, *kwongin* for *tvungen,* &c."—*Atk.*

TWILT. *va.* To beat.
The same as *quilt,* qv.

TWINE. *va.* To whine.
Worsaae (Danes and Northmen) refers our word to Dan. *tvine,* a dial. form, I presume, of *hvine.*

TWINTER. *sb.* A two-year-old sheep.
Holst. *twenter,* a two-year-old sheep, Fris. *twinter-dier,* an animal two years old, Ang.-Sax. *twy-winter,* duos annos natus. Our ancestors reckoned age by winters.
"And in a tawny tabard,
Of twelf wynter age."—*P. Pl.*
Similarly, we have *thrinter,* a three-year-old sheep.

TWIST. *sb.* A feeder, an eater.
Lonsd. *twist* is rendered by Peacock "a great eater," as in the phrase, "He's a rare *twist.*" The word by itself, however, I think means simply "eater," from Ang.-Sax. *gewistan,* to feed, feast, Ang.-Sax. *wist,* Old Norse *vist,* food. We may presume an Ang.-Sax. *gewista,* feeder; whence, by the interchange of *cw* or *gw* with *tw* (see *twill*) comes our *twist.* In Cumberland the word is sometimes used in the sense of appetite, which may probably arise from "he's a rare twist," (in which way the word is most generally used), being taken to be "he has" instead of "he is."

TWIST. *vn.* To whine, to be peevish or out of temper.
Clev. *twisty*. peevish. Dan. *tvist*, Dut. *twist*. strife, disagreement. squabbling, Dan. *tviste*, Dut. *twisten*, to quarrel, squabble.

TWITCH-BELL. *sb.* The ear-wig.
Twitch seems to be from Ang.-Sax. *twig*, two, double, in reference to the forked tail of the insect. The ending *bell*, as also in *warble*, (the name of an insect), seems to be a contraction of *beetle*.

TYLE. *va* and *n.* To weary, distress, wear out.
"I's *tyled* to death wid this kurn."—*Gibson*. *Tyle* may perhaps be for *tewl*, as a frequentative of *tew*. which we use in the same sense, as in "I's fairly *tewed* to death." See *tew*.

U.

UDDER-GATES. *adv.* Otherwise.
Udder-gates is other *ways*. See *gate*.

UNHOMED. *adj.* Awkward, unlikely. — *West. and Cumb. Dial.* Perhaps from Dut. *komen*, convenire, decere, with the negative prefix.

UNKET. *adj.* Strange, unknown.
Clev. *unkard, unkit*. Sco. *unco*. Eng. *uncouth*. "Uncowth, extraneous, exoticus."—*Pr. Prv.* Ang.-Sax. *un-cuth*, unknown, strange.

UNKOES. *sb.* Wonders, news.
The origin seems to be the same as above *unket*.

UP. *va.* To lift up. To upset.
Old Norse *yppa*, Dan. *yppe*, elevare, Ang.-Sax. *uppian*, to rise up.

URCHIN. *sb.* The hedgehog.
Sco. *hurcheon*. "Orchen, a lytell beest full of prickes, herison,"—*Palsg*. The derivation seems to me to be involved in considerable uncertainty. On the one hand we have Lat. *ericius*, Span. *erizo*, Fr. *herisson*, the idea in which is seen in Ital. *riccio*, something rough or prickly, Fr. *herisser*, to set up his bristles. And on the other, Gael. *uircean*, a little pig, whence in the Dict. of the Highland Soc. is derived our *urchin*. And the Bret. *heureuchin*, hedgehog, which seems to be a compound word, Corn. *harow*, rough, bristly, and Bret. *hoch*, pig, Welsh

hwcan, little pig, thus corresponding with *hedgehog* (properly *edge-hog*, Ang.-Sax. *ecg*, point), and *porcupine* (prickly pig). Then Rouchi (patois of Hainault) has *hirchen*, hedge-hog, the connections of which seem uncertain. And lastly, we have the Ang.-Sax. *erscen*, which seems to be from *ersc*, park, warren. Among these various forms I cannot undertake, with anything like certainty, to propose an origin for our word.

URLED. *adj.* Stunted, dwarfed. See *urlin*.

URLIN. *sb.* A stunted or dwarfish person.
Clev. *urling*, a dwarfish child or person, one who through sickness or other cause has not grown properly. North. *urled*, starved with cold.—*Hall*. Sco. *worling*, a feeble and puny creature. We may perhaps think of Dial. Swed. *örla*, to swoon, lose the senses, also to become wild or unmanageable, *örling*, a madcap. The latter sense would seem to accord with that of Old Eng. *wyrlyng* (if that word be the same as ours)—

"God forbede that a wylde Irish *wyrlyng*
Shoulde be chosen for to be theyr kyng."
MSS. Soc. Ant.

Or perhaps *url* may be a frequentative from Ang.-Sax. *eargian*, to be dull, inert, timid, Old Norse *ergias*, in pejus mutari.

URPH. *sb.* A miserable, diminutive child or person.
Perhaps from *yrf* in Old Norse *yrflingr* or *yrmlingr*, a little worm (Germ. *wurm*, worm, signifying figuratively a poor little child). Or, from the frequent change of *g* final into *f*, from Ang.-Sax. *earg*, weak, timid, helpless. Comp. Crav. *arfe*, fearful.

V.

VAMP UP. *va.* To furbish up, repair temporarily.
Literally, to put on a new upper leather, from *vamp*, the upper leather of a shoe.—*Wedg.*

VINE. *sb.* A *vine-pencil* is a black-lead pencil. See *calevine*.

W.

WARBLE. *vn.* To sway to and fro.
Low Germ. *wabbeln*, Bav. *waibeln*, Dut. *weifelen*, to waver, move to and fro.

WAD. *sb.* Black-lead or plumbago.
Probably for *wag*, from the frequent interchange of *d* and *g*. Ang.-Sax. *wæcg*, a mass of metal, black-lead being found, as in the famous mine at Borrowdale, in masses or lumps of pure metal. Another word for black-lead, now obsolete, would seem to have been *collow*. See *calevine*.

WAD-EATER. *sb.* India-rubber, from its erasing the marks made by *wad* or black-lead. See *wad*.

WAFF. *sb.* A puff of wind.
Welsh *chwaf*, a gust. Dan. *vifte*, Swed. *vefta*, to waft.

WAFF. *sb.* The bark of a small dog.
"Wappynge (of houndys) or barkynge.—*Pr. Prv.* Goth. *vopjan*, Old Fris. *wepa*, Strl. *vapia*, to cry, Ang.-Sax. *wæflan*, to babble.

WAFFLE. *vn.* To waver, be undecided.
See *wabble*.

WAFFLER. *sb.* A fickle, uncertain person.
Dut. *weyfeler*, homo vagus, inconstans, vacillans.—*Kil.* See *wabble*.

WAITS. *sb.* Nightly musicians who used to play in the streets at Christmastide. "Wayte, waker, vigil."—*Pr. Prv.* Old Norse *vakta*, Old High Germ. *wahten*, Germ. *wachten*, to watch, or keep awake.

WALE. *va.* To beat, cudgel.
Probably from Old Norse *völr*, Swed. *val*, a stick ; Wel. *gwial*, a rod, twig.

WALKER. *sb.* A fuller.
Ang.-Sax. *wealcere*, Dan. *valker*, a fuller.

WALLOP. *va.* and *n.* To dangle loosely. Also to beat.
Swiss *valple*, vacillare.—*Idiot. Bern.* "*Wallop* bears the same relation to *wabble* that Swiss *swalpen* does to Germ. *schwappelen*, to splash or dash to and fro like water, or Old Eng. *walmynge* to *wamelynge* of the stomach. (*Pr. Prv.*)—*Wedg.*

WALLOW. *adj.* Weak, faint, tasteless, insipid.
Dut. *walghen*, to nauseate, to loathe. See *welsh*.

WAMMEL. *vn.* To rock to and fro.
Dut. *wemelen*, Low Germ. *wümmeln*, to shake to and fro ; Welsh *gwammalu*, to waver.

WAN. Won. Pret. of win.

WANDY. *adj.* Long and flexible, as a wand.
Old Norse *vöndr*, a rod, wand.

WANDLY or WAANLY. *adv.* Gently, carefully.
" ' Come, luiv,' quo I, ' aw'll *waanly* take thee down.'
' Stand off, thou gowk,' she answered, with a frown."
Ewan Clarke.
Sco. *waynd*, to care, be anxious about. Ang.-Sax. *wandian*, vereri, revereri, Old Norse *vanda*, to do a thing attentively or carefully, *vandlega*, sollicite.

WANG-TOOTH. *sb.* A grinder.
Ang.-Sax. *wang-toth*, a grinder, from *wang*, the jaw.

WANKLE. *adj.* Weak, infirm, tottering.
Ang.-Sax. *wancol*, unsteady, Dut. *wankelen*, to totter, stagger. Formed by taking the nasal, on *waggle*, Germ. *wackeln*, Dut. *waggelen*, &c.

WAP. *sb.* A bundle of straw.
Old Norse *vefja*, involucrum, Ang.-Sax. *wæfan*, to envelope.

WARE. *vn.* To expend.
Old Norse *verja*, to spend, to trade, Welsh *guariau*, to spend, disburse.

WAR-DAYS. *sb.* Working days, all days but Sunday.
Suio-Goth. *hwardag*, Dan. *hverdag*, an ordinary day.

WARISON. *sb.* The belly.—*Hall.*
See *warishin*.

WARK. *sb.* Pain, aching.
Ang.-Sax. *wærc*, Old Norse *verkr*, pain.

WARN. *va.* To summon to a funeral.

WARN. *va.* To deny, forbid, keep off.
Ang.-Sax. *wyrnan*, to refuse, forbid, hinder, Old Norse *varna*, prohibere, obstare, Old Sax. *warnian*, recusare.

WARN. *va.* To assure, to warrant.—*Dick.*
North. *warn*, to warrant.—*Hall.* Old Fris. *wernja*, to warrant ("verbürgen, sicherheit geben."—*Richt.*) I have never, however, myself, heard the word used in such a way as to be certain that it was not a contraction of *warrant*.

WARRIDGE. *sb.* The withers, or shoulders, of a horse.
Atk. collates *warridge* with Germ. *wither rist*, withers. But we may perhaps find a connection with Welsh *gwar*, the nape of the neck, the part just below the neck, Corn. *gwar*, neck, *guarac*, that which is bent. The Old Norse *sviri*, Ang.-Sax. *sweor*, Old Eng. *swire*, neck, seems to be from the same root.

WARP. *va.* To lay eggs.
Old Norse *verpa*, Suio-Goth. *wārpa*, Swed. *vărpa*, to lay eggs. The primary meaning is to cast or throw.

WARRISHIN. *sb.* Store, provision.
" See a *warrishin* of sooins an' yal."—*Dick*. *Warrishin* seems to be from the same origin as *wares*, goods, merchandise, on which Wedgwood observes that the radical meaning seems to be provisionment, stores, from the root *ware*, to look, observe, take notice of. "The development of the signification is especially clear in Finnish"—*warata*, to be provident, *warasta*, provisions, stores. Comp., also, Swed. *matwaror*, provision of meat, *fiskwaror*, provision of fish. The above shows the more remote origin of our word, but it is, in all probability, immediately derived from Fr. *garnison* (orig. *guarnison*), itself of Teutonic origin. The *n* is lost in Eng. *garrison*, which is the same word as our *warrishin*, in the restricted sense of the supply of soldiers (perhaps originally general supplies) for a fortress. Then the Scotch has *warison*, in the sense of guerdon or reward; we find also in Cornish, no doubt a relic of Old English use, *weryson* or *gueryson* in the same sense; it appears to be the same word with a variation of meaning. The *West. and Cumb. Dial.* has *warison*, the stomach and its contents, in a sense again somewhat divergent. The Lonsd. *warish*, to recover from sickness, Old Eng. *waresche*, to cure, to heal, though from the same general origin, do not seem to be immediately connected with our word, but to be from the Fr. *guerir*, to heal, a development in another direction of the same root *ware*, and a corresponding sense to which is found in Lapp. *warres*, sanus, bene valens.

WATH. *sb.* A ford in a river.
Old Norse *vad*, Old Swed. *wad*, Swed., Dan. *vad*, a ford, a place through which one can *wade*. Hence Ital. *guado*, Fr. *gué*, ford.

WATTER-BRASH. *sb.* A rising of acrid saliva into the mouth. *Brash* is connected by *Atk.* with Old Eng. *brake*, Dut. *braecken*, to vomit. It occurs to me, however, as not improbable that it may be by transposition for *barsh*, Fris. *barsck*, Germ. *barsch*, bitter, acrid. Or from a corresponding noun.

WATTER-GOIT. *sb.* A place in a stream across which a pole is laid, to prevent trespass of cattle. Ang.-Sax. *gyte*, an overflowing, Dut. *waeter-geute*, alluvies—the reference being to the raising of the water by means of the obstruction.

WATTER-JAW'T. *adj.* Applied to potatoes that have been spoiled by being left too long in the water after boiling. *Jaw't* or *jawed* seems to be most probably from Old Norse *galladr*, spoiled, defective, from *galli*, fault, imperfection, the *l* being dropped as usual.

WATTER-TEE. *sb.* The water-wagtail.
Tee in the above seems to be for *tit*, a small bird. See *moor-tidy*.

WAUR. *comp. adj.* Worse.
Ang.-Sax. *wærra*, Dan. *værre*, Swed. *värre*, Lapp. *wärr*, worse.

WAX. *vn.* To grow, increase in stature.
Ang.-Sax. *weaxan*, Old Norse *vaxa*, Germ. *wachsen*, to grow.

WAX-KERNELS or WAXEN-KERNELS. *sb.* Glandular swellings in the neck, popularly supposed—whence their name—to be more common among those who are *waxing* or growing. Ang.-Sax. *cyrnel*, kernel.

WAZE. *sb.* A pad for the head, to carry weights upon.
Crav. *wais*, a wreath of straw or cloth worn on the head, to relieve the pressure of burdens. Sco. *weasses*, a species of breeching for the necks of work-horses. *Waze*, or wreath of straw.—*J. K.* Fris. *waase*, padding under a woman's dress, *waask* (diminutive), a pad for the head, to carry weights upon, Low Germ. *wase*, a sod of turf, whence (from its frequent use for that purpose) the diminutive *waseke*, a pad for the head, to carry weights upon (*Hamb. Idiot.*), Swed. *vase*, sheaf, Suio-Goth. *wase*, Old Norse *vasi*, a bundle of small twigs, Ang.-Sax. *wase*, Old High Germ. *waso*, turf (whence Fr. *gazon*), Germ. *wasen*, sod, turf, clod, Prov. Germ. *wase*, bundle of brushwood.

WEAR. *va.* To turn or stop cattle or sheep.
Ang.-Sax. *werian*, Old Norse *verja*, Germ. *wehren*, to check, restrain, keep off.

WEASAND. *sb.* The gullet or windpipe.
Ang.-Sax. *wæsend*, the windpipe, from *hweôsan*, to blow, wheeze.

WEATHER-GO. *sb.* The end of a rainbow seen in the morning in showery weather.—*Dick. Weather-gall*, the lower part of a rainbow when the rest of the arch is not seen.—*West. and Cumb. Dial.* Crav. *weather-gall*, a secondary or broken rainbow. Sco. *weather-gaw*, part of one side of a rainbow, appearing immediately above the horizon, viewed as a prognostic of bad weather. Isle of Wight *water-geal*, a secondary rainbow.—*Hall.* Germ. *wasser-galle* or *regen-galle*, "a part of a rainbow, an imperfect rainbow, of which only a part is seen."—*Adelung.* Old Norse *haf-gall*, a rainbow on the sea, portending a storm. Wachter's explanation of Germ. *wassergall*, splendor pluvius, referring to Ang.-Sax. *gyl*, splendid, does not seem to me very satisfactory. If we take weather to be used in the sense of foul weather or storm, which is one of the meanings of Old Norse *vedr*, and which, as *Jam.* observes, has the sanction of ancient use in Scotland, and which appears to be the obvious meaning in Lonsd. *weather-breeder*, "a sudden fine day of extraordinary beauty, followed often by rain and storm;" the most natural explanation of *gall* would seem to be that of "presage," from Ang.-Sax. *galan*, to foretell. Thus *weather-gall* would be, like the Old Norse *vedr-spaer*, "that which foretells bad weather," as the Germ. *wasser-gall* and Isle of Wight *water-geal* would be that which foretells wet.

WEBSTER. *sb.* A weaver.
Ang.-Sax. *webestre*, a female weaver. The distinction of sex seems at an early period to have been lost. See *dyster*.

WEEKY. *adj.* Moist, juicy.
Old Norse *vökva*, madefacere, *vökvi*, humour; Dut. *wack*, udus, humidus, laxus, mollis, *weeken*, to soak, steep, Low Germ. *wêk wäder* mild weather, thaw.

WEEL. *va.* To select, to pick out.
Old Norse *velja*, Dan. *vælge*, Swed. *välja*, to choose, to elect.

WELL. *va.* To weld.
Swed. *välla*, Germ. *wellen*, to join two pieces of iron by heat. "From Germ. *wallen*, Dut. *wellen*, Ang.-Sax. *weallan*, to boil. The process of welding is generally named from the word for boiling in other languages."—*Wedg.*

WELSH. *adj.* Insipid, tasteless.
Referred by Jamieson to Dut. *gaelsch*, insipid. But it may be rather a contraction of *wallowish*, nauseous (*Hall.*), which, again, from *wallow*, flat, insipid. Comp. *valg*, tasteless, insipid (*Aasen*), and also Dut. *walgen*, to nauseate."—*Atk.*

WELT. *va.* To upset, to turn over.
Ang.-Sax. *wealtiau*, Old Norse *velta*, to turn, roll over.

WELTS. *sb.* The ribbed tops of stockings, &c.
Welsh *gwald*, hem, border.

WENTS. *sb.* Narrow lanes in the towns of Cockermouth and Workington. *Went*, in the sense of a passage, "ane dern went," a dark passage, occurs in *Doug. Virg.* It seems to be the same word as *wynd*, used in Scotland for an alley or lane, and which *Jam.* refers to Ang.-Sax. *wendan*, Germ. *wenden*, to turn, "as turnings from a principal street." Rather, it seems to me, from Ang.-Sax. *wendan*, in the sense of ire, procedere, as *passage*, that through which one *passes*, and as *alley*, from *aller*, to go.

WENTIT. *adj.* Turned sour.
The word properly denotes simply "turned." Ang.-Sax. *wendan*, Old Norse *venda*, to turn.

WEYT. *sb.* A vessel formed of a wooden hoop covered with sheepskin, used for lifting grain in the barn. Sco. *wecht*. Jamieson particularises two different kinds of *wecht*, one for winnowing the grain, and the other for simply lifting it. In the former sense he suggests his derivation from Germ. *wechen, wehen*, to blow, Belg. *wayer*, "more properly *vecher*," a fanner or winnower. In the latter sense we might think of Ang.-Sax. *wegan*, Old Norse *vega*, to lift; whence Ang.-Sax. *wegd*, Low Germ. *wecht*, Dan. *vægt*, Eng. *weight*, that which is lifted. In any case both words are probably from the same origin.

WHAMP or WAMP. *sb.* A wasp.
It seems uncertain to what extent our word is coincident with Eng. *wasp*, more especially as the etymology of *wasp* remains to be accurately defined. Wedgwood, collating other names of the insect, (as Gael. *speach*, from *speach*, to bite, sting), says "there can be little doubt that it comes from a word signifying to sting." Perhaps Sansc. *vis*, to pierce, which from its derivatives *visan*, poison, Lat. *virus* (Eichoff), seems to have had more especially the sense of stinging. But there is also another strongly-marked characteristic from which the wasp might take its name, and that is, its peculiar conformation, or, in other words, its thin waist. And in the Welsh *gwasgu*, to press or squeeze, whence *gwasg*, the waist, " the place where the body is squeezed in," (*Wedg.*), we seem to have at all events a noteworthy comparison with *wasp*. Our word *wamp*, if it be not simply a variation of *wasp*, (comp. *clamp* with *clasp*), may, changing *n* euphonically into *m*, be compared with Welsh *gwanu*, Gael. *guin*, Corn. *gwane*, to pierce or sting, whence Welsh *gwenynen*, Corn. *gwanen*, a bee. Williams finds the root in Sansc. *vân*, to pierce; which, if, as seems probable, it

is also the root of *venenum*, Welsh *gwenwyn*, Corn. *guenoin*, poison, seems, like *vis*, to have the sense of stinging. But in this case again, we have the Bret. *gwana*, Ir. *geinnim*, to press, squeeze, suggesting an etymon in the other direction. Still, on the whole, the former seems the more probable derivation, and we may think of *wasp* and *wámp*—if not simply variations of the same word—as parallel words derived from two collateral roots signifying to sting.

WHANG. *sb.* A thong, a leather strap, a slice of something tough, as cheese. Ang.-Sax. *thwang*, Suio-Goth. *twänge*, a thong.

WHANE. *va.* and *n.* To stroke down caressingly. Also to coax, to wheedle. Lonsd. *whane*, to coax, entice. Clev. *whally*, to stroke the back of an animal gently; also to obtain one's ends by caressing or wheedling. *Whane* and *whally* seem to be parallel words; the latter, as *Atk.* has it, from Old Norse *væla*, to take in, impose upon, and the former from Ang.-Sax. *wægnian*, of the same meaning.

WHANTLE. *va.* To fondle.—*Hall.*
Seems to be a frequentative from Old Norse *vanda*, to do a thing attentively or carefully, (see *wandly*). If not for *whannel*, as a frequentative of above *whane*.

WHAT! *intj.* An often-used expletive. "*What*, Jemmy! how's thou?"—*Dick.*

"I caw'd to sup cruds wi' Dick Miller,
An' hear aw his cracks an' his jwokes;
The dumb wife was tellin' their fortunes—
What! I mud be leyke udder fwoks."—*Anderson.*

"'What!' quod the preest to Perkyn,
'Peter, as me thynketh,
'Thou art lettred a lytel.'"—*P. Pl.*

Ang.-Sax. *hwæt*, what! lo!

WHEEN. *sb.* A certain limited quantity, a little.
Sco. *quhene*. Ang.-Sax. *hwêne*, somewhat, a little, Germ. *wenig*, Low Germ. *weenig*, a little, a few.

WHEEZLE. *vn.* To wheeze, breathe with difficulty.
A frequentative from Ang.-Sax. *hweosan*. Old Norse *hvæsa*, to wheeze.

WHELK. *va.* To beat or thump.
"Whele or whelke."—*Pr. Prv.* A modification of *wale* or *weal.* See *wale.*

CUMBERLAND DIALECT. 167

WHEMMEL. *va.* and *n.* To overturn, overwhelm.
Dut. *wemelen*, to whirl, turn round. *Whemmel* is the original form of *whelm*.

WHEWT. *sb.* "A few *whewts* o' snow."—*Dick. Supp.*
The meaning seems to be a whiff. Welsh *chwyth*, blast, Ang.-Sax. *hweotha*, breeze.

WHEWTLE. *sb.* A low whistle.
Clev. *whewt*, *whewtle*, to whistle. Sco. *quhew*, to whistle. Welsh *chwyth*, blast, *chwythu*, to blow, *chwythell*, whistle. Ang.-Sax. *hweotha*, a breeze.

WHICKFLU. *sb.* A whitlow.
"The true form of the word (whitlow) is probably preserved in N.E. *whick-flaw*, a *flaw* or sore about the quick of the nail."—*Wedg.*

WHICKS. *sb.* Young thorns planted for growing.
Properly *quicks*. Ang.-Sax. *cwic*, alive.

WHIDDER. *vn.* To tremble, shudder.
Old Norse *hvidra*, cito commoveri, "cognate with which is probably Ang.-Sax. *hweotherung*, a murmuring, *hweotheran*, to murmur."—*Atk.*

WHIDDERER. *sb.* A strong and stout person.
Lonsd. *witherer*. Lanc. *witherin*, large, powerful. Davies refers to Welsh *uther*, terrible, but I prefer Ang.-Sax. *swithra*, one strong or skilful, from *swith*, strong, powerful, great.

WHIG. *sb.* Whey kept for drinking. "If suffered to become sour, aromatic herbs are steeped in it."—*Dick.* Ang.-Sax. *hwæg*, *hweg*, whey. Or perhaps rather Welsh *chwig*, whey fomented with sweet herbs.

WHILE. *adv.* Until.
"Wait *while* I come." "The traces of this usage—which is of constant occurrence, and very striking—or of the origin of it, rather, may be occasionally met with in early texts. Thus in Northumb. Gosp. Matt. 1. 24 ; he ne cunnade hea tha huile hia gecende hire frumcende sunu ; and he knew her not the while she brought forth her first-born son. * * * No doubt our *while* is the remains of an elliptical mode of expression, equivalent to during the time or space (*hwile*) before."—*Atk.*

WHILK. *pron.* Which.
Ang.-Sax. *hwilc*, Old Norse *kvilikr*, Germ. *welcher*.

WHILLIMER. *sb.* A very poor kind of cheese, said to have been originally made in the township of Whillimoor. But Lonsd. *winnymer*, also signifying a very poor cheese, seems to throw a doubt on the above explanation. And Lonsd. has also in the same sense *whangby*, a puzzling word, which seems to be from *whang*, a thong or slice of something tough, as cheese; and yet, from its ending *by*, would seem to indicate the name of a place.

WHIM. *adj.* Soft, noiseless, quiet, running smoothly. Lonsd. *wheam*, soft, quiet, mild, smooth, sheltered. Clev. *whimly*, softly, gently, stilly. Crav. *wheem*, smooth, calm, unruffled, applied to the surface of water unruffled by a breeze. *Wheam*, smooth, sheltered, impervious to the wind.—*Brock.* Halliwell has *wheam*, snug, convenient, *North.*; and *wheamly*, slily, deceitfully, *Linc.* Atkinson finds the general root in Ang.-Sax. *cweman*, to satisfy, please, delight. But there is a further suggestion which seems to me worth making respecting this word. In most of its meanings it coincides exactly with Eng. *calm*, and it appears further as if it might contain the same root. Now *calm* comes to us from the Romance through the French, and its primitive meaning (see *Wedg.*) "seems to be heat," Port. *calma*, heat, Prov. Sp. *calma*, the heat of the day. Now the question which occurs to me is whether our word *whim* or *wheem*, in the sense of calm, may not be in a similar manner derived from Ang.-Sax. *wilm* or *welm*, signifying heat. Comp. Ang.-Sax. *hwem*, a corner (sheltered place?)

WHIN. *sb.* Furze or gorse.
"Properly waste growth, weeds, but now appropriated to gorse or furze."—*Wedg.* Welsh *chwyn*, weeds, Swed. *hven*, bent grass, Old Norse *hvönn*, angelica, common in a wild state in Iceland, Norw. *kvanne.*

WHIN-COW. *sb.* A stem of furze or gorse.
See *ling-cow.*

WHINGE. *vn.* To whine,
Suio-Goth. *wenga*, plorare, Dial. Swed. *hvinka*, to whine, lament, Low Germ. *wingern*, to moan, whine.

WHINNEY, WHINNER. *vn.* To neigh.
Lat. *hinnio*, Fr. *hennir*, to neigh, imitative of the sound.

WHINTIN. *sb.* A dark slate-stone found on Skiddaw.
Sco. *quhin-stone.*

WHIRR. *sb.* Old and curdled butter-milk.
Perhaps properly *whirf*, from Ang.-Sax. *hwirfan*, Old Norse *hverfa*, to turn. Or from Welsh *chwerw*, bitter.

CUMBERLAND DIALECT.   169

WHISHT! *intj.*   Hush! silence!   It is sometimes used as an adjective. "As *whisht* as a mouse."—*Dick.* Swed. *wysch*, interjection of nurses lulling children to sleep (*Serenius*), *wiszja*, to hush to sleep. Old Norse *hviska*, Dan. *hviske*, Fris. *wiske*, to whisper, are probably allied, the general origin being onomatopœic, representing "a slight sound, such as that of something stirring, or the breathing or whispering of some one approaching."—*Wedg.*

WHISK. *vn.*   To move smartly or quickly.
Germ. *wischen*, to do anything with a light quick movement. Fin. *huiskata*, to run to and fro, Lapp. *swisko*, a switch.

WHISK. *sb.*   The game of whist.
Whist is generally derived from the interjection enjoining silence, in reference to the rapt attention which it requires. If not from *whisk* as above, in the sense of light, rapid movement, as that of dealing cards.

WHITE. *va.*   To cut or whittle anything, such as a stick.
Ang.-Sax. *thwitan*, to cut.

WHITEFISH. *sb.*   Flattery, cajolery.
Clev. *whiteheft*. The prefix *white*, as in *whitefish*, *whiteheft*, seems to be a similar word to the Sco. *white*, hypocritical, dissembling, in which Jamieson finds "an evident allusion to the wearing of white garments, as an emblem of innocence, especially by the clergy in times of popery." The ending *fish* (comp. Sco. *feese*, to flatter), may possibly be from Swed. *fjäsa*, to fondle, cajole. Or it might be the same as Germ. *fischen*, to fish, which, in a metaphorical sense, means to get by cunning.

WHITTLE. *sb.*   A knife.
Ang.-Sax. *hwytel*, a large knife.

WHITTLEGATE. *sb.*   The privilege, accorded to clergymen and schoolmasters, of using a knife and fork at the tables of their various parishioners, as a means of eking out their scanty stipends. "The custom still (1858) exists in one or two fell dales."—*Dick.* See *whittle* and *gate.*

WHY. *sb.*   A heifer.
Old Norse *quiga*, Dan. *quie*, a heifer.

WIDDERFUL. *adj.*   Cross, fretful, contradictious.
Ang.-Sax. *wither*, contrary or opposed, *witherian*, to resist, oppose. Germ. *widerwillig*, reluctant, cross-grained, *widrig*, cross, adverse.

Widdy, Withy. *sb.* A band of platted willows.
Ang.-Sax. *withie*, a twisted rod, Swed. *vidja*, willow, twig.

Wiggin. *sb.* The mountain ash.
Another name is *witch-wood*. Ang.-Sax. *wice*, the mountain ash, from *wiccian*, to use enchantment, to bewitch. All the various names of this tree, which, among the Northmen, was sacred to Thor, as *wiggin*, *witch-wood*, and *roan-tree*, seem to be connected with the supposed efficacy of its wood in spells and incantations. See *roan-tree*.

Wilk. *sb.* The bark of a young dog when in close pursuit.—*Dick*. The idea seems to be that of a short, sharp, half-choked sound, and it seems probable that *wilk* is a parallel word with *wherk*, to make a noise in breathing. Old Norse *querk*, the throat, Dan. *hværke*, to choke. Comp. Sco. *quhilk*, short cry of a gosling, and Old Norse *quakla*, suspirare.

Willey. *sb.* A child's night-dress.—*Hall*.
Sco. *wilie-coat*, an under-vest, generally worn in winter. Ruddiman's derivation from Eng. *wily*, "because by its not being seen, it does, as it were, cunningly or slily keep men warm," is absurd enough. The following extract from Spalding, quoted by *Jam.* in his *Addenda*, shows that it was formerly used in the same sense as our *willey*. "But she (the Queen) gets up out of her naked bed in her night *waly-coat*, bare-footed and bare-legged." The origin, on which *Jam.* remarks as "quite uncertain," is, I take it, to be found in Old Norse *hvila*, Dan. *hvile*, Swed. *hvila*, to rest, repose, go to sleep, Old Norse *hvila*, bed, *hvila-vod*,' bed-sheet. The word is found also in the Celtic, as Welsh, Corn. *gwely*, Bret. *gwele*, bed, Bret. *gweleden*, a shift or under-garment. *Wilie-coat*, then, of which our *willey* is a contraction, means simply sleeping or night-dress.

Will. *vn.* To doubt, to consider, to deliberate, as "I *wills* whether to gang or nit."—*Dick*. Sco. *will*, adj., uncertain how to proceed. *Jam.* refers to Old Norse *villa*, to lead astray. The Old Norse *væla*, one of the meanings of which is to consider, turn over in the mind, seems to suit best with the meaning of our word.

Wineberries. *sb.* Red and white currants, ribes.
Old Norse *vinber*, a grape, Suio-Goth. *winbær*, "nuncupamus ribes, ex quadam cum uvo similitudine (*Ihre*), Germ. *weinbeer*, grape. The term *currant* itself, now applied to the fruit of various ribes, properly applies to the small grape brought from Corinth. "By a similar confusion the red currant was in Turner's time called a raisin-tree."—*Prior*.

WINJE! *intj.* "A gladsome expression of surprise or wonder. *Winje*, wife, what a berry puddin !'—*Dick.* Apparently related to Ang.-Sax. *wyn*, joy, pleasure.

WIN IN. *va.* To get in the crop.
Ang.-Sax. *winnan*, to labour, to toil, to acquire by labour.

WINNEL-STRAW. *sb.* The stem of the couch grass.
Ang.-Sax. *windel-streawe*, straw for platting.

WINNICK. *sb.* Something very small.
Seems a diminutive of *wheen*, qv.

WINSOME. *adj.* Pleasant, lovable.
Ang.-Sax. *winsum*, pleasant.

WINTER-PROUD. *adj.* Applied to winter wheat when of too forward growth. Lonsd. *proud*, luxuriant. Welsh *pryddhau*, to become luxuriant.

WISE-LIKE. *adj.* Wise, prudent.
Ang.-Sax. *wislic*, wise, prudent.

WISHY-WASHY. *adj.* Trifling, worthless.
Dut. *wisjewasje*, fiddle-faddle, Vulg. Germ. *wischiwaschi*, tittle tattle, *wisch*, trash.

WISK. *sb.* A slight and short shower.
"The syllable *whisk* represents the sound of a light or fine body moving rapidly through the air. * * * Hence Germ. *witschen*, *wischen*, and Eng. *whisk*, to do anything with a light, quick movement."—*Wedg.*

WITCH-WOOD. *sb.* The mountain ash.
See *wiggin.*

WIZZENT. *adj.* Dried up, withered.
Ang.-Sax. *wisnian*, Old Norse *visna*, to wither, dry up, Swed. *wissnad*, dried up, withered.

WO, WAW. *sb.* Wall.
Lonsd. *wogh*. Sco. *wauch, waw*. Though it would be quite in accordance with the ordinary rule of our dialect to derive *wo* or *waw* from *wall*, Ang.-Sax. *weall*, yet the form of the corresponding northern words seems to point rather to Ang.-Sax. *wâg, wah*, Fris. *woch, woge*, Old Norse *veggr*, Dan. *væg*, Swed. *väg*, wall, for their common origin.

WOKE-RIFE. *adj.* Sleepless, watchful.
Ang.-Sax. *wacce*, watchfulness, and *rife*, abundant.

WORTS, ORTS. *sb.* The refuse of fodder left by cows.
N. Fris. *orten*, to leave remnants in eating, Low Germ. *orten*, to pick out the best and leave much remnants, Dut. *oor-aete*, reliquiæ fastiditi pabuli.—*Wedg.*

WRAMP. *sb.* A sprain.
Dut. *wrempen*, to twist the mouth, *rimpe*, a wrinkle, fold, twist, Ang.-Sax. *hrympelle*, a wrinkle.

WRECKLING. *sb.* A feeble, unhealthy child; the smallest and weakest of a litter. Sco. *wrig*, of the same meaning. Fris. *wräk*, Jutl. *vrägling*, a small, feeble person, Swed. *vrak*, refuse, something worthless, *vråke*, to reject.

WROWKE. *va.* To stir up roughly.
"I olas liked John, but I cared so laal for Grace at I cud ha' tean her an' *wrowkt* the fire wid her,"—said by a Cumberland woman of her children (*Gibson*). Old Norse *hrekja*, pellere, propellere, Fris. *wreka*, to use force to, to wrench. Or Dut. *rukken*, to tear, pull, tug.

WUD. *adj.* Mad, furious.
Ang.-Sax. *wud*, mad, furious, insane, Dut. *woeden*, to be wild or mad.

WUMMEL. *vn.* To wriggle or worm into a hole.
"He'll *wummel* hisself intil t' creuktest rabbit whole i' Siddick," —said of a terrier (*Gibson*). Low Germ. *wümmeln*, to wabble, Dut. *wemmelen*, to drive round, whirl, thence to bore with an augur. "Parallel forms are Fr. *gimbelet*, Langued. *jhimbelet*, a gimlet, *jhimbla*, to twist."—*Wedg.* *Wummel* is another form of *wammel*.

WUN. *vn.* To dwell, inhabit.
Ang.-Sax. *wunian*, Dut. *wonen*, Germ. *wohnen*, to dwell.

WUNS! *intj.* An exclamation of surprise or annoyance.
"The breyde, geavin aw roun her,
   Cries '*Wuns!* we forgat butter sops.'"—*Anderson.*
Seems to be a profane expression, like *Ods wuns*. At the same time it may be observed that *wann* is used as an interjection very much in the same manner in Low Germ. (*Hamb. Idiot.*)

WURSLE, RUSSLE. *vn.* To wrestle.
Ang.-Sax. *wræstlian*, Fris. *wrassele, wrustle*, Dut. *worstelen*, to wrestle, Old Norse *russla*, contrectare.

WYKE. *sb.* The corner of the mouth.
Old Norse *vik*, recessus, Dan. *mundvig*, the corner of the mouth.

Y.

YAN, YEN. One.
Old Norse *einn*, Dan. *een*, Ang.-Sax. *an*, one, "S. Jutl. *jen*, which corresponds almost exactly in form and sound with our *yan*, is especially note-worthy."—*Atk.*

YADDLE. *vn.* To prate, to chatter.
Dan. *jaddre*, to babble, prattle. Or perhaps the same as the Clev. *yaffle*, Dan. *ævle*, to prate, chatter.

YAKKER-SPIRED. *adj.* "When the malting process is too long continued, and both root and sprout are visible, the barley is *yakker-spired*, and injured for malting."—*Dick.* Crav. *spire*. to shoot up luxuriantly. Dan. *spire*, germ, sprout, Swed. *spira*, bud, shoot, sprout. The prefix may be the Dut. and Germ. *achter*, behind, in reference to the sprouting from the bottom as well as from the top.

YAL. *sb.* Ale.
Ang.-Sax. *eala*, Old Norse *öl*, Suio-Goth. *öl*. "The pronunciation of this word suggests a Scand. origin, inasmuch as Ang.-Sax. *eale* presents a long syllable or sound in contrast with the shorter and sharper sound of the word in either of its three northern forms."—*Atk.*

YAL-JAW'T. *adj.* Partially intoxicated, worse for ale.
Sco. *jute*, to tipple. Perhaps from Ang.-Sax. *geótan*, Dut. *gieten*, Swed. *gjota*, to pour, to smelt.

"For each was at a slwote a *smelter*."—*Stagg.*

But see *watter-jaw't.*

YALLA-YOWDERIN. *sb.* The yellow-hammer.
Sco. *yeldring*. *Yewle-ring* (Cotg.) seems the more proper form, from Ang.-Sax. *geole*, yellow, in reference, as *Jam.* suggests, to the yellow ring which, at least partly, adorns the neck of this bird." Hence *yellow-yowderin* is tautologous.

YAMMER. *vn.* To talk fast and wildly.—*Dick.*

"Furst deal about he gat spead yace,
An' crew an' *yammered* sair than."—*Lonsdale.*

Brockett explains it "to complain, to whine," which seems to be the original sense. Dut. *jammeren*, Germ. *jammern*, Dan. *jamre*, to wail, to lament, Ang.-Sax. *geomrian*, to groan, lament.

YAP. *sb.* A troublesome, mischievous child.
Clev. *yap*, a troublesome, cross, or crying child, also a cur. Atk. refers to Dial. Dan. *jappe*, or *hiappe*, to be over hasty in

action or speech. Comp. also Low Germ. *jappen*, to snap. But perhaps the word may be the same as *yelp*, Old Norse *gjalpa*, obstrepere, Fr. *japper*, to yelp.

YAR. *adj.* Rough, harsh.
Welsh *garw*, Corn. *garow*, Gael., Ir. *garbh*, rough, sharp, fierce. Hence probably the river names *Garry*. *Yare*, *Yarrow*, in the sense of violence.

YARK. *va.* To beat soundly.
Seems to be the same word as *jerk*. "To *yerk*, *jerk*, or whip." —*J. K.* Atkinson, remarking that the Linc. Gloss. gives both *yack* and *yark* with nearly coincident senses, suggests Old Norse *hiacka*, *jacka*, to beat, as the common origin of both. Comp. also Flem. *jacken*, flagellare scutica.—*Kil.*

YAT, YET. *sb.* A gate.
Old Fris. *iet* for *gat*, Ang.-Sax. *geat*, gate.

YAUD, YAD. *sb.* A mare *(Gibson)*, an old mare *(Dick)*.
"Fra Tindal Fell twelve pecks she'd bring;
She was a *yad* fit for a king."—*Anderson.*
Lonsd. *yode*, a riding horse, Crav. *yaud*, a horse, North. *yaud*, a horse or mare (*Hall.*) Sco. *yad*, "properly an old mare," (*Jam.*) Halliwell makes it the provincial form of *jade*. But it is in fact, as I take it, the more correct form, the origin of both being to be found in Old Norse *jalda*, a mare (used only in poetry), Dial. Swed. *jälda*, a mare, with which Rietz, I think rightly, collates Eng. *jade*. In this case the special sense of a mare as distinguished from a horse, which the word has with us, would be the right one.

YEDDER. *sb.* A long rod or wand used in hedging.
Ang.-Sax. *eder*, a fence or hedge. Hence *stower* and *yedder*, a mode of fencing with rods or twigs fastened to upright stakes. See *stower*.

YERDFAST. *sb.* A stone fast in the earth, and just visible at the surface. Old Norse *jard-fastr steinn*, Dial. Swed. *jordfast sten*, a stone fixed deeply in the earth.

YETLIN. *sb.* A small iron pan.
Sco. *yettlin*, of or belonging to cast-iron, *yet*, to cast metals. Ang.-Sax. *geôtan*, Dut. *gieten*, to melt, to cast metals. Hence *yetlin*, something made of cast-metal.

YOLLER. *vn.* To shout, to halloo.
Probably the same as *goller*, qv.

YOUER, YOWER. *sb.* The udder.
Old Norse *jûgr, jûr,* Dan. *yver,* Dial. Swed. *jur, jaur,* Norw. *jur,* Ang.-Sax. *uder.* "The remarkable correspondence between our word and the Scand. forms cannot fail to be more striking when the sound of the N., Swed. and Dan. *fv* and *v* are taken into account."—*Atk.*

YOOL, YAWL. *vn.* To weep, cry, to howl as a dog.
Low Germ. *jaulen,* applied to the long-continued whining of children, and the noise made by dogs when tied up.—*Danneil.* See also *gowl,* of which the above might be another form, as *yat* for gate.

YOPE, YAUP. *vn.* To shout, to whoop.
Clev. *yope* is explained by *Atk.* as meaning to yelp, of which it is taken to be simply another form. But the way in which our word is used suggests rather a connection with Eng. *whoop.* Old Norse *œpa,* to shout, Ang.-Sax. *wop,* cry.

YOWE-YORLING. *sb.* The earth-nut.
Yorling seems to be a contraction of *yerthling* or *earthling.* I am unable to suggest an origin for the prefix *yowe.*

YUCK. *vn.* To itch.
Clev. *uke.* "Ichyn or ykyn or gykyn, prurio."—*Pr. Prv.* Dut., Dan. *jeuken,* Germ. *jucken,* to itch.

YULE. *sb.* Christmas.
Old Norse *jôl,* Ang.-Sax. *geôl,* Fin. *joulu.*

YUR. *sb.* The corn-spurry plant. Spergula arvensis.
Sco. *yarr.* "Abbreviated from *yarrow,* and applied to a very different plant, from both having been confused under the name of milfoil."—*Prior.*

ADDITIONS AND CORRECTIONS.

ASLEY. *adv.* "As *asley*, as willingly, as soon that way as the other."—*Dick.* *Asley* would seem to be the Old Eng. *as lief*, as willingly, Ang.-Sax. *leóf*, dear, *leófre*, rather, more willingly, *liever*. In this case, *as asley* is redundant.

BARNACLES. *sb.* Irons put on the nose of a horse to make him stand quiet. Also an old name for spectacles. "Bernak for horse, chamus."—*Pr. Prv.* Wedgwood takes the latter sense to be the original one, referring to Lang. *borni*, blind, *bernikal*, one who sees with difficulty, *berniques*, spectacles.

BEARD. *va.* To lay projecting brushwood over the edge of a wall. Sp. *barda*, coping of straw or brushwood for the protection of a wall, Fr. *barder*, to bind or tie across, overcross, or athwart, *bardeau*, a shingle or small board such as houses are covered with (*Cotg.*). The origin of the word, which seems to be derived more immediately from the French, may be Old Norse *bord*, edge, brim.

BRANGLE. *vn.* To wrangle.
Sco. *brangle*, to confound, throw into disorder. Perhaps from Old Norse *brengla*, to distort.

BRANKS. *sb.* A kind of halter having a nose-band which tightens as the horse pulls. Gael. *brangas* or *brancas*, a halter.

BUCKELT. *adj.* "A saw or anything is *buckelt* which has lost its pliancy from being over-bent."—*Dick.* Goth. *bjugan*, Old Norse *buga*, Dut. *booghen, boghelen*, to bend.

BUMMELKITE. The black or bramble berry.
Icel. *bimbult* (pron. *bumbult*), to feel uneasy (*Cleasby*), seems to be the same word as that quoted from Haldorsen.

CALEEVER. *vn.* To prance, kick about in an ungainly manner. Perhaps connected with Old Norse *klifra*, Dan. *klavre*, to clamber, in the idea of sprawling, spreading the hands and feet. Compare also Old Norse *klaufi*, an awkward and clumsy boor, *klaufilegr*, awkward, clumsy.

O

CASH. *sb.* Friable strata.
>Span. *cascar*, Fr. *casser*, to break, Ital. *casco*, old, decaying. The word, however, notwithstanding its more close resemblance to the above, may be of Teutonic origin, Ang.-Sax. *cwisan*, to crush, Goth. *quistjan*, to spoil, decay, go to ruin, connected by Benfey with Sansc. *cish*, to cut. Comp. Eng. *quash*.

CONK. *sb.* The nose or profile.
>Perhaps, assuming the *n* as phonetic, to be connected with Gael. *coc*, to cock or stick up apruptly, *coc-shron*, a cocked-up nose.

COWT-LWORD. A pudding made of oatmeal and lumps of suet. The derivation of *lword* from *lard*, suet, is inconsistent with the pronunciation, which implies a word formed with a long *o*. Moreover, Dickinson, in his Supplement, gives the alternative *cow't leeady*. I must leave the latter part of the word unexplained.

CRONK. *sb.* The cry of the raven.
>Old Norse *krunk*, cry of the raven.

CUTTLE. *vn.* To chat or gossip.
>Like *cutter*, a frequentative from Ang.-Sax. *cwiddian*, Dut. *kouten*, to talk.

CUVVIN. *sb.* A periwinkle or sea-snail.
>Clev. *cuvvin*, Lonsd. *kewin*. Old Norse *kúfungr*, a periwinkle, from *kúfr*, convexity.

DIRL. *vn.* To give out a tremulous sound.
>Dut. *drillen*, motitari, Swed. *drilla*, to shake or quiver with the voice. Another form of *thrill*.

DOLLOP. *sb.* A large lump.
>Atk. cites Old Norse *dolpr*, a shapelessly fat brute. Comp. also Wel. *talp*, mass, lump. But possibly from Corn. *duilof*, Wel. *dwylaw*, the two hands, Wel. *dwylofaid*, the full of both hands, in a similar way to *gowpin*.

FAW. *sb.* An itinerant potter or tinker.
>The name has been derived by some from Johnnie Faw, the leader of the gipsies. But it seems a question whether he might not rather derive his surname from his occupation. One might possibly think of Old Norse *farri*, land-louper, vagrant, *r* final being almost mute in English.

GALE. *sb.* Wild myrtle.
>Ang.-Sax. *gagl*, wild myrtle.

ADDITIONS AND CORRECTIONS.

GALLOWS. *sb.* A person of bad character.
Ang.-Sax. *galga-môd*, wicked, "gallows minded."

GAUM. *va.* To understand, comprehend, give attention to. Ang.-Sax. *geomian*, Old Norse *geyma*, Norw. *gauma*, to give heed, pay attention. Dick. gives this word (whence *gumption*) in his Supp.

GAVEL-DYKE. *sb.* An allotment of fence liable to be maintained by a farm not immediately adjoining. Ang.-Sax. *gafel*, tribute, Wel. *gavael*, Gael. *gabhail*, holding, tenure. The origin is probably Celtic, Gael. *gabh*, Wel. *gafaelu*, to take, hold. We have the same word apparently in *runnin cavvel*, applied to a particular kind of occupancy of undivided common lands (see *run-rig*), and which seems equivalent to running (or changing) tenure.

GAVELOCK. *sb.* An iron crow-bar.
Ang.-Sax. *gafeloc*, Old Norse *gaflok*, a javelin, Wel. *gaflach*, a fork. The origin seems to be Celtic, and the same as that of the preceding word.

GELD-GRUND. *sb.* Ground devoid of minerals.
Dial Swed. *gall grund*, unproductive ground.

GIS. *intj.* A call to swine.
I have suggested Old Norse *gris*, a little pig. Comp. also Corn. *guis*, Bret. *gwiz*, an old sow.

GLEAD. *sb.* A kite.
Ang.-Sax. *glida*, Old Norse *gledi*, a kite.

GOE. *sb.* A spring or wet place in a field.
Crav. *gall*. Prov. Germ. *gölle*, puddle, Suio-Goth. *göl*, a marsh, Wel. *gwl*, wet.

GOLLICK. *sb.* A deep cut or wound.
Corn. *golye*, Bret. *goulia*, Wel. *gwelio*, to cut, wound.

GULL. *sb.* A mess for sick cattle, gruel for calves.
Wel. *gwlyb*, soft or liquid food, gruel, *gwl*, wet.

HACKER. *vn.* To stammer.
Comp. also Dan. *hakke*, to which Worsaae (*Danes and Northmen*) refers our word.

HALE-WATTER. *sb.* A heavy shower.
Old Norse *helli-skur*, a heavy shower, from *hella*, to pour.

HAP. *va.* To wrap, cover up.
   I have supposed a lost verb. Cleasby has *hyppa*, to huddle on the clothes, and *hjúpa*, to put in a shroud, both corresponding to a considerable extent with *hap*, which has rather the sense of a loose covering, as with bed-clothes.

HASK. *adj.* Harsh.
   Old Norse *heskr*, harsh (*Cleasby*).

HECK AND REE. Ancient terms used in guiding horses to right or left, and now only used in reference to an obstinate person or horse who will "nowther *heck* nor *ree*."—*Dick.* "The Northumberland *heck* is the Icelandic *hoegr* (pron. *haikir*)."—Gould (*Scenes in Iceland*). Swed. *höger*, right.

HEFTIN. *sb.* A beating.
   Heft would seem, like *quilt*, to be formed as a secondary verb from Old Norse *hæfa*, to hit.

HELSE. *sb.* A rope to put round a horse's neck in place of a halter. Old Norse *helsi*, a collar, from *hals*, the neck.

HIDE. *va.* To beat.
   To "give one a *hiding*," is a slang term of general use. Old Norse *hýda*, to beat, *hýding*, a flogging, from *húd*, the skin.

HIKE. *va.* To throw in the arms, as nurses do children. Perhaps more probably from Old Norse *hjúka*, to nurse, than from the origin before assigned.

HIPE. *va.* One of the modes of throwing an adversary in wrestling. Yorks. *hipe*, to strike with the head or horns. Dial. Swed. *hypa*, to strike, *hyp*, a heavy blow.

HOOSIN. *sb.* The husk of a nut.
   Dut. *hulse, huysken*, husk. Old Norse *hauss*, the skull.

HOBTHRUSH. *sb.* "A hobgoblin having the repute of doing much useful work unseen and unheard during the night, if not interfered with, but discontinuing or doing mischief if crossed or watched."—*Dick.* "A local spirit, famous for whimsical pranks. In some farm-houses a cock and bacon are boiled on Fassen's eve (Shrove Tuesday); and if any person neglect to eat heartily of this food, Hobthrush is sure to amuse himself at night with crammiug him up to the mouth with *big-*

chaff."—Brockett. Hence the following, addressed satirically to a greedy eater :—

> For aw's weel seer Hobthrush 'll neer
> Ha thee to chowk wi kaff, mun.—*Lonsdale.*

Atkinson's suggestion that *hob* is the same as the Goth. *alb*, Old Norse *alfr*, elf, seems to carry with it a good deal of probability. Comp. *Oberon*, the king of the fairies, with *Albruna*, the wise woman of the Germans in Tacitus (*alb*, elf, and *rûn*, mystery, secret knowledge). The only objection seems to be that if *thrush* be, as suggested by W. Grimm (*Deut. Myth.*), connected with Old Norse *thurs*, giant, hobgoblin, the word would be tautologous. Unless we might think rather of a connection with Old Norse *thruska*, mulier laboriosa. Or with Goth. *thwairs*, Dut. *dweersch*, athwart, Ang.-Sax. *'thwyreslic*, perverse, Old Norse *thriötska*, contumacia, Swed. *tresk*, perverse, wilful—in the one case giving the sense of an industrious, and in the other that of a perverse or self-willed elf—both of which are in accord with the description given of *Hobthrush*.

HOLT. *sb.* A peaked hill covered with wood.— *West. and Cumb. Dial.* Ang.-Sax. *holt*, a wood, Old Norse *holt*, properly a wood, coppice, Germ. *holz*, wood, lignum. In Iceland, where trees are rare, the word denotes a stony hill, as opposed to a marsh or ley (*Cleasby*).

HOW. *adj.* "*How* neet," applied to the dead of the night. Clev. *holl*, the depth of winter, sometimes applied to the dead of night.

> Wi monny mair see Meggy Hoop,
> Wi her bit sarkin linen
> At keep'd her feckly thro th' *how* doup,
> Wate weel reet constant spinnin.—*Stagg.*

Here we have *how*, as in Clev., applied to the depth of winter— *doup* being probably the same as Sco. "doup of the day," the latter part of the day, applied to the season of the year.

HUKE. *sb.* The hip.
Comp. Swed. *huka*, to sit squat. We do not find the noun from which our word is directly derived.

HULLERT. *adj.* Coagulated, as blood.
The Celtic words I have referred to may probably be cognate, but the word most nearly concerned is, I take it, the Ang.-Sax. *hwelan*, to become foul or putrid, *heolfer*, clotted blood.

HUMMEL MITTENS. *sb.* Woollen gloves without any division but for the thumbs. Similar gloves are worn by the Norwegian peasants. *Hummel* I take to be the same as *huvvel*, q.v., from the frequent interchange of *m* with *v* or *f*.

ADDITIONS AND CORRECTIONS.

HUVVEL POKE. *sb.* A cap for protecting a sore finger.
Clev. *huffle, huvvil,* a protection for a sore finger. Old Norse *hufa,* cap, hood, Dial. Swed. *huv,* a covering, hood.

JOWET. *sb.* A term of effeminacy. "Thou's a feckless *jowet.*"—*Dick.* Probably from the French *jouet,* toy, plaything.

KAYTER. *adj.* Friendly, agreeable.
Perhaps connected with Old Norse *kæta,* to gladden.

KEMPS, CAMPS. *sb.* Hairs in wool.
The true origin of this word, for which various explanations have been offered, is, there seems little doubt, to be found in Old Norse *kampr,* beard, whisker, moustache (*Cleasby*).

KEP-JOPE. *sb.* A child's pinafore.
Kep, in our dialect, is to catch, and *jope* is to spill. Hence *kep-jope* is that which catches what is spilt (and so protects the clothes).

KES-FAB. *sb.* A cheese vat.
Properly, I think, *kes-fat,* Old Eng. *fat,* Ang.-Sax. *fat,* a vat, Gael. *fiadhan,* a cheese vat.

KIND. *adj.* Friendly, intimate.
"Knoweth me *kyndly.*"—*P. Pl.*
Atkinson, comparing the above with our "him and me's varra *kind,*" refers to Norw. *kjend, kent,* well acquainted, and observes that our word "retains an—perhaps the—ancient sense which has passed away from the current speech."

KIPPERT. *adj.* Partly cured (of fish).
There seems to me to be considerable doubt as to the correctness of Jamieson's derivation of *kippered* from *kipper,* a spawner, on account of foul fish having been originally used for the purpose. The word is applied to other fish, as herrings. It may be rather from Old Norse *kippa,* a bundle drawn on a string, *fisk kippa,* a line of fish on a string, *kipra;* to wrinkle, draw tight.

KYPE. To fall off, give up, die.
Cleasby adduces a verb, *kopa,* to fall off from age or the like, which seems to be the parallel to our *kype,* rather than Germ. *kippen.*

KYPT. *adj.* Bent or twisted.
"A saw is said to be *kypt* or *buckelt* when it is twisted."—*Dick.* Of these two words the one (*buckelt*) is probably Teutonic; the other seems more probably Celtic. Comp. Wel. *cyftino,* to contort, from *cyf*=Lat. *cum.*

LALDER. *sb.* Foolish talk.
   Wel. *llol*, foolish talk, *llolio*, to babble, prattle, Sansc. *lal*, to prate. Our word, I think, may probably be properly *laller*, the origin being onomatopœic. See *lal*.

LASHINS. *sb.* Abundance.
   Old Norse *hlass*, Dan. *læss*, a cart-load, Old Norse *hlessing*, load, freight. Hence *lashins* is the same as *loads*, similarly used in the sense of abundance.

LECK. *sb.* A hard sub-soil of gravel and clay.—*Dick.*
   Apparently from the Wel. *llech*, Gael. *leac*, a flag, flat stone.

LED-FARM. An additional farm on which the occupier does not reside. One might think of Ang.-Sax. *lid*, Dan., Swed. *led*, limb, joint, in the idea of a *led* farm as an attached farm. But more probably, I think, *led* is to be referred to Old Norse *leiga*, Dan. *leje*, Swed. *lega*, to hire, to rent—as a record of the old time when Cumberland was occupied by a race of freeholders living on their own lands, and when a rented farm was the exception.

LEEVE-TALE. Easy to sell or dispose of.
   Dut. *lief-talligh*, acceptus, gratus, gratia valens.

LILLY. *va.* To fondle, caress, cajole.
   Old Eng. *loll*, to fondle. North. *lill*, to ease pain. *Lilly* might be the same as the Dan. *lefte*, to caress, pay court to, cajole. If not from *lull*, in the sense of soothing, Norw. *lulla*, to sing to sleep, &c.

LEEND. *sb.* A shelter from the wind.
   Ang.-Sax. *hlèo*, shelter, Old Norse *hlyja*, to shelter, *lygn*, calm. Dut. *luw*, shelter from the wind. Hence *lee*, in nautical language. Allied to *log* and *lownd*.

MANK. *vn.* To nod the head.
   Perhaps from Swed. *maka*, to move, taking the nasal.

METLAM CORN. *sb.* A toll of corn payable to the lord of the manor. Perhaps properly *metlan* or *metlin*, Old Norse *meta*, to tax. But as Jamieson has a word *meteham* or *metham* with the meaning of manor, it may be a question whether ours is not the same word with a phonetic *l*, *metlam* corn thus being simply *manor* corn.

MORLAN. "There are three annual fairs held at Keswick, the chief of which is on the 2nd of August, called *Morlan* fair, in the language of the country."—*Hutchinson.* The word seems to be compounded of Wel. *mawr*, great, and *llanw*, flood—"it being a rainy season, and they expect a flood."—(*Hut.*)

MORTAL. *adv.* Much, very, used as an intensitive, as "*mortal* fine." Carr may, I think, be right in deriving *mortal* from *mort*, a large quantity. It might originally be a noun, like *hantel*.

MOOT-HALL. *sb.* A town hall.
Old Norse, *môt*, Ang.-Sax. *gemot*, a meeting. In Norway *môt* is a town meeting, as opposed to *thing*, a county meeting (*Cleasby*).

PEEL-HOUSE. *sb.* A place of defence in the border wars, a small fortress. Wel. *pill*, a fortress, a secure place. The original idea would seem to be that of a stockade, from *pill*, a stake.

PLUTTERY, PLEUTERY. *sb.* Lumber, rubbish.
Swed. *pultar*, rags, Low. Germ. *pulten*, rags, *pulterig*, ragged (*Richey*), Germ. *plunder*, rubbish (originally rags.) Similarly, from Germ. *lumpen*, rag, *lumperei*, trifle, trumpery. And from Swed. *lumpor*, rags, *lumpen*, paltry. I am inclined, from the analogy of the above, to think, though Wedgwood's derivation is different, that the present word is the origin of Eng. *paltry*.

PLOY. Employment.
This seems to be the same as the word *plough* in the following:

> Of preieres and of penaunce
> My *plough* shal ben herafter.—*P. Pl.*

POAP. To grope, walk as one in the dark.
Comp. also Wel. *palfu*, to grope gently, probably cognate with Lat. *palpare*.

PUNDER. *vn.* To crowd, press.
Ang.-Sax. *pyndan*, to hinder, shut in, impound.

RAG. *sb.* Hoar frost.
Dial. Dan. *rag*, fog or mist.

RAISE. A cairn, heap of stones.
Old Norse *hreysi*, a heap of stones (*Cleasby*).

RAMPS. *sb.* Wild garlic, *allium ursinum*.
Ang.-Sax. *hramsa*, Dan. *ramse*, Swed. *ramslök*. From *ram*, rank, strong smelling. The Gael. *creamh*, wild garlic, seems to be an allied word, the initial *c* representing an aspirated *h*, as in Ang.-Sax. *hramsa*, now lost.

RAMSHACKLE. *adj.* Rude, wild, uncouth.
Perhaps from Old Norse *ramskakkr*, quite wrong, absurd.

REED. *va.* To strip. " Butchers *reed* the entrails of slaughtered animals to obtain the fat."—*Dick.* Old Norse *hrjoda*, to strip, Swed. *reda*, to clear, to disentangle.

RID. *va.* To clear away trees from land.
Another application of the preceding word. Old Norse *riodr*, a place cleared of wood, Dan. *rydde*, to grub up, Bav. *rieden*, to clear away, root out, *rieder*, riddings, places cleared of wood.

RIFT. *vn.* To belch.
My supposition of a secondary verb formed from the noun is unnecessary, as Cleasby has the verb itself, Old Norse *reypta*, to belch.

RIPPLE. *sb.* A slight scratch.
A diminutive of *rive* or *rip*, to tear, scratch, Swed. *repa*, to scratch, &c.

ROAN. *sb.* The roe of fish.
Old Norse *hrogn*, Dan. *rogn*, roe, spawn.

ROOP'T. *adj.* Hoarse, as with shouting.
Clev. *roupy*, hoarse from the effect of, cold, *rouped up*, to be rendered hoarse. Sco. *roup*, to shout, *roupy, roopit*, hoarse. Jamieson derives *roopit*, hoarse, from *roup*, to shout, Old Norse *hrôpa*. Atkinson connects it with the same root as *raven*, collating Dut. *raven*, Dial. Dan. *ræbbe, ræppe*, to croak. *Roopt* may in fact, as it seems to me, be *raw-oopt*, from Ang.-Sax. *hreow*, Old Norse *hrâr*, Swed. *rä*, Eng. *raw*, and Old Norse *ôp*, Ang.-Sax. *wop*, shout, cry—*roupt* thus being *raw*, or *rough voiced*.

ROOSE. *va.* To praise, flatter.
Old *hrôsa*, Dan. *rose*, to praise.

ROOSTY. *adj.* Rough in manner.
Probably connected with Old Norse *hraustr*, strong, hearty, *hryssingr*, coarseness, brutality, Swed. *rusta*, to make a riot or disturbance, Eng. *roister*, &c. See *royster*.

SAFE, SEF. *adj.* Certain. " He's safe to be drowned."
Lanc. *sef.* Seems probably to be, as Davies has it, from Welsh *sef*, certain.

SAMMIL. *sb.* A kind of conglomerate gravel.
A word in use in the lake district. From *sam*, implying combination. See *ham-sam*.

SCABBLE. *va.* To rough dress stone for building.
Crav. *scapple.* Probably a frequentative of Ang.-Sax. *scapan*, Old Norse *skapa*, Dan. *skabe*, to shape, to *scabble* being to shape roughly.

SCOPY. *adj.* Thin of soil.
Crav. *scaup*, a thin soil. Perhaps allied to *scoop*, Dut. *schop*, Low Germ. *schuppe*, a shovel, Boh. *kopati*, to hack, dig, *scopy* being that which is readily *scooped*. Or perhaps, taking the word as properly *scalpy*, to be connected with Sco. *skelve*, to separate in thin layers, Gael. *sgealb*, to split, splinter, *sgealb chreag*, a splintered or shelvy rock, Bret. *skalfa*, to split, separate.

SCROO. *sb.* A slide.
Gael. *sgiorr*, to slide.

SHANGLE. *va.* To fasten a tin can to a dog's tail.
A nasalised form, I take it, of *shackle*.

SHAW. *sb.* A copse of natural wood.—*Dick.*
Old Norse *skôgr*, Dan. *skov*, a wood.

SHORPEN. *vn.* To shrivel by heat.
Old Norse *skorpna*, to shrivel or wrinkle, *skorpinn*, shrivelled, wrinkled, contracted.

SHUGGY. *sb.* A swing.
Clev. *shuggy-shaw*, Sco. *shuggie-shue*. Swiss *schuggen*, to jog, Wel. *ysgogi*, to wag, shake to and fro.

SIB. Akin.
Ang.-Sax. *sib*, alliance, relationship.

SICKER. *adj.* Sure.
And *siker* thu miht hider comen.—*Layamon.*
Dan. *sikker*, Swed. *säher*, Dut. *zeker*, sure.

SKAITCH. To beat with a stick.
Scutch, to strike with a thin switch, which is often done to snakes.—*Hunter.*
We have *scotched* the snake, not killed it.—*Macbeth.*

ADDITIONS AND CORRECTIONS.

SKREED. *sb.* A narrow strip.
The same as Eng. *shred*, by transposition for *sherd*. Old Norse *skarda*, minuere, incisuram facere, Dut. *schroode*, shred, Gael. *sgraid*, *sgrait*, shred, rag.

SKRIKE (O' DAY). *sb.* Break of day.
Dut. *krieken van den dag*, break of day. "The sudden appearance of a brilliant light is represented by the sound of an explosion, and a sparkling or broken glitter by the sound of crackling."—*Wedgwood*.

SMATCH. *sb.* A smack, slight savour.
Ang.-Sax. *smæccan*, Dut. *smaken*, Swed. *smaka*, to taste.

STARBENT. *sb.* The *juncus squarrosus*.
Old Norse *stargresi*, Dan., Swed. *stargräs*, coarse grass, carex.

SWARF. *vn.* To swoon.
Perhaps, taking a phonetic *r* from Ang.-Sax. *swefan*, to fall asleep, or into a state of insensibility.

TEUTLE. *vn.* To trifle.
Would seem to be a frequentative of *tute*, q.v., unless we may connect it with Wel. *twtial*, to loiter.

THUMMEL-POKE. *sb.* A cap for a sore finger.
Old Norse *thumall*, thumb.

TOUP. To overturn.
I have connected our word *coup*, to upset, with Goth. *kaupatjan*, to strike. The following table, intended to show the connections of our two words *coup* and *toup*, shows some other instances of this interchange of meaning :—

Cumb. *coup*, to fall, to upset. Cumb. *toup*, to fall.
Sansc. *kûp*, to fall. Sansc. *tup*, to strike.
Greek κυπτειν, to fall. Greek τυπτειν, to strike.
Goth. *kaupatjan*, to strike.
Lat. *cubare*, to lie down.
Gael. *cub*, to bend, crouch.

With the insertion of a liquid.
Wel. *cwympo*, to fall, to fell. Wel. *twmpio*, to fall, to drop.
  Wel. *twmpian*, to strike.
  Old Norse *tumba*, to fall.

With the prefix of s.
  Swed. *stupa*, to fall, to drop.

Trunlins. *sb.* Large or round coal.
Crav. *trunlin*, a large coal. Wel. *turn*, round, Ang.-Sax. *trendel*, a circle. Hence the idea is the same as that in "round' coal.

Worchit, Orchit. *sb.* Orchard.
Ang.-Sax. *weorteard*, *ortgeard*, Old Norse *jurtagardr*, a yard or inclosure for *worts* (vegetables).

Yerth, Yurth. *sb.* Earth.
Ang.-Sax. *earthe*, Old Norse *jörd*, Dan., Swed. *jord*. (*J* in the above Scand. words is sounded as our *y*.)

OBSOLETE AND OTHER TERMS FOUND IN THE NAMES OF PLACES.

BESIDES the words at present in use in the district, there are many obsolete terms now existing only in the names of places. Some of these, and notably those of Celtic origin, have probably been out of use for many centuries, while others still survive in kindred dialects, and it is therefore reasonable to suppose have not been long out of use in our own. The connection, then, between the nomenclature of the district and the living speech of the people is so intimate that a chapter on local etymology is an appropriate supplement to a glossary of the dialect.

The tendency among men to "call their lands after their own names" is strongly characteristic of the Teutonic race, and in England, as in Germany, a large proportion of the names of places are derived from the names of the men who founded them. In Cumberland a great part of these names date from the division of the soil among the followers of the Conqueror, of which Denton gives us many of the particulars. Thus Dovenby* was called from Dolfin,

---

* There is also a place called *Dolphenby*, near Penrith. And the name Dolfin is found on the Runic inscription discovered in Carlisle cathedral.

the son of Ailward; while Ailward the father gave his name to Ailwardby, perhaps the present *Allerby*. *Gamelby* took its name from Gamel, lord of Bothel—*Melmerby* and *Ousby* (formerly Ulfsby), from Melmor and Ulf, the sons of Halden or Halfden. *Ponsonby* has its name from one Ponson in the time of Stephen, and *Moresby* from one Maurice. *Allonby* is said to have been founded by Alan, second Lord of Allerdale. *Longwathby*, formerly called Long Waldeofby, may have been founded by Waldeof, son of Gospatrick, to whom Allerdale was given by Meschines. And *Boothby* may probably have been founded by Bueth, who also gave his name to *Bewcastle* (Buethcastle), in the same part of Cumberland. The post-fix in all these cases is the Danish *by*, a village.

Some of the above names, as Ulf, Gamel, Dolfin (Old Norse Dolgfinnr) are distinctively Scandinavian. Melmor, though in company with Danish names, seems to be itself more probably Celtic, and may, as was the name Nial, have been borrowed by the Northmen from the Celts. On a stone at Kirk Michael, in the Isle of Man, is an inscription in Scandinavian runes—"Mal Lumkum raised this cross to his foster-father Malmor." This, described by Worsaae as "a Norwegian inscription with purely Gaelic names," seems to give further evidence as to the adoption of this name by the Northmen. Bueth, who founded *Bewcastle*, and as I have suggested, *Boothby*, and Gil (Gisil), his son, who gave his name to *Gilsland*, seem to have been

Northmen, though the names themselves are not exclusively Scandinavian. So also Harold, probably contained in *Harraby*. *Ireby*, which corresponds with Iurby in the Isle of Man, may, as suggested by Worsaae of the latter, be from the Danish name Ivor.

Botchard, who founded Botchardby (now *Botcherby*) in the time of Rufus, was, we are told, a Fleming. *Roberby* (Robertby) and *Rickerby* (Richardby) are probably derived from Norman names, as also *Aglionby*, though the name here contained (Aglin or Agelin), is, like the two former, of Teutonic origin. *Maughonby* and *Tarraby* (formerly Terriby) contain names, Maughon and Terry, also probably Norman. Horn, found in *Hornsby*, is the name of one of the heroes of ancient romance.

The well-known Danish name Ketil is found in *Kelton*, formerly Ketilton. Perhaps also in *Keswick* (for Kelswick = Ketilswick). Among the Northmen themselves the name seems to have been frequently contracted into Kel; thus the names Thorketil and Hrossketil appears as Thorkel and Hrosskel. Another derivation is however practicable, as elsewhere stated. The Danish name Thurstan is found in *Thurstan's water*, the old name of Coniston lake, and in *Thrustonfield*. Brother also, in *Brother's water*, may be from Broder as a Scandinavian name, among others that of a Danish king of Dublin. Low, in *Loweswater*, is a name rather probably of Danish origin (O. N. *logi*, Dan. *lue*, Cumb. *low*, a flame. The Danish name Rafn (raven) is probably found in *Renwick*, formerly Ravenwick, and

Einar in *Ennerdale*. Also Ragnar in *Rannerdale*, Arni (eagle) in *Arnside*, Hamill in *Ambleside;* these three names, however, are not exclusively Scandinavian. Silver, in *Silverhow*, *Silverdale*, &c., may be from the name Sölvi, whence Sölvadalr in Iceland. And in *Honister crag* we may find the old Northern name Högni, whence Högnastadr in Iceland. *Honister* might be a contraction of Honistader, but more probably it may be the same as Högnasetter* in Shetland, where also Högni is found as a man's name in a charter of the 14th century. Olafur, at present one of the most common Christian names in Iceland, is found in *Ulverston* (Taylor, *Words and Places*), and possibly also may be that found in *Overwater*. Orm, a distinctively Scandinavian name (= A.S. *worm*, serpent), perhaps retained in our present name Oram, is found in *Ormathwaite*, *Ormesgill*, &c. So also Ulf (= A.S. *wulf*, wolf), in *Ulleswater*, *Ulpha*, &c.

The word *how* (O.N. *haugr*, a sepulchral mound), is found in many cases coupled with a Scandinavian name, we may presume that of the warrior whose grave it was. Thus we have *Gunner's how* from Gunnar, *Cornhow* from Korni (comp. Kornahaug in Norway), and *Loadenhow* from Lodinn (hirsutus); the last-named was opened in the last century, and the remains of the warrior found therein.

---

* This name occurs in the Roll of property belonging to the Monastery of St. Michael at Bergen, among other possessions in Shetland. "On Scottish and Irish Local Names," by Prof. Munch, in the *Memoires des Antiquaires du Nord*.

Butraldi (stumpy) is also an old Danish name found in *Buttereld keld*, near Bow Fell, in Cumberland.

Elter and Devoke, in *Elterwater* and *Devokewater*, are names probably Teutonic, but not especially Scandinavian. The latter may be the same name as that found in *Cumdevock*, so we have elsewhere in England Comb Basset, Comb Martin, &c., similarly compounded with names of men. *Glassonby* and *Lazonby* (formerly Leysingby) also contain names probably Teutonic—the latter perhaps the same as the present Germ. Lessing. Dagsa, in Dagsa's stone, now *Dalston*, seems to be a name of the early Saxon class.

Mr. Kemble (Saxons in England) has referred to the names indicative of family settlements in various parts of England. These names sometimes consist of a nominative plural in *as*, as in Hastingas, "the Hastings;" sometimes of a genitive plural in *a*, with *ham*, *tun*, &c., appended, as in Herelingatun, "the town of the Herelings," now Harlington. *Ing* in the above is the Ang.-Sax. *ing*, son, descendant, as in Billing, son or descendant of Bil or Bila. Names of this class, so common in some parts of England, are, as Kemble remarks, scarce north of the Humber. And in the sparsely occupied mountain districts of Cumberland and Westmorland especially, the names are those rather of individual occupancy than of family settlements. Kemble notes in Cumberland the following as being probably of this class, viz., Distingas as found in *Distington*, Hanesingas in *Hensingham*, Irthingas in *Irthington*, Weorcingas in *Workington*, Camcringas in

Cammerton, Hearingas in *Harrington*, and Rotingas in *Rottington*. From this list must be deducted *Irthington*, which takes its name from the river Irthing, on which it is situated, and not from a family settlement. And for Hearingas we must substitute Hæferingas, the name of *Harrington* having originally been Haverington. We may add to the list Aldingas as found in *Aldingham*, and Frisingas as found in *Frisington*. The three which I have added are all found by Kemble in other counties of England. We have also *Snellings*, which might represent an ancient Snellingas as a nominative plural "the Snellings." But it seems to me as probable that it may simply be from the name Snelling as a possessive, equivalent to "Snelling's property," like *Rawson's* and other names of places in the district. The above, it should be observed, are to some extent speculative; it is only in cases where we have the Anglo-Saxon form of the word as preserved in charters or elsewhere that anything like certainty is to be attained. Mr. Kemble has two lists, the former consisting of names thus historically tested; and the latter, among which are the Cumberland examples, of names which seem formed in an analogous way.

This tendency to call their lands after their own names, perhaps to some extent a sign of want of imagination, seems to have been less common among the Celtic races; I only know of three names in Cumberland which seem to be thus formed; *Carlisle*, the capital, which may be probably called from its founder Luol; *Cardurnock*, formerly Caerdronack, in which there seems a probable Celtic name, Gael. *dornach*, champion, pugilist, or *druinneach*, a druid; and *Gilgarron*, which, as elsewhere noted, is probably from the name of a Scoto-Irish saint. The name of *Dunmail raise* (properly Dumnail raise), which there does not seem any reason to doubt, is from a British king of Cumberland, would seem—*raise* being a characteristic Scandinavian word—to have been given by the Northmen.

On the whole, then, I take it that the names of ancient proprietors in the district, a decided preponderance of which are unquestionably Scandinavian, will be found to be in accordance with the distribution of the words of the dialect in the next chapter.

In the following list of obsolete and other words found in the names of places I have included Westmorland and that part of Lancashire north of the sands, as being subject generally to the same conditions as Cumberland, so far as regards the character of their local names.

ARK. As in *Pavey ark, Mickle ark, Arkholme.*
> Perhaps from Ang.-Sax. *hearg*, Old Norse *hörgr*, Old High Germ. *haruc*, a heathen altar or place of worship. In provincial Norse *horg* is a dome-shaped hill (*Aasen*), which might be simply the meaning in the case of mountains, as *Pavey ark*. Still, if *Pavey* be, as seems rather probable, from O.N. *pauft*, a lurking fiend according to Cleasby, a dark and mysterious corner according to Haldorsen, it would seem to imply something more in accordance with the former meaning. The ending *ergh* in *Mansergh* and *Sizergh*, would seem to be from the above *hearg*, an altar, and might tempt to a mythological speculation, as suggesting Mannus and his son Tiw (High Germ. *Zio*), the mythic ancestors of the Teutons, if we could account for a High Germ. form like Zio, as the name of a deity.

BLEN. Wel. *blaen*, top, summit, extremity.
Blencogo and *Blencow* may be from Wel. *goch*, *coch*, red. Or from *coeg*, empty, perhaps in the sense of void of wood. *Blindcrake* (formerly Blencreye) is probably from *craig*, rock. *Blencathra*, the ancient name of *Saddleback*, may be, I think, from Wel. *cader*, Gael. *cathair*, seat or chair, in allusion to the peculiar form of its summit. Hence of meaning somewhat analogous to that of its other name *Saddleback*. From a similar origin James (*Welsh Names of Places*) derives the name of Cader Idris, on one of the rocks of which there is, he says, an excavation like a chair.

BLITTER. In *Blitterlees*, near Silloth.
Comp. *blittert*, torn by winds, Germ. *blättern*, to come off in scales. This is very suitable for the locality in question, a range of sand-hills constantly stripped or peeled by the wind.

BOTEL. BOL. Ang.-Sax. *botel*, a house, dwelling.
Hence probably *Bothel* and *Bootle*. The word in the Scandinavian tongues is contracted into *ból*, whence probably *Bowscale* (*scale*, a wooden hut) and *Bowness*, formerly Bolness (*ness*, a promontory).

BREAK. As in *Mellbreak*.
Old Norse *brekka*, a slope, a gentle acclivity. "As a law-term in Iceland the hill where public meetings where held and laws promulgated" (*Cleasby*). Common in names of places in Norway and Iceland.

CAER. Wel. *caer*, fortified place, city.
Respecting *Carlisle* and *Cardurnock* see p. 194. *Caer Mote*, a hill on which are the remains of entrenchments, is evidently from the above and *mote*, a little hill. Jamieson derives *mote* from Ang.-Sax., Old Norse *môt*, conventus hominum, a meeting, "applied to a little hill, because anciently conventions were held on eminences." But Chevallet (*Origine et formation de la langue francaise*) refers French *motte*, an eminence, to a Celtic source, Sco., Ir. *mota*, a hill, the correctness of which seems very doubtful.

CAM. Ang.-Sax. *camb*, Old Norse *kambr*, a crest, ridge.
Frequent in local names in Iceland, "of hills rising like a crest" (*Cleasby*). Hence *Cam Fell*, *Catsty cam*, &c.

CARROCK. Wel. *careg*, a rock.
Hence *Carrock Fell*, *Castle Carrock*, &c.

COVE. Ang.-Sax. *cofa*, a cove, recess.
Hence *Red cove* and *Kepple cove* on Helvellyn, the latter perhaps figuratively from Ang.-Sax. *cepla*, a basket.

CRAG. Gael. *creag*, Wel. *careg*, a rock.
I introduce this as the only Celtic word applied in names of places which, if not exactly current, is at least, I think, understood in the dialect. *Thrang crag*, near Elterwater, is the site of an extensive slate-quarry, and probably derives its name from this source, *thrang* meaning busy, crowded.

DUN. Gael., Corn. *dun*, a hill.
Dundraw seems probably from the above and Wel. *derw*, oaks.

DURRAN. In *Durran hill*, near Carlisle.
Perhaps from Wel. *duryn*, beak, snout, whence Davies derives *Durn*, "a projecting point or ledge of land," in Lancashire.

EARTH. Old Norse *jörd*, earth, used also in the sense of a farm or estate. Hence may be *Hawks earth*, Haukr, hawk, being a Scandinavian proper name.

EY. Ang.-Sax. *eah*, an eye, whence figuratively an island. Sw. *ö*. Hence *Walney* and *Fouldrey* (Icel. *foldir*, fields, the local name of a grassy oasis in West Iceland). (The small islands on the lakes are called *holms*.) Some isolated hills in Cumberland seem to be formed from the above *ey*, in a sense equivalent to that of island, e.g. *Moutay* and *Binsey*.

FORCE. A water-fall. See *ant*, p. 46.
Airey force might be from Wel. *eirig*, splendid, whence the Scotch and Lanc. *eery*. But more probably, I think, from Wel. *eirwi*, a water-fall, to which has been added the Scand. *force*. *Scale force* might be from Old Norse *skâl*, bowl, cavity, in reference to the hollow in which its waters are received. But more probably I think—the shoot being high, and the volume of water small—from *scale*, to disperse, separate, in a sense somewhat akin to that of the *Staubbach*, "dust-fall," in Switzerland.

FORTH. As in *Gosforth, Galeforth*.
Old Norse *forath*. Icel. *forœthi*, a pit, abyss, in modern use a fen or morass, which would seem the most probable meaning in *Gosforth*, "goose fen."

GALE. Old Norse *geil* (pron. *gale*), a narrow lane or glen. In Iceland the straight road leading to a farm. "Every Icelandic homestead was approached by a straight road *(geil)*"—Dasent, *Bnt. Njal.* Obsolete in the dialect, but common in names of places.

GLEN. Wel. *glyn*, Corn. *glen*, valley, glen.
Unknown in the dialect, but found in names of places. *Glencoin*, perhaps from W. *cogan*, bowl. *Glenridding*, perhaps from

W. *rhedyn*, fern. If the station *Amboglanna* be, as seems to be the opinion of the best authorities, the present Burdoswald, the name may be taken to be from *ambo*, water, river, and the above *glen*, a valley, appropriate to the situation of the station, looking down upon the Irthing flowing in a deep glen below.

HALL. In *Hall Fell, Hawl gill.*
Old Norse *hallr*, a slope, hill; also a boulder. Hall, as a man's name common among the Northmen, derived by Cleasby from *hallr*, a boulder, may intermix.

HAMMER. Old Norse *hamarr*, a crag standing out like an anvil. *Hammer scar*, Grasmere. Common in local names in Norway, as *Hammer fell*, &c.

HEST. Old Norse *hestr*, Dan. *hest*, horse.
Hest Fell in Cumberland compares with *Hesta Fell* in Iceland, "a horse-shaped crag."—*Cleasby*. There is also a *Hesten Fell* (*the* horse fell) in Norway. *Hesket* may be *hest-cote*, a shed or shelter for horses; one place of that name is in the midst of Inglewood forest. We have also *Hestholm* (*holms*, pasture land by a river).

HOPE, OP. As in *Hope, Hartsop, Greenup*.
Sco. *hope*, a slanting hollow between two hills; also a small bay. The latter seems the original sense, Old Norse *hôp*, a small land-locked bay or inlet. Found in local names in Iceland, as *Vestrhôp*.

JAW. Old Norse *gja*, a rift or chasm.
Sco. *geow*. Hence the *Jaws* of Borrodale?

KIL. Gael. Ir. *cil*, a church.
From this origin I take to be *Gilcrux* and *Gilgarron* in Cumberland, and not from *gill*, a ravine, which never occurs as a prefix. *Gillcrux* (pron. Gillcroose) seems to be from Welsh *crwys*, cross, "the church of the cross." *Gillgarron* is no doubt the same as Kilgarran in Pembrokeshire, Kilkerran in Ayrshire and Connemora, Kilkiaran in Islay, from St. Ciarran, the apostle of the Scotto-Irish.* Then we have also *Culgaith*, another form of the same, the latter part of the word being perhaps Wel. *gaith*, open.

KIRROCK, KIRK. A circle of stones of the kind generally known as druidical. It would seem evident that the *kirrock* was associated with the idea of sacredness. While in some cases we find one of these circles surrounded by graves; in other cases we have the individual grave-mound encompassed

---

* Taylor, *Words and Places*. Bannister, *Cornish Names*.

by its own circle of stones, by which it would seem that the odour of sanctity was supposed to be communicated to it—thus bringing, as it were, the church-yard to the grave. Hence, I presume, the origin of *Kirkbarrow*. *Kirkstone Pass* may, I think, derive its name from a *kirrock* on the summit, which was cut through in making the road across it, rather than from any imaginary resemblance of its rocks to a church. In a previous work (*Northmen in Cumberland and Westmorland*) I suggested that this word *kirrock* or *kirk* might be the original of our *kirk* or *church*,* the ordinary derivation of which from the Greek is not satisfactorily accounted for. On this subject a number of communications appeared some time ago in the *Times* and the *Guardian*, and among others one from Prof. Max Müller, who, admitting the difficulty with respect to the ordinary derivation, held that no less difficulty attended the one in question, and observed that we ought as a first step to know the origin of the Cumberland word. It seems highly probable that the meaning is simply *circle*, and that the word is the same as the Lat. *circus* (Wel. *cwr*, circle, *cwrc*, curvature, Gael. *car*, a bend, a turn, Ang.-Sax. *cerran*, *cirran*, to bend, turn, *cyr*, a bend, a turn). A word similarly formed from the same root would seem to be found in the *churka* or rotatory gin of India. But if *Cat kirk* (in Westmorland) be, as seems probable, like the many *Cat stones* in Scotland, from Celtic *cad*, *cat*, war, battle, in the supposition of the graves of those who fell in some battle, it would be rather in favour of a Celtic origin for the word. I would only observe further that from the parallel form *cal* or *kil* (Wel. *call*, what goes or turns round, Wel. *cylch*, circle, Bret. *kilia*, to turn, *kelch*, circle), might in a similar sense be derived the ancient Celtic word *kil* for a church in Scotland and Ireland, usually presumed to be the same as Lat. *cella*, Eng. *cell*.

KNIPE. Old Norse *gnipa*, a sharp peak.

Hence *Knipe scar*. *Great Knipe* and *Little Knipe* in Westmorland. Comp. *Knipenborg* in Norway.

KNOCK. Wel. *cnwc*, bunch, knot. Dut. *knoke*, knot.

Hence *Knock pike* near Appleby, &c.

KNOT. Old Norse *knutr*, Dan. *knud*, a knot, excrescence. *Hardknot* compares with *Hartenuten* (the hard knot), a mountain in Norway. *School knot*, in Westmorland) may be from Skúli, a Scandinavian proper name (signifying protector).

LAN. Wel. *llan*, church.

The only name in which this word seems to occur is *Lanercost*. Probably the oldest record in which the name is found is the

---

* This idea I since find to have been previously broached by Lloyd in Baxter's *Glossarium Antiquitatum Britannicarum*.

Runic inscription on a rock near Bewcastle, whereon it appears, according to the rendering of the Rev. J. Maughon, as Llanerkasta. "Can the name denote," he adds, "the church over the cyst?" Perhaps rather from the name of some Saint.

LATTER. In *Latterbarrow, Whinlatter, Latrigg*?
The O.N. *látr* signifies a place where animals lay their young. Eng. *litter*. *Látrbjarg*, in Iceland, might then compare with our *Latterbarrow*. The Gael. *leitir* signifies the side of a hill, but a Celtic origin would hardly, as it seems to me, be consistent with the compounds in which our word occurs.

LUND. Old Norse *lundr*, Dan., Sw. *lund*, a grove, especially a sacred grove. Hence *Hoff lund*, in Westm., O.N. *hof*, a temple. Cleasby refers to this origin *Gilsland*, in Cumb., but it is by no means clear that it is from this origin, and not from *land*, terra.

MAINS. As in the *Mains*, near Carlisle. Also *Redmain* and *Dalemain*? Sco. *mains*, the farm attached to the mansion on an estate, formerly held by the proprietor himself. Derived by Skene from Fr. *domaine*. Or possibly, from Fr. *mener*, Old Fr. *mainer*, to manage, from *main*, the hand, as we speak of having land in one's "own hand."

MELL, MEAL. Old Norse *melr*, a kind of bent grass growing on sandy soil, hence a sandhill covered with such grass. This word has been superseded in the dialect by the Celtic *bent*, but appears to be found in several names of places, as *Eskmeals, Meala* near Allonby, both places answering to the above description, and *Meal rigg*, "a narrow strip of fertile land surrounded by mosses" (*Hutchinson*), probably also in *Mealy syke*. "The *Meales*, the name of sand-banks at Hunstanton" (*Norfolk Words*, by A. Gurney, Phil. Soc.) *Mell Fell*, which corresponds with *Mel Fel* in Norway, might perhaps be assigned to this origin rather than the word previously mentioned. Common in local names in Iceland, as *Melar*, perhaps, seeing that *r* final is mute in English, the same word as our *Meala* (plur. sandbanks).

MERE. Ang.-Sax. *mere*, a lake.
Hence *Windermere, Buttermere, Thirlemere* (probably from its long and narrow shape, A.S. *thirlian*, to drill, to bore).

MIRE. Old Norse *myrr*, Icel. *myri*, a bog.
Hence *Sour mire* (see *sour*), *Mire house, Cardew mire*. The O.N. *kjarr-mýrr* signifies a marsh grown with brush-wood. But *dew* in Cardew seems rather probably to be from O.N. *dý*, also signifying a marsh or bog, and it would rather seem as if

mire had been added as a later word, when the meaning of *dew* came to be forgotten. Found in many names of places in Norway, as *Rossemyr*, "horse mire."

MAN. As in the *Old Man* at Coniston.
Dr. Whittaker makes this a corruption of the Celt. *alt maen*, lofty hill. There is also a mountain in Appenzell called *Alt Mann*, which Obermüller similarly ascribes to a Celtic origin. It seems to me, however, very uncertain whether the name may not be similar to that of the *Mönch*, the *Jungfrau*, &c.

NAB. Ang.-Sax. *cnæp*, Old Norse *knappr*, a knob.
Hence *Nab scar*, Rydale, and the *Knab* on Windermere. Comp. *Knaben* (*the* Knab, in Norway).

NESS. Ang.-Sax. *næs*, Old Norse *nes*, a promontory.
Hence *Bowness*, formerly Bolness, O.N. *bol*, a dwelling, and *Skinburness*, perhaps from Skinnabiorn, the name of a Northman in the Landnamabók of Iceland.

ODD. As in *Hodbarrow point*.
Would seem to be most probable from Old Norse *oddi*, N. Fris. *odd*, a point or tongue of land. Peacock has *odd*, a small point of land, a promontory, as a word in use in Lonsdale.

ORREST. Ang.-Sax. *orrest*, Old Norse *orrosta*, a battle.
Hence seem to be *High orrest*, *Near orrest*, and *Orrest head*, near Windermere, marking, it would seem, the various points of some considerable fight.

OUSE. In *Ouse bridge*, at the outlet of Derwentwater.
Old Norse *óss*, out-let of a river or lake.

PEN. Wel., Corn. *pen*, end, top, summit.
Hence the *Pen* in Duddon valley. *Penruddock* seems probably to be from W. *rhwdog*, red. *Penrith* has also been explained as "red hill." Or one might possibly think of Corn. *ryth*, open, plain, flourishing, taking *Penrith*, beyond which lay Inglewood forest, as the "end of the plain or open country." Or again, we might think of Gael. *rath*, circle, in reference to the remarkable circle called King Arthur's round table. On the whole, however, the first suggestion is perhaps the most probable.

RAY or WRAY. Old Norse *vrå*, Dan. *vraa*, a corner.
The word *wros*, in the sense of corners, occurs in the romance of Havelock the Dane. Hence *Wray*, on the Lancaster and Carlisle Railway, *Wray*, on Windermere, *Birkwray* (*birk*, birch), *Elleray* (*eller*, alder), *Dockwray* (O.N. *dökkr*, dark?), &c.

S

Ross. As in *Rosley, Rosthwaite*, &c.
: Old Norse *hross*, horse. At *Rosley* is held the principal horse fair in Cumberland, whence perhaps the name (*ley*, pasture, plain).

SCALE. Old Norse *skali*, a wooden hut, corresponding with Sco. *shiel*. Hence probably *Scaleby* (*by*, a village), *Seascale*, near the sea-shore, *Lonscale*, O.N. *laun*, Eng. *lone*, &c.

SCARTH. Old Norse *fjall-skard*, a gap in a mountain.
: Hence *Scarf-gap*, properly Scarth gap, a pass in the Lake district (*th* and *f* interchanging as in other cases previously noted). Also *Balder scarth*, in Westmorland, from Balder as a Teutonic name. Comp. *Skarv Fell*, in Norway, and *Vikarskard, Evarskard*,, &c., in Iceland, compounded, like *Balderscarth*, with proper names.

SCAW. Old Norse *skagi*, a promontory.
: Hence *Sca Fell*, and *Scaw*, a hill behind Red pike. Comp. *Skaw*, a promontory on the Isle of Unst. And *Skagen*, "*the* Scaw," at the northern extremity of Jutland.

SCRAT, SCRATCH. Old Norse *skratti*, a goblin or evil spirit, whence our "old Scratch." Hence probably *Skratta Fell*, in Iceland. And W. Grimm (*Held. Sag.*) observes that in the Fornm. Sög. mention is made of a rock called *Skratta skar*, "geniorum scopulus." From a like origin might be *Scratch meal scar*, in Cumberland, taking *meal* to be from the O.N. *mella*, which has the meaning both of a chasm and also of a female spirit or goblin, in either of which senses the word would seem applicable.

SEAT. Swed. *sät*, seat, residence. Or perhaps the Old Norse *sætur*, a summer pasture. Hence *Seatollar*, in Borrowdale, perhaps from the Scand. name Olvar, *Seatallan*, from the name Allan, &c. Also perhaps *Honister*, see p. 192.

SIDE. As in *Ambleside, Ormside, Arnside*.
: The meaning in the above, which all seem compounded with the names of men (Hamall or Amal, Orm, Arn or Arni) would seem to be that of a seat or location, perhaps on the hill side.

SOUD. Old Norse *saudr*, a sheep.
: *Souter fell* may perhaps be the same as *Sauda fell*, in Iceland, signifying "sheep fell." We have also *Souty how, how*, a hill.

SOUR. Old Norse *saur*, dung of cattle. Crav. *saur*, urine from the cow-house, &c. Obsolete in our dialect, but found in the names of places, as *Sour mire*, descriptive of a puddle of the sort often found around a farm. *Sowerby* might be from the same origin, but as we find *Saur* as the surname of a Northman in the Landnamabok, and *Saurbær* (*bær=by*) as the name of a place, it might be, like most of the other names in *by*, from the name of a man.

STAPLE. Dut., Swed. *stapel*, a pile, a heap, whence, in the sense of a collection of things for sale, a market. *Ainstable* may be from Agin or Ain, a Teutonic proper name (*Förstemann*, *Altd. Namb.*).

STICKLE. Ang.-Sax. *sticel*, Old Norse *stikill*, a sharp point or peak. Hence the two pikes of Langdale, *Harrison stickle* and *Pike o' stickle*.

STOCK. As in *Greystock*, *Linstock*.
Ang.-Sax. *stoc*, Old Norse *stokkr*, a stock. The meaning may be that of a place protected by a stockade, corresponding with Celt. *pil*. There is near Stockport, in Lancashire, an ancient British encampment called the *Peel*, whence Stockport (*stock=* Celt. *pil*), may take its name.

STRAND. Old Norse *strönd*, Dan., Swed. *strand*, shore, strand. Hence the *Strands* on Wastwater. Common on the lakes and fjords of Norway.

STRATH. Gael. *strath*, a valley.
Langstreth, a dale diverging from Borrowdale, seems to be the only name in the district in which this Celtic term is preserved.

THORP. Ang.-Sax. *thorpe*, Old Norse *thorp*, Dan. *torp*, Germ. *dorf*, a village, a collection of houses. Scarcely known in Cumberland, it becomes more frequent as we advance into Westmorland, till in Yorks. and Linc. it becomes very common. Comp. *Hackthorp*, in Westm., with *Hakantorp*, in Sweden.

THWAITE. Old Dan. *thveit*, *thvet*, " an isolated piece of ground."—*Worsaae*. Fris. *tved*, a place cleared of wood, also a boundary between two fields, Low Germ. *twyte*, a narrow lane. I take the meaning in our district to be that of a place cleared of wood, A.S. *thwitan*, to cut. Common in the southern part of Norway, where we have *Braathveit*, *Birkethveit*, *Esketvet*, *Brattethveit*, corresponding with our *Braithwaite*, *Birthwaite*, *Ashthwaite*, *Branthwaite* (O.N. *brattr*, Cumb. *brant*, steep). *Ormathwaite* is from the Dan. name Orm. *Armthwaite*, formerly Ermonthwaite, from the ancient German name Ermin or Armin (the Arminius of Tacitus). *Bassenthwaite* can hardly be, as generally supposed, from the fish called *bass* found in the lake. It may rather, like *Bassingham* and *Bassingthorpe*, in Linc., be from a proper name. Not however, I think, from Dassingas as the name of a mark or family clan, to which Kemble places the above, but from Bassing (son of Bass), as an individual name. *Lownthwaite* is probably from *loun*, calm, in opposition to its neighbour Windy hill. *Satterthwaite* might be from Sæter, as the name of a deity (whence Saturday). But perhaps more probably from Satter (Ang.-Sax. *sætere*, seducer?), still in existence as a family name. *Finsthwaite* also is probably from *Finn* as a man's name; there are several Northmen bearing this name in the Landnamabok. *Legberthwaite* seems possibly to contain a reference to the *lögberg*, rock of law, where the legislative court was held.

WATER. There seems a certain amount of probability that *water*, in the names of our lakes, is due to the Old Norse *vatn*, which is the usual word for a lake in Iceland, and (in its modern form *vand*) in Norway. And that it has been changed into its present form by the influence of the current speech. The names of lakes in the north of Scotland ending in *vat* are supposed by Worsaae to be from the above origin. And there is one *Watten lochs*, in Caithness (which seems to have escaped his notice), wherein the original form is preserved. *Watendlath*, formerly *Watenlath*, on a small sheet of water above Borrowdale, may also be from the same origin, "the barn by the water" (*lath*, a barn). Some of our names in *water* are conjoined with a Scand. name, as *Ullswater* (Ulf's water), *Thurstan's water*, perhaps also *Brothers water*, *Lowes water*, *Leathes water*, and *Skeggles water*. Also possibly *Over water*, from the Norse name Olver, or the present Icel. Olafur. Compare with these *Gisla vatn*, *Hiardar vatn*, *Reidar vatn*, &c., in the Landnamabók of Iceland.

WICK or WYKE. Old Norse *vik*, Dan. *vig*, a bay.
Hence *Blowick*, "blue bay," *Sandwick*, &c. I have suggested, p. 191, that *Keswick* may be from the Dan. name Ketill. Comparing another place, *Kelswick*, in Cumb., with *Kjolsvik* and *Kjelsvik*, in Norway, another derivation may seem open, from *keld* or *kel*, a fountain, or O.N. *kjöll*, a boat or barge, the latter perhaps the more probable.

WITH. Old Norse *vidr*, Dan., Sw. *ved*, a wood.
As the ending of names of places, *with* in the north of England shows the Scand. form as compared with Saxon *wood* in the south. Thus *Skirwith*, in Cumb., is the equivalent of *Sherwood* in the south, probably from A.S. *scěran*, O.N. *skera*, to cut. *Colwith*, near Elterwater, seems to be from O.N. *kolvidr*, "coal wood," *i.e.*, wood for making charcoal. *Skipwith*, in Yorks., is "ship-wood," wood suitable for building ships. *Blawith*, near Coniston, signifies black or dark wood. (Comp. Blaskog, "dark wood," in Iceland.)

River-Names of the District.

In this district, as elsewhere generally throughout England, we find that while the names of towns and villages, and most of the terms descriptive of the features of the soil, are Saxon or Scandinavian, the rivers still retain their original Celtic names. Indeed the same remark applies generally to the whole of Europe, the river-names of which, the more that they are investigated, show more clearly the marks of a common origin. There may be, as is the case in Germany, in many instances the suffix of a Teutonic word for a river to the original name. And in a few cases in our district there is reason to believe that the whole of the word is of Teutonic origin.

The river-names of the district may, as to their form, be classed generally under three heads—

1st—Those that contain simply the primitive from which they are derived, as the *Bure*, the *Esk*, the *Vent*, the *Gelt*, the *Ive*.

2nd Those which have the ending *a* affixed, as the *Rotha*, the *Greta*, the *Bratha*. There is reason to believe that this is the Old Norse *â*, a river, corresponding with the Old High Germ. *aha*, Germ. *ach* and *au*, which is similarly affixed to many river-names of Celtic origin in Germany, as the *Donau*,

Rodau, Rodach, &c. The ending *er* in many northern river-names may be only the same word, as from the mute pronunciation of *r* final in English there is no difference in sound between *Rotha* and *Rother, Calda* and *Calder.*

3rd—Those which contain the ending *en,* as the *Eden,* the *Ellen,* the *Marron.* This has been by various writers supposed to be a contraction of the Celtic *avon,* Manx *aon,* river. In cases where the former part of the word is an adjective or contains an epithet, this is in all probability the case. Thus the *Carron* (ant. Corabona), is no doubt *cor-avon,* a small stream. But when the former part of the word is itself a Celtic appellative, as in the Eden (Obs. Gael. *ad,* Sansc. *ud,* water), I think that this termination is simply formative. Now *avon* itself is not a primitive form; the primitive form is *av* or *ab* (Obs. Gael. *abh,* Sansc. *ab, ap,* water), and *en* is added as a phonetic termination, to round off, as we might say, the word. And just in the same way that Obs. Gael. *abh* forms Avon, so, I take it, does Obs. Gael. *ad* form *Eden.*

Then there are a few cases of endings in *el* and *et,* as in *Petterill* and the *Lyvennet*; these may perhaps be diminutives.

I have divided the following names into two classes —those which contain simply an appellative, or a word signifying water, a river; and those which contain an epithet referring to some special quality, as, for instance, the character of its course, or the clearness of its waters.

To those who have traversed the Lake district, and drunk from its limpid streams, the number of names expressive of clearness or transparency will not be a matter of surprise.

APPELLATIVES.

IVE. Obs. Gael. *abh*, Sansc. *ab, ap*, water.
: The above contains the simple form whence *Avon* and *Evan* in Eng. and Sco., *Ebro* (ant. Iberus), in Spain, and *Ebr(ach)* in Germany.

EHEN. Wel. *avon*, Manx *aon*, river, from the above root *ab*. Comp. *Aune* and *Inney*, Engl., *Ihna* and *Inn* (Aenus of Tacitus) in Germany.

ESK. Wel. *wysg*, Ir. *uisg*, Gael. *uisge*, water.
: Comp. *Exe, Ash, Usk* in Eng. and Wales, *Esque* in France, *Axe, Ahse*, and *Ischl* (ant. Iscala) in Germany.

WIZA. Probably the same word as the last, with the ending *a*, a river (*Wisga*), by contr. *Wiza*). The *Weissach* in Germany (ant. Wizaha), is referred by Förstemann to *wiz*, white. It may, however, contain the same Celtic word as ours, adapted to a meaning by the Germans.

EDEN. Obs. Gael. *adh*, Sans. *ud*, water, Wel. *eddain*, to flow, glide.

BURE. Gael. *bior*, water, Bret. *bera*, to flow.
: Comp. *Bere*, Dorset—*Barrow*, Ireland—*Bar, Bere*, France—*Behr*, Germany, &c.

LEVEN, LINE, LUNE. Wel. *llion*, a stream, *llifo*, to flow, Obs. Gael. *lu*, water, Sansc. *li*, to be liquid. Comp. *Lion*, Scot.

LYVENNET. The same as the above, with *et*, perhaps a diminutive—*Lyvennet* = the little Leven.

LEATHE. Wel. *lleithio*, to moisten, *llyddo*, to pour, Gael. *lith*, a pool, Goth. *leithus*, Ang.-Sax. *lidh*, liquor. Comp. *Lid*, Engl.—*Leitha*, Germ.—*Lidden*, Engl., *Leithan*, Scotl.

LIDDLE. The same as the above, with *el*, perhaps a diminutive.

GOWAN. Wel. *gover, guuer*, Corn. *gover, gower*, a brook.
: *Gowan* seems to be the same word as *gower*, with an alternative ending. Comp. *Gouw*, Holland, and *Gowin(aha)*, the old name of the Jahnbach in Germany.

COCKER, COCKLEY BECK. Gael. *caochan*, a small stream (a primitive *caoch* may be implied). Comp. *Cock beck* in Yorks.—*Coc-brôc* (Cod. Dip.)—*Coquet*, Northd.—*Kuchelbach*, Germany.

STOCK. The small stream which forms Stockgill-force. The word, as it stands, has no connection with any other river-name, and there seems no doubt that the *t* is intrusive, and that the word should be properly *Sock*, corresponding with the *Soch* in Wales, *Suck* in Ireland, the *Sow* in Engl., and the *Save* or *Sou* in Germany. The origin is then to be found in Sansc. *sava*, water, *su*, liquere, Wel. *sug*, moisture, Gael. *sugh*, moisture, also a wave, billow. There is a tendency in Teutonic speech to strengthen such Celtic words by the introduction of *t*—e.g., Wel. *syth*,* Ang.-Sax. *stith*, firm, stiff, Ir. *sruamh*, O.N. *straumr*, Germ. *strom*, Eng. *stream*. The same is found also in the Romance language, as Gael. *sil*, Lat. *stillare*, to drop, distill. Comp. also Wel. *seren*,, Lat. *(a)strum*, Ang.-Sax. *steorra*, Eng. *star*. It is to this principle we owe *Stour* as a river-name in England, *Streu*, *Stry*, in Germany, and *Stura* in Italy ; it is the same as the Bret. *ster*, a river, from Sansc. *sru*, to flow, with a phonetic *t*. Hence also the classical Danastris, the *Dniester*, and the Ister, which latter, though Gr.mm's explanation is different, I take to be simply the word *ster*, a river ; with, as in a(strum), a phonetic initial.

BELA. Ir. *biol*, *buol*, water.
Comp. the *Boyle*, Ireland, of which, according to O'Brien, the Irish form is *Buol*. Also the *Peel*, Isle of Man.

SARK. Seems to be from the primitive form found in Sans. *sru*, to flow, whence Sansc. *srota*, Ir. *sruth*, a river. Comp. *Soar*, England—*Serre*, France—*Saar*, Germany. The ending may be the Obs. Gael. *oich*, river.

DACRE. Wel. *daigr*, a drop, Gael. *deoch*, drink.
In the Old Norce *deigr*, moist, Icel. *daugg*, rain, Eng. *dew*, a similar sense is found, and we may thus perhaps get the sense of water. The *Docker*, in Lanc., is the only similar name I find, and that may perhaps be from a different origin, Gael. *doich*, rapid. On the whole, this seems a word about which there may be some doubt as to whether the place Dacre is named from the river, or *vice versâ*.

SPRENT. Old Norse *spretta*, to sprinkle, Cumb. *sprint*, *sprent*. This is one of the few names which seems to be of Teutonic origin.

---

* "It seems that the Celtic nations were unable to pronounce an initial *s* before a consonant, or, at least, that they disliked it."—*Science of Language*. The Bret. seems to some extent an exception.

CRAKE. "Cryke of watyr, scatera."—*Pr. Prv.*
Dut. *kreke*, a crooked water-course, Old Norse *krakja*, to wind, to turn. The word then might either mean simply a stream, which is one of the senses of Eng. *creek;* or it might mean a winding stream. In any case, this word seems to be, like the last, of Teutonic origin. Davies' derivation from Wel. *crec*, a sharp noise *(Races of Lancashire)* does not seem to me suitable.

PETTERILL. The word contained herein seems to be *Pedder* or *Petter*, as in the *Pedder*, Somers.—*Pedr(ede)*, Cod. Dip., now the Parret, and the *Pader* (ant. Patra), in Germany. The Wel. *pyddu*, to run or spread out, *pydew*, well, spring, are the only suitable words that I find. The A.S. *pidele*, a thin stream, whence *Piddle* as the name of several small streams *(Kemble, Cod. Dip.)*, may be allied.

IRK (in Lancashire). Irish *earc*, water.
There are in Wales many streams with the name of *Jurch*, which Lhuyd derives from Wel. *iwrch*, a roebuck, from their bounding along the hill side. But I think the above in every way preferable.

DUDDON. Wel. *diod*, drink, Ir. and Obs. Gael. *dothar*, water, with which we may perhaps connect Lap. *dadno*, river. Comp. the *Dude* in Germany, and the *Dodder* in Ireland.

NENT. Wel. *nant*, *nannau*, a brook, Gael. *nigh*, to bathe, to wash. Comp. *Nen*, Northampton—*Nenagh*, Ireland —*Nenny*, France.

MITE. The Wel. *mwydo*, to soak, to moisten, Sansc. *miditas*, fluid, Lat. *madidus*, O. N. *móda*, a river, seem sufficiently to set forth the sense of water as contained in the above.

MINT. I am rather inclined to take this to be the same word as above *(Mite)*, taking the nasal. Or otherwise we may refer to the Gael. *min*, soft, gentle, small.

RIBBLE. "The name of this well-known river," says Mr. Davies, "has much perplexed antiquarian philologists." There is a river in Denmark called the *Ribe;* and *Ribe* and *Ribble* seem evidently to correspond with Lat. *rivus* and *rivulus*. It would seem probable that *rivus*, which contains simply the root *ri*, to flow (Sansc. *ri*, Gr. ρεω), with an euphonic rounding (as Cumb. *div* for *dee*), may have had its representatives in the Celtic tongues.

ELLEN. This contains the primitive root *al* or *il*, to move, to go, whence are formed Gael. *ald* or *alt* (older form *aled)*, and the Old Norse *elfa*, Dan. *elv*, a river. Comp. the *Ilo*, *Allow*, England—*Ille*, *Éllé*, in France—*Alle*, Germany—*Alne*, *Allan*, *Ilen*, in Great Britain—*Aulne*, in France, &c.

T

THE FOLLOWING I TAKE TO BE DERIVED FROM THE
CLEARNESS OF THEIR WATERS.

LIZA. Wel. *llwys*, clear, pure, Gael. *las*, to shine, cognate with Lat. *luceo*, &c. Comp. *Lez*, in France—*Lesse*, in Belgium—*Ljusne*, in Sweden, &c.

BRATHA. Ir. and Obs. Gael. *breath*, clear, pure. Comp. *Broth(ock)*, in Scotland—*Brett(ach)*, in Germany, &c.

LOWTHER. Wel. *glawdd*, brightness, lustre, *gloewder*, clearness. Comp. *Lauder*, in Scotland—*Lauter*, in France.

VENT. Old Celt. *vind*, Wel. *gwyn*, Germ. *fionn*, Ir. *finn*, clear, pure. Comp. *Wente*, in Yorkshire—*Finn*, in Ireland—*Finnan*, in Scotland.

WINSTER. The origin of this name is very uncertain. It might be from *vind*, as above, and Bret. *ster*, a river, whence the *Alster* in Denmark, *Elster* in Germany, and probably the ancient *Cestrus, Danastris*, and *Ister*. There is a river in Norway called the *Vinstra*, which may be the same word. The objection to that is that there is no analogous name, so far as I am able to make out, in England. It might be (though that would be contrary to the general rule) from the place *Winster*, upon its bank (O.N. *stadr*, a place, town).

WINDERMERE seems also somewhat uncertain. It might be from the above Old Celt. *vind*. Or it might be from *Winder* as the name of a man, found in some other names of places, and still existing in the district.

KENT. Wel., Ir., Bret., Obs. Gael. *can*, pure, clear, Sansc. *cand*, to shine, Lat. *candeo*. As in the case of Wel. *gwyn*, Corn. *wyn*, from the older Celt. form *vind*, the present Celtic *can* has no doubt dropped the dental, which is still retained in the river-name *Kent*. Comp. *Cann, Kenne, Cain*, in England and Wales.

THE FOLLOWING I TAKE TO BE DERIVED FROM THE
TORTUOUSNESS OF THEIR COURSE.

WAVER or WEAVER. Wel. *gwibio*, to rove, to wander, *gwib*, serpentine course. Old Norse *vâfa, vippa*, gyrare. Comp. *Weaver, Vever* in England, *Wipper* in Germany, &c.

BLENG. More properly, I take it, *Blegen*, from Wel. *plygu*, to fold, to bend, Wel. *plyg, blyg*, Corn. *pleg, blec*, a fold, a bend. Comp. the *Blegno* or *Blenjo* in Switz., Canton Tessin. In these cases the termination *en* may be a contraction of *avon*.

KEER. Gael. *car*, twisting, bending.
Comp. the *Keiru*, Merion.—*Kerr*, Middlesex—*Cher*, in France, &c.

IRT. Wel. *gwryddu*, to wreathe, to turn.
Sansc. *irat*=Lat. *errans*, wandering. Comp. *Ourt* (Urta ant.), in Belgium—*Irati*, Spain, &c.

IRTHING, from its ancient name *Urtius*, would seem to be the same as above.

DERWENT. Among the various derivations proposed, that of Baxter from Wel. *dyrwyn*, to wind, seems to me, on comparing the various allied names, the most suitable. Comp. *Trent* (ant. Treonta), the *Durance* (ant. Druentia), the *Drewenz*, Germ., and the *Trento* (ant. Truentius).

THE FOLLOWING SEEM TO TAKE THEIR NAMES FROM
THE SOUND OF THEIR WATERS.

GRETA. Old Norse *gráta*, (pret. *grêt*), to wail, or weep with noise. This name probably bears marks of a Northern adaptation, but as the Welsh has *grydio*, to scream, *grwytho*, to murmur, perhaps cognate with the above, it is very possible that the Norsemen did nothing more than assimilate to their own form a previous Celtic word with the same meaning.

GELT. Förstemann takes the word *gelt* in German river-names to mean "loud sounding." Old Norse *gella*, Icel. *gelta*, to yell. The Welsh has also *gwylo*, to weep, Ir. *guil*, so that, as in the case of the last word, we may have an original Celtic word adapted by the succeeding race. But it may be a question whether the Wel. *gwyllt*, rapid, is not the word here concerned. Comp. *Geltn*(*ach*), *Geltbach*, Germ.

NADDEN (Lancashire). Bamford, in his glossary of South Lancashire words, explains *Nadden* as "na din," *i.e.*, the silent river ! On which Davies remarks that Bamford had evidently never seen the river in question, which is in fact a noisy, brawling stream. Davies refers it to Wel. *nadu*, to cry, to howl, which is probably correct, so far as the immediate origin is concerned. But we may carry the investigation somewhat farther back, and refer to Sansc. *nadi*, whence Hind. *nuddy*, a river, from *nad*, sonare, the only appellative, as far as I know, similarly derived, the general origin of such appellatives being a primitive root signifying to move, to go.

There remain a few names of rivers derived from various characteristics of their course or properties of their waters.

ROTHA, RATHAY. Probably from the rapidity of their current. Wel. *rhedu*, to run, to race. Hence Zeuss derives the ancient *Rhodanus*, now the Rhone. Comp. *Roth* in Germ., *Rodden* in Shrops., *Rother* in Sussex, &c.

MARRON. Probably from Wel. *marw*, Gael. *marbh*, dead, slow, still, Gael. *marbh-shruth*, a still or tranquil stream. In this case the ending *en* is probably a contraction of *avon*.

CALDEW, CALDA, or CAUDA, and CALDER. *Calda* seems to be the same name as the *Kaldá* in Iceland. One of the two streams which form it is called *Cald beck*,* and rises on Cold Fell. Hence, when it becomes a river, it still retains the title, *Calda*, cold river, O.N. *á* river. The *Calder*, the main stream of which also rises upon a Cold Fell, I take to be the same name. But though the name *Cauda*, as it stands, is almost without doubt a relic of the Northmen, it may, as I have taken to be the case in other instances, have been founded upon a previous Celtic name. The most striking characteristic of this river is its liability to sudden rise and fall, and in the Wel. *codi*, to swell, would be a very appropriate etymon.

EAMONT. Originally called *Eamot*, rises in Ulleswater, and after a short course falls into the Eden. The place of junction, Old Norse *ámot*, "meeting of rivers," may have given the name to the whole river.

I conclude this chapter with some remarks on the name of the *Solway Frith*, which has been referred by Prichard to the Caledonian tribe of the Selgovæ, who occupied the territory to the north of the frith. This opinion, which has also been adopted by the late Mr. F. L. B. Dykes (*Notes and Queries, July 21, 1860*), is,

---

* Caudebec (in Normandy) the same name as Cawdbeck in the Lake District, and the Kald bakr in Iceland."—*Taylor*.

according to my view, scarcely in accordance with the general character of our local nomenclature, more particularly when we take into account the unquestionably Scandinavian origin of *frith*. I have before suggested that the name, which appears in Leland as *Sulway*, may be from Old Norse *sulla*, miscere, confundere, Eng. *sully*, in reference to the floating sand which gives to its waters a turbid appearance. The root-meaning of O.N. *sulla*, probably originally *sumla*, seems to have been simply mixture, from *sam*, signifying combination. Or we might take *sul* as another form of *swell* (O.N. *sullr*, swelling), in reference to the "swell" with which the tide comes in. "During ebb tide much of the frith is a naked flat, and may occasionally be crossed in some places; but the tidal wave, especially during spring tides, returns very suddenly, and with great violence, so that accidents to shipping have repeatedly happened" *(Dict. of Geog.* A. K. Johnston). In the case of either of the preceding derivations, the ending *way* might be presumed to be the O.N. *vogr*, a bay, "voe" in Sco. local names. On the whole, however, I think the presumption is rather in favour of *Solway* as derived from a personal name, like so many of the other place-names of the district. No word seems to have been more frequently coupled with a personal name by the Northmen than *fiördr*. The Landnamabök of Iceland gives us a very great number of such names, one of which, *Sölva fiördr*, from the name Sölvi, might point to the original of *Solway frith*.

GENERAL OBSERVATIONS.

My aim in the present chapter is to collect and to compare the results already obtained, and to present something like an approximate estimate—first, of the Celtic element as compared with the Teutonic, and secondly, of the Scandinavian as compared with the Anglo-Saxon and kindred tongues. And further, briefly to particularise the phonetic, grammatical, and other peculiarities of the dialect.

Of the words of the dialect which I have passed under review I take a proportion of about four in a hundred to be probably, and about an equal proportion to be possibly, derived from the Celtic. With regard to the latter, it would probably be correct to say that in many cases the words are derived both from the Celtic and the Teutonic. For in the struggle for supremacy, it seems only reasonable to suppose that a word which was common to both the contending tongues would be ensured of preservation. When, therefore, as in the case of *loover*, an opening in the roof to let out the smoke, referred by one writer to a Celtic, and by another to a Scandinavian origin, we have a word which may be assigned to two different sources; instead of referring it arbitrarily to either, it would seem more reasonable to ascribe its existence to the concurrence of the two. And though the dialect which, on the whole, largely preponderates must, in that point of view, have the stronger claim, yet there may be other considerations, such as the circumstances under which the word is found in other dialects, which may tend to restore the balance of probability. Thus, the word *crow* or *creuh*, a pig-sty, might be derived either from a Celtic or from a Scandinavian origin. But if the word is not found in the Yorkshire dialects, which are the strong-hold of the Norse tongue, but is found in the Lancashire, which contains a more considerable Celtic admixture, this fact must to a certain extent weigh in determining the origin.

It may not be without interest to carry the comparison a little further with a view to ascertain whether the distribution of the words of the dialect may not assist, however feebly, to throw a ray of light upon the relations which subsisted between the subjected race and their masters.

In the first place—so far as the words descriptive of the physical characteristics of the country may serve to indicate the ownership of the soil, a nomenclature distinctly Scandinavian would seem to prove that it had passed away from its original owners to their Northern invaders. The words *by* and *thorp*, a village, *fell*, a mountain, *how*, a hill, *force*, a waterfall, *tarn*, a small lake, *wath*, a ford, *dowp* and *wick*, a bay, *gill*, a small ravine, *with*, a wood, *lund*, a grove, *thwaite*, a clearing, *carr*, a low, damp grove, *flow*, a bog, characteristic Scandinavian words, most of them living terms of the dialect, and all of them of constant occurrence in the names of places, distinctly assert the occupation of the district by the Northmen. And though, as shown in the preceding chapter, no inconsiderable number of Celtic terms still survive in the names of places, there is scarcely one of these terms in living use in the dialect. And it is not an unusual thing to find the ancient Celtic appellative conjoined as a proper name with the word of present use which has superseded it. Thus we have Airey Force, which seems in all probability to be from the Welsh *eirwy*, a water-fall, coupled with the Scandinavian *force*.

Among the terms connected with agriculture there seems, as might naturally be expected, a considerable sprinkling of Celtic words. But here again it is to be observed that while the general terms descriptive of the stock and the property of the farm are, with scarcely an exception, Teutonic, and to a considerable extent Scandinavian, the Celtic terms are generally those having reference to some individual peculiarity. Such are *garron*, a tall awkward horse, *boly*, a horse with white legs and face, *dog pig*, a castrated boar, *crock*, an old ewe, probably *crobs*, the worst lambs of the flock, *mug sheep*, sheep with white faces. For a cow given to striking we have three different terms,—*putty-cow*, *dumpy-cow*, and *bunsin-cow* — the first Celtic, the second Scandinavian, and the third Anglo-Saxon or Frisian: here we have all the principal constituents of the dialect represented. So also for a cow without horns we have four different words, *cowie, cowt cow, doddy,* and *polly,* of which the first and second, which are variations of the same word, are Scandinavian, the second Frisian or Saxon, and the third, though it is also capable of a derivation from a Low German source, may again be Celtic (Wel. *pwl,* blunt). For a milk-maid's cushion for the head we have three words, *sop, boss,* and *waze,* of which the first is most probably Celtic, the second Saxon or Frisian, and the third the same. The terms *aird,* high, and *bent,* bleak, descriptive of the situation of land, also *leck,* a hard sub-soil, and *scopy,* thin of soil, seem to be Celtic. It is rather curious, and possibly significant, that all the words descriptive of inferior land, seem to be Celtic. And the *brob* or *brog,* twig or straw carried in the mouth on the hiring day by those wanting to be engaged as servants, is appropriately Celtic. Then there are several other words common to both the Celtic and Teutonic, as *crow* or *creuh,* a pen or sty, *ark,* a chest for meal, *creel,* a basket, *rean,* a boundary, &c.

It will be found that many words descriptive of personal peculiarities, more especially with reference to physical characteristics, and containing generally something of a ludicrous or sarcastic sense, seem to be of Celtic origin. Thus we have *brusey,* a coarse fat person, *brannigan,* a puffy child, *gayshen,* an emaciated person, *garrick,* an awkward person, *rappack* and *craddagh,* a troublesome child. Also *crag,* the jaw, *crow* and *paw,* the hand, *conk,* the nose or profile, *doose,* a slap with the hand, *game leg,* a hurt or crooked leg, all words applied with a sense more or less of humour or ridicule. But on the other hand, while many words sarcastically referring to personal features are Celtic, those referring to mental crassness, of which there are a considerable number, are, with scarcely an exception, Teutonic. It is the race which rules that gives the words expressive of stupidity.

It might naturally be expected that many of the words describing the simple and common articles of diet would be from the Celtic, and we have accordingly *sowens, bannock, botcher, soss, gulls, cummt milk, lithy* (thick, as with meal), &c. The names of some of the common household utensils, as *gully*, a large knife, *geggin, noggin,* and *piggin,* vessels or measures, probably *girdle*, a baking plate, &c., may also be referred to the Celtic. Our word for small coal, *chillipers*, seems to have a Celtic origin, and it is noticeable that also in Lancashire small coal has a name of Celtic origin, *grummil*, referred by Davies to Welsh *gremial*, to crash. May we look upon it as the type of the condition of a subject race, fain to take up with the leavings of their masters?

Then there are some words probably adopted from the Latin through the Celtic into the Teutonic prior to the settlement of our ancestors in the British Isles; referred to by Dr. Guest (Proc. Phil. Soc. 3, 169), among which may be probably *kale*, greens, *chibies*, onions, perhaps *saim*, grease.

The mercurial temperament of the Celt may be exemplified in *tantrums*, fits of passionate excitement, and the converse *doldrums*, low spirits or melancholy. And their superstitions in *dobby*, *boggle*, and *boman*.

Mr. Davies has remarked of the dialect of Lancashire that various words of a coarse or obscene meaning are of Celtic origin. We have two, *dunnecan*, a privy, and *bandylow*, a prostitute, which seem to be so derived. Perhaps also *giglet*, *jillet*, or *jilt*, which seems to have contained originally a somewhat stronger sense of ignominy than at present. Can we account for the retention of such words on the same principle as that which gives rise to the phrase *fille de joie*, and causes the ruling race in India sometimes to describe certain things by native expressions?

There is one word, *filly-fair*, an annual festival at Arlecdon, in which, as in the case before-mentioned of Airey Force, we seem to have retained a forgotten Celtic word in conjunction with the living word of the same meaning.

The proportion which I have assigned to the Celtic in our dialect is considerably larger than that (one and a half in the hundred) assigned by Mr. Atkinson to the dialect of Cleveland. It might be assumed that this difference is mainly owing to the proximity of Scotland, but it will be seen that it is only to a limited extent to be accounted for by this cause. For, while out of a hundred Celtic words in our dialect I find twenty-four common to the Cleveland, there are not more than thirty-seven which are common to the Scotch, leaving thirty nine to be otherwise accounted for. Out of these a few may be found in some other of the English dialects, and especially that of Lancashire, but the greater part seem to be peculiar to our own. And it is to be noted that while those words which are common to Scotland prevail more especially, as might be expected, in the Northern part of the county, those which are peculiar to our own dialect are found chiefly, as appears by the classification of Mr. Dickenson, in the centre of the county.

Large as unquestionably is the amount of the Scandinavian element in our dialect, the proportion of words which I am able to make out as distinctly traceable to that source is not more than twenty in the hundred. This falls so very far short of the proportion (forty in the hundred) assigned by Mr. Atkinson for the dialect of Cleveland, founded on a partial scrutiny, that I am rather disposed to think—after making allowance for the thorough knowledge of the Scandinavian idioms which might enable him to adjudicate in cases where I should not—that a scrutiny of the whole vocabulary would hardly have given the same result. I refer only to cases of absolute proof—the *probabilities* are on the side of the preponderating dialect, and his general conclusion that "wherever the Cleveland dialect diverges from the ordinary or standard language, it is indebted to the Scandinavian tongues and dialects for certainly not less than sixty per cent. of such divergencies," may not be far from the truth. And what applies to Cleveland will not be far from the mark in the case of Cumberland.

I have already referred to the words descriptive of the physical features of the country as essentially Scandinavian. So also to a very great extent those descriptive of the stock and property of the farm. Thus we have *lathe*, a barn, *midden*, a dung-hill, *leah*, a scythe, *gripe*, a fork, *why*, a heifer, *yaud*, a mare, *gimmer*, a two-year-old ewe, *cushy*, a pet or familiar name for a cow, *shot*, a half-grown swine, *gaut*, a boar pig, &c. The word *led* farm, a farm on which the occupier does not reside, I have taken to be from the Old Norse *leiga*, Dan. *leje*, to rent, as a reminiscence of the old time when each man occupied his own land, and a rented farm was the exception. So Cleasby has *leigu-ból* and *leigu-jörd*, similarly meaning a rented farm. There is a noteworthy resemblance between our term *fire-house* for the inhabited part of a farm-stead, and the *eld-hús* (fire-house) formerly in Iceland the principal room in the mansion, and in modern use the kitchen. Possibly also the word *down-house* for a kitchen (*West. and Cumb. Dial.*) may be connected with O. N. *elds-daunn*, smell of fire.

The traveller in Norway cannot fail to note many expressions the counterpart of those which are in use with us. Thus we say of butter that is of two colours that it is *randit*, i.e., marked in stripes, the Norwegian *randut*. "The husband at first declined assisting us, as he was very *traeng*," (Oxonian in Norway)—this is precisely our *thrang*, i.e., busy.

One of the traces of Scandinavian inflections referred to by Garnett is the dropping of a final *d* after a liquid, as in *grun* for *ground*, *fun* for *found*, &c. Another seems to be the elision of *w* in such words as *soop* for *sweep* (O. N. *sôpa*), *sump* for *swamp* (Dan., Swed. *sump*), *sooal* for *swivel*, &c. A third may be found in the introduction of *v* before a vowel, as in *tiv* for *to*, *div* for *do*, *frav* and *frev* for *fra* (from), " genuine descendants from the Scandinavian *frâ*, still pronounced *frav* in Iceland" (*Garnett*). Another phonetic tendency in our dialect is the change of *g* final into *v* or *f*. Thus Burgh, the name of a village, is pronounced Bruff. And Barf, the name of a mountain, is, no doubt, properly Barg, Ang.-Sax. *beorg*, Old Norse *bjarg*, Germ. *berg*, mountain. Atkinson compares this tendency of the Northern dialects with the change which has taken place in the Scandinavian tongues, *e.-g.*, Old Dan. *plôg*, Mod. Dan. *plov*, plough, Suio-Goth. *agn*, Mod. Dan. *avn*, Cumb. *awn*, the beard of barley, Old Norse *skôgr*, Mod. Dan. *skov*, Cumb *shaw*, a wood, &c. A general relic of Scandinavian influence throughout the Northern dialects is to be found in the change of long *o*, as in *home, rope, stone*, into long *a* or *ai*, as *hame, raip, stane*. But there is, in Cumberland as in Yorkshire, a notable variation in the pronunciation of the words thus formed with a long *a*. Thus, as well as *stain, hame, raip*, we have *styen* or *steean*, *hyem*, *reeap*. Mr. Atkinson shows from Kok that the same peculiarity is to be found at the present day in the dialect of South Jutland, and that it is moreover to be found in Old Danish writings of the 15th century, e.-g. *stien* for *sten*, stone, *dielle* for *dele*, Cumb. *deeal*, share, division. The Cumberland dialect introduces a similar vowel sound before *oo*, as in *greeuv* for *groove*, *leeum* for *loom*. Words which in Old Norse are formed with an accented *ô* take this form in our derivatives—thus *leeuf*, the palm of the hand, O. N. *lófi*. But neither of the above sounds are confined to words of Scandinavian origin. The Cumberland dialect, moreover, introduces the sound of *oo* in words formed with a long *o*, as in *roo-ose* for *rose*, *noo-ote* for *note*. This gives the same sound as *w*, by which it is usually represented, as *rwose* and *nwote*. Another peculiarity is the introduction of *y* before words beginning with *a* or *e*, as in *yak* or *yek*, oak, *yakker*, acre, *yel* for ale, *yan* or *yen* for one. This is also a peculiarity of the Jutland dialect, as also of certain Norse dialects. Thus Jutland *jen* for *en*, one, which *(j* having the sound of our *y)*, is identical with our *yen*.

It has been suggested by Cleasby that the prevalence of *a* (Old Norse *â* = on), instead of *be*, as in *afore*, *ahint*, *atween*, *aside*, instead of *before*, *behind*, *between*, *beside*, in the Northern dialects, may be attributed to Scandinavian influence, the preposition *be* being unknown in the Scandinavian idiom. The use of *at* for *to*, as the sign of the infinitive, is a distinctive token of Scandinavian influence. This, observes Mr. Dickenson, is nearly obsolete in Cumberland now, though common in the last century. How suggestive is this —how many interesting characteristics of our dialect may also have perished in the last century or two?

For the time when men begin to take note of these peculiarities is necessarily also the time when they begin to pass away.

The apparently ungrammatical forms "I is," "thou is," are, as noted by Garnett, in exact accordance with the practice of the Danes, the verb substantive being respectively inflected as follows—

Danish.	*Cumberland.*
Jeg er	I is
Du er	Thou is
Han er	He is
Vi ere	We are
I ere	Ye are
De ere	They are

There is however an irregularity to be noted in regard to the third person plural, for though a Cumbrian never uses *is* with *they*, yet he does so with any noun. Thus he would say, "Oats *is* varra dear at present," but in replying to the same remark he would say "they *are*," not "they *is*."

So in the future we say "I's go," "Thou's go," or "Thou'st go," "We's go," for "I shall go," "Thou shalt go," "We shall go." The analogy of our dialect seems rather in favour of the supposition *(Dr. Guest, Phil. Soc., 2, 227)* that we have here a contraction of the Northern auxiliary *sud*, "I's go" being "I *sud* go," which, indeed, is often used as an alternative expression.

As "certainly Scandinavian," Mr. Atkinson classes the following particles. Of these, two, *helder* and *hine*, I have never met with in our dialect, though *hine* is given as a Cumberland word by Ray, and of a third, *parlous*, the Scandinavian origin seems to me to be at least doubtful.

> *Aback*, behind, in the rear of. O. N. *âbak*.
> *Amell*, between. O. N. *âmilli*.
> *Amid*, among. O. N. *âmedal*.
> *At*, to. O. N. *at*, apud, cum, quod attinet ad.
> *An*, than. O. N. *an*, Sw. *än*.
> *An*, if. O. Sw. *æn*.
> *At*, that. O. N. *at*, Sw. *att*.
> *At efter* afterwards. N. *atefter*, D. *efter at*.
> *Fra, frav*, from. O. N. *frâ*.
> *Fur*, for. O. N. *fyr, fyrir*.
> *I, iv*, in. O. N. *î*.
> *Off*, from (as a foal off yon meear). D. *af*.
> *Intil, intiv*, into. Sw. *intill*.
> *Till, tiv*, to. O. N. *til*.
> *Wi, wiv*, with. O. N. *vid*, D. *ved*.
> *Helder*, rather, in preference. O. N. *helldr*.
> *Inoo*, presently. D. *i et nu*.
> *Backlings*, backwards. D. *baglængs*.
> *Parlous*, greatly, terribly. D. *ferlich*.
> *Sae*, so. Sw. *sa*, D. *saa*.
> *Sair*, very, exceedingly. D. *saare*.
> *Hine*, be off, away with you. D. *hedan*.

"The peculiar Northern interjections *a! eh!*" Mr. Atkinson goes on to say, "and the adverbial forms in *som*, as *what-som, how-som* (in *whatsomever, howsomever*)—compare Dan. *hvadsomhelst*, &c.—are almost certainly Scandinavian, and so also are the assentative and negative particles *ay, neya*, (Sw. *nej*, &c.), not to mention other less obtrusive forms."

The objection which has been raised that there is no trace in the Northern dialects of what is at present

x

one of the most distinctive features of the Scandinavian tongues, the form of the definite article, which is universally post-positive and coalesces with its noun,* has been dealt with by Mr. Atkinson. He shows that the definite article is not uniformly post-positive, and does not uniformily coalesce with its noun—that the South Jutland dialect is at present in this respect an exception, and quotes Molbech and Grimm to prove that in the oldest Danish writings this practice does not exist, and that it is in fact "one of later introduction and originally unknown in the Northern speech."

I may also quote Prof. Stephens *(The Old Northern Runic Monuments of Scandinavia and England)* who observes that "the post-article, the passive in *s*, and all other such provincial nostrums, were either unknown in Scandinavia A.D. 800–900, or were only very slowly creeping in."

The proportion of words in our dialect derived from the Norman-French I make out to be about two and a half in the hundred, which corresponds pretty nearly with that assigned by Atkinson to the dialect of Cleveland. Of these, some are characteristically found in the terms relating to sporting, as *dub*, to prepare a cock for fighting, *foil*, the scent of a hare or fox, *piley*, a white game-cock with some black feathers, *herrinshew* or *heronsew*, the heron, &c. Some articles of food, as *frummety*, *haggis*, *powsoddy*, *figsue*,

---

* As in the name of the Danish newspaper Dagblad*et*, the daily sheet.

and some articles of furniture, as *aumry*, *truncher*, probably *doubler*, may also be referred to this origin. The words *jome*, a window or door-post, *jeest*, a joist, *gimmers*, cupboard hinges, as also *plash*, to trim a hedge, and *beard*, to protect a wall with a coping of brushwood, seem to indicate the introduction by the Normans of improved ideas of comfort and neatness in the dwelling and its surroundings.

I have to deal, in the last place, with some general characteristics of the dialect. I may note the tendency to the introduction of a phonetic *r*, most common in words beginning with *st*. Thus *scrow*, *strunts*, *strunty*, *straddelt*, for *scow*, *stunts*, *stunty*, *staddelt*. So also *sharps* for *shaups*, *cherts* for *cheets*, *purdy* for *puddy*, &c. This tendency our dialect shares with the Scotch, and hence Jamieson has sometimes been at a loss to account for a word which a comparison with the Cleveland or other Northern dialects enables us to explain. The dropping of *l*, as in *fowthy* for *fulthy*, *fotter* for *falter*, &c., is a predominant feature in the Northern dialects generally, but is carried to a greater extent with us than in the others, *e.g.*, we have *how* for Clev. *holl*, deep, hollow, *goe* for Crav. *gall*, spring, wet place, *know* for *knoll*, hill, *pow* for *pool*, &c. We seem, indeed, to deal sometimes in the same way with *m*, if *caw't*, twisted, awry, be, as seems probable, for *cam't*, Wel. *cam*, crooked. Our pronunciation of *find*, *bind*, *wind*, *clim*, with a short vowel, instead of, as in English, a long one, and of *spreed*, *treed*, instead of *spread* (spred), *tread* (tred), is in correct accordance with the root. The guttural sound of *gh*, the loss of which in English Mr. Earle (Philology of the English Tongue) attributes to French influence, was "formerly, and even within memory," observes Mr. Dickenson, a feature of our dialect.

I have already (see *ne*) referred to our use of a special word as an assent to a negation. While as a direct negative we use generally *neah* or *naa;* in assenting to a negation we use *nee*, whether simply a different pronunciation or not I am unable to express an opinion. Also to our use of *min* as a vocative of *man*, used only in familiarity, and generally with a tinge of reproof or contempt. "Hoot, *min!* thou kens nout aboot it." Halliwell gives this also as a Westmorland word, but its use is so general with us that I am rather surprised to find it apparently restricted to these two counties.

The partiality of our dialect for alliterative expressions, as *ham-sam, hurdem-durdem, how-strow, hay-bay, helter-skelter, havey-skavey, hapshy-rapshy,* &c., is noticeable—the idea expressed in all these words being that of confusion or disorder.

Of old plurals we have, besides *owsen*, four, *een, kye, shoon,* and *housen,* the last not in general use, but occurring in the sense of a range of buildings; *childer* also is sometimes heard. And, as elsewhere through the Northern dialect, we dispense with *s* as the sign of the genitive. Thus, "that's Billy meear," not Billy's meear, a peculiarity to be found in P. Pl. and other works of Northumbrian origin.

GENERAL OBSERVATIONS.

Another peculiarity which our dialect (with the exception, according to Dickenson, of the north-east of the county) has in common with other Northern dialects, in the contraction of the definite article into *t'*, as in I'se *t'* rwose o' Sharon and *t'* lily o' *t'* valleys.* Peacock indeed, comparing our "at give *t'* bairn *t'* breast" with the corresponding Swed. *at gifva barnet bröstet*, has advanced the theory that our definite article is not *t'* but *'t*, and that it is in fact the same as the Dan. and Swed. *et*, the only difference being that instead of being post-positive, as barn*et*, bröst*et*, it is pre-positive, *et* barn, *et* breast. This theory however, though at first sight it might seem plausible, Mr. Atkinson has shown to be altogether untenable.

In the formation of its preterites our dialect shows considerable variations from the standard language. Thus we have *see, seed; sell, selt; come, com; creep, crap; bring, brong; beat, bet; spreed, spred*, &c. Also *split, splat; stick, stack*, &c. So also in the past participle we have *get, gitten; come, cummen* or *cumt; stand, stooden; brest, brossen; find, fand* or *fun*, &c.

---

* Much as we are indebted to Prince Lucien Bonaparte for the dialectic investigations which he has set on foot, I cannot help thinking that the subject selected for the purpose, (the Song of Solomon), is singularly ill-adapted for the purpose of drawing out the fine degrees of difference between cognate dialects. As a poetical composition it is removed from the every-day ideas of the people, and in most of the versions it will be found that very many of the expressions, instead of being careful illustrations of nice distinctions, are simply the arbitrary renderings of the writer's judgment.

Of words which we still retain in their original sense, but which have become changed in the standard language, are *bounce* in its original sense of striking (as a *bunsin* cow); *stop*, in its original sense of stuffing or cramming; *angry*, in its original sense of painful; *sad*, in its original sense of heavy; *rid*, in its original sense of rooting out; and *plod* (ploat), in its original sense of wading or plunging through wet.

Mr. Davies has remarked (Races of Lancashire) that there are instances in which a clearer correspondence is to be traced with the Sanscrit than with the languages more directly related. So also in the Scottish language. Take, for instance, the word *cummer*, a young girl, of which no co-relative seem to be found in the languages immediately cognate (*cummer*, a gossip, being a different word), but which has its exact correspondent in the Sanscrit *kumári*, of the same meaning. So also in Cumberland we have some words, such as *nous*, which in sense and in form are nearer to the Sanscrit than anything we find in the languages immediately cognate. Such words seem also to be *toup* and *coup*, which, as the central points in their respective groups, see p. 187, may put in a claim to the dignity of the highest antiquity.